Coloured by History, Shaped by Place

New Perspectives on Coloured Identities in Cape Town

Edited by Zimitri Erasmus

KWELA BOOKS
and SA History Online

This book forms part of the Social Identities South Africa Series, and has been produced with the financial assistance of the National Research Foundation, and of the Delegation of the European Commission through the CWCI Fund

Published jointly by Kwela Books and South African History Online

Kwela Books
28 Wale Street, Cape Town 8001;
P.O. Box 6525, Roggebaai 8012
Kwela@kwela.com

South African History Online
P.O. Box 11420, Maroelana 0161
Info@sahistory.org.za
www.sahistory.org.za

Cover design by Liam Lynch and Omar Badsha
Photograph on cover by Ledochowski
Set in 10 on 13.5pt Garamond
Printed and bound by NBD, Drukkery Street, Cape Town, South Africa
First edition, first printing 2001

ISBN 0-7957-0136-5

SISA

Social Identities South Africa
General Editor: Abebe Zegeye

The identities of South Africa and its citizens have been undergoing crucial changes since 1994, when the first democratic elections resulted in the demise of statutory apartheid. This has led to an emerging ethos of democratic rule among all citizens of South Africa. But, although changes in South African society are clearly visible in increased social mobility, migration, access to jobs, training and educational and general reform in South Africa, the nature and influence of the identities being formed in response is as yet less clear. The SISA project aims to determine the nature of some of these new identities.

The project is shaped by research that indicates the South Africans, while going through flux and transformation in their personal and group identities, have a shared concern about the stability of their democracy and their economic future.

Titles in the SISA Series jointly published by Kwela Books and South African History Online:

Social Identities in the New South Africa
After Apartheid – Volume One
Edited by Abebe Zegeye

Culture in the New South Africa
After Apartheid – Volume Two
Edited by Robert Kriger and Abebe Zegeye

Kala Pani
Caste and Colour in South Africa
Rehana Ebr.-Vally

Coloured by History, Shaped by Place
New Perspectives on Coloured Identities in Cape Town
Edited by Zimitri Erasmus

The I of the Beholder
Identity formation in the art and writing of Breyten Breytenbach
Marilet Sienaert

Contents

Notes on Contributors

Zimitri Erasmus is a senior lecturer in sociology at the University of Cape Town. She received her PhD in the field of development and cultural change at the University of Nijmegen, the Netherlands. Her research interests include the deployment of identities in contexts of social transformation, managing organisational change, and strategies for anti-racist practice. She has published on the politics of 'race' and culture in South Africa.

Sean Field is Director of the Centre for Popular Memory at the University of Cape Town. He received his PhD in social history from the University of Essex, UK. He is currently editing a book on oral histories of forced removals in Cape Town. His research interests are in oral history, life stories and the recording, interpretation and dissemination of popular memories.

Pumla Dineo Gqola teaches in the Department of English and Classical Culture at the University of the Orange Free State. She received her MA in colonial and postcolonial literature from the University of Warwick, UK. Her research interests include South African literature and culture, Caribbean literature, slave narratives, Feminist/Womanist theory and postcolonial theory.

Heidi Grunebaum has recently joined the Direct Action Centre for Peace and Memory as Research and Education Director. She is a writer, critic and peace activist who has written and published on Holocaust survivor testimony, Jewish identity in Africa, the Truth and Reconciliation (TRC) process, memorialisation, and social responsibility in South Africa. She received her MA in French language and literature from the University of Cape Town and is currently reading for her PhD at the University of the Western Cape where she teaches part-time in the English Department.

Adam Haupt is the editor of friedjam.com, a digital music download website and e-zine. He also spins yarns for the marketing department of kalahari.net. He received his MA in English at the University of the Western Cape. He has lectured in English literature, media studies and communication science at the University of the Western Cape, the University of Stellenbosch and Cape Technikon. During his spare time he performs in the spoken word outfit, *colony*.

Cheryl Hendricks, formerly of the University of the Western Cape, received her PhD in government and international relations from the University of South Carolina, USA. She received her MA in southern African studies from the University of York, UK. Her research interests and publications are in the fields of government and politics in sub-Saharan Africa, identity politics, gender and 'race', nationalism and ethnicity.

Shamil Jeppie is a lecturer in the Department of Historical Studies at the University of Cape Town. His research focuses on the histories of Sudan and South Africa. He completed his PhD as a Fullbright Scholar at Princeton University, USA and recently spent time at Oxford University, UK, as a Chevening post-doctoral scholar.

Desiree Lewis is a senior lecturer in English studies in the School of Language, Culture and Communication at the University of Natal (Pietermaritzburg). She has published on southern African writing and popular culture, and feminist theory and politics. Her doctoral work at the University of Cape Town examined the writings of Bessie Head.

Thiven Reddy completed his PhD at the University of Washington (Seattle). He lectures in political studies at the University of Cape Town and currently holds a Commonwealth Fellowship at the University of Bristol, UK. He is author of *Hegemony and Resistance: Contesting Identities in South Africa* (Ashgate, 2000). His current research is in the field of dominant political parties and democratic transition in deeply divided societies.

Steven Robins is a senior lecturer in the Department of Anthropology & Sociology at the University of the Western Cape. He completed his PhD at Columbia University, New York. He has published on the cultural politics of land, development discourses, memory and identity in post-apartheid South Africa, the politics of Holocaust memory and South African-Jewish identities, the politics and ethics of memory in the Truth & Reconciliation Commission (TRC) and cultural landscapes of the post-apartheid city.

Crain Soudien is professor at the School of Education, University of Cape Town. He teaches in the fields of sociology and history of education. His research interests include 'race', culture and identity, school and socialisation, school effectiveness and urban history. He is co-editor of two books on District Six and helped establish the Disctrict Six Museum in Cape Town in 1989. He was educated at the University of Cape Town and holds a PhD from the State University of New York at Buffalo, USA.

Acknowledgements

Many people contributed to the process of preparing this book for publication.

The University Research Committee at the University of Cape Town and Isandla Institute funded the conference, held at the University of Cape Town in June 1998, which marked the beginnings of this book project. Special thanks go to Edgar Pieterse for his assistance in conceptualising this project. Invaluable editorial and publication support was provided by the Social Identities South Africa 2000 project, funded by the National Research Foundation. Special thanks go to Abebe Zegeye, Rehana Vally, Robert Kriger and Rachel Stewart.

Contributors who participated in the conference would like to thank Ali Rattansi, Françoise Vergès, Isabel Balseiro, Teresa Barnes, Zine Magubane, Crystal Jannecke and Theaster Gates for critical intellectual engagement with their work. We are further indebted to Zoë Wicomb, David Goldberg, Denis Constant Martin, Kenneth Parker and Françoise Vergès who kindly offered to read and comment on the chapters of the initial manuscript.

I thank Colleen Crawford-Cousins, Robert Berold, Marion Wertheim, Ruth Buckingham and Shamil Jeppie for much needed moral support during my preparation of the manuscript for publication. Many thanks go to all contributors for their unfailing commitment to and support during this project. Special thanks go to Andries du Toit for his unfailing love and support.

Zimitri Erasmus
Cape Town

Editor's Note

There is no such thing as the Black 'race'. Blackness, whiteness and colouredness exist, but they are cultural, historical and political identities. To talk about 'race mixture', 'miscegenation', 'inter-racial' sex and 'mixed descent' is to use terms and habits of thought inherited from the very 'race science' that was used to justify oppression, brutality and the marginalisation of 'bastard peoples'. To remind us of their ignoble origins, these terms have been used in quotation marks throughout.

Zimitri Erasmus

Introduction[1]

Re-imagining coloured identities in post-Apartheid South Africa

Zimitri Erasmus

Hou jou linne binne (Keep your linen hidden). *Hou jou koek in jou broek* (Keep your fanny in your panties). *Vroeg ryp, vroeg vrot* (Early to ripen, early to rot). Such expressions abound in coloured communities in South Africa. They stipulate the bounds of sexual behaviour for young coloured women. Such expressions are considered undignified in my family. With our roots in the rural outback, the family's journey to the city, combined with a Protestant work ethic, has made it now middle class and 'respectable'. Although not said in quite the same way, the message of my family was that girls who 'came home with babies' were 'not respectable'. Many of my peers as a matter of fact were 'not respectable'. The price for coming home pregnant was clear: my father would disown me. In my imagination, informed by countless examples in my community, this meant living on the streets, consigned to the fate of being a 'half-caste outcast'. These were the possibilities in my young life: respectability or shame.

Today, looking back, I can see how these possibilities were shaped by the lived realities not only of gender and class but also of 'race'. I can see how respectability and shame are key defining terms of middle class coloured experience. For me, growing up coloured meant knowing that I was *not only* not white, but *less than white*; *not only* not black, but *better than black* (as we referred to African people). At the same time, the shape of my nose and texture of my hair placed me in the middle on the continuum of beauty as defined by both men and women in my community. I had neither 'sleek' hair nor *boesman korrels*.[2] Hairstyling and texturising were (and still are) key beautification practices in the making of womanhood among young coloured women. In my community practices such as curling or straightening one's hair carried a stigma of shame. The humiliation of being 'less than white' made being 'better than black' a very fragile position to occupy. The pressure to be respectable and to avoid shame created much anxiety. These were discomfiting positions for a young woman to occupy.

Over the years I have seen how this discomfort is among the conditions of being coloured. Being coloured often means having to choose between blackness and whiteness. When one lives aspects of both these cultural identities having to choose one means the denial of some part of oneself. This is not easy especially when one's actions are judged in these stark racial terms. Being coloured means being the privileged black and the 'not quite white' person. It means a distinction between being 'sleek' or *kroes* haired, and between being *kris* (Christian) or *slams* (a derogatory term for Muslim). Being coloured is about living an identity that is clouded in sexualised shame and associated with drunkenness and jollity.

This book examines (and plays with the boundaries of) the disconcerting, discomfiting meanings that have grown around urban coloured identities. It grew from a conference held at the University of Cape Town (UCT) in June 1998. I organised this event with the help of Edgar Pieterse in response to the worn and inadequate conceptualisations of coloured identities that circulated in Cape Town in the aftermath of 'the coloured vote' for the National Party in the April 1994 democratic elections. The purpose of this conference was to explore modes of analysis that moved beyond interpretations of the vote simply as a vote against liberation or evidence of a 'slave mentality'.[3] It aimed to provide 'safe space' for thinking about coloured identities – a space less encumbered by the presence of the canon of colonial knowledge production still in place at UCT, and free also from the pressures of political correctness and politeness. The participation of Ali Rattansi and Françoise Vergès[4] facilitated this exploration, already initiated by all participants – those presenting papers, discussants and performing artist Lueen Conning (as she then was[5]), from Kwa-Zulu Natal. At the time, Lueen Conning's well known theatre production, *a coloured place*, had recently graced the stage of the Nico Malan Theatre in Cape Town. We had the privilege of both her presence and seeing her perform an extract from her work at the conference. The conference proved to be stimulating, raising interesting ideas and discussion.

This book is the result.[6] Insisting on the possibility and multiplicity of 'coloured places', this book attempts to rethink what it means to be coloured in post-apartheid South Africa. It explores the making of coloured subjectivities[7] in a way which scrutinises established boundaries of black and white, African and European, progressive and reactionary. It argues that coloured identities are not based on 'race mixture' but on cultural creativity, creolized formations shaped by South Africa's history of colonialism, slavery, segregation and apartheid. This conceptualization undermines the common sense view that conceives colouredness as something produced by the mixture of other 'purer' cultures. Instead, it stresses the ambiguity and ceaseless fluidity of coloured identity formations while remaining conscious of the conditions under which they are produced.

This book attempts to challenge both the erasure and the reification of coloured identities. It calls for an acknowledgement of coloured identity as part of the shifting texture of a broader black experience and warns against claims of moral authority based on the deployment of fixed groups for the purposes of exclusion. This approach is partially shaped by changes in political and social science theory from an emphasis on structure and political economy towards an acknowledgement of the constitutive role of the discursive and the multiplicity of subject positions. It does not, however, reduce identity formation to mere multiplicity without politics. In the context of post-apartheid South Africa we need to acknowledge the fluidity and the openness of identity – but not at the cost of imagining a rainbow-land where our relations with one another are not shaped by the past, by new configurations of 'race', or by emerging class and/or regional and broader politics on the continent.

Coloured by History attempts to create a space for voices until recently lost in debates centred around a black-white reductionism. This rigidity too often assumes that someone's politics can be read off the colour of her skin with little attention to her everyday practices – and that no matter what colour her skin really is, she has to be essentially either on the side of black or of white. This reductionism further assumes that blackness and whiteness are themselves given, coherent and homogeneous identities.

This text is not a comprehensive study of coloured identities in South Africa. It adds to existing historical works, community case studies and examinations of cultural practices. Among its many limitations are its focus on the western Cape and the absence of a rural focus, analyses of the regional diversity in articulations of coloured identity, and comparative analyses with similar formations elsewhere in Africa and the world. Its strength lies in its revelation of the complexity and specificity of coloured identity formations, of coloured identities not as 'lack' but as a positive 'presence'. The book also argues for an affirmation of coloured identities without resorting to the ethno-nationalism of organizations such as the *Kleurling Weerstandsbeweging*[8] or the romanticization of District Six (Wicomb 1998, 94).

The need for moving beyond the replication of binary categories encourages a dialogue with history. This is a process which should concern itself, among other issues, with survival of the dislocation and brutality of the colonial encounter and with opening debate about understanding all forms of identification. It is our hope that this collection will contribute to this process.

A new terrain

The essays in this volume, drawn from a variety of disciplines and with a focus on various issues, chart a conceptual space for imagining coloured identity. This introduction provides the reader with a map. I begin with a brief overview of how coloured identities have been and continue to be conceptualised in official and popular discourse. I explore the ways in which the racial discourses in South Africa have made it impossible to see colouredness as an identity that could be understood and respected on its own terms. I show how it has always been understood as a residual, in-between or 'lesser' identity – characterized as 'lacking', supplementary, excessive, inferior or simply non-existent. Discomfort among some coloured people with the idea of being coloured has resulted, on the one hand, in attempts to reconstruct a sense of purity based on claims to ethnicity and indigenous roots, or on the other, a complete denial of this identity. These negative characterizations and denials have contributed to the marginalization and trivialisation of coloured identities in relation to processes of building a national identity in post-apartheid South Africa. The key task of this introduction is to create the framework for an alternative understanding in order to make possible the re-imagination of coloured identities. I draw on the work of Edouard Glissant, a prominent writer and intellectual of the Caribbean. He engages critically with the ideas of negritude and Afrocentrism. There are four pillars to my argument.

First, coloured identities are not about 'race mixture'. Attempts to define these identities in terms of mixture buy into notions of 'race purity' that can be traced to nineteenth century European eugenicists. Since cultural formations involve borrowing from various cultural forms, and thus all identities could be seen/read as culturally hybrid,[9] it should not be difficult to conceive of coloured identities as such, rather than in terms of 'race mixture' or 'miscegenation'. They are cultural formations born of appropriation, dispossession and translation in the colonial encounter.

Second, coloured identities are distinguished not merely by the fact of borrowing *per se*, but by cultural borrowing and creation under the very specific conditions of creolization. I here use creolization to refer to cultural creativity under conditions of marginality. Creolization involves the construction of an identity out of elements of ruling as well as subaltern cultures. This *bricolage* does not invalidate such identities. Although it is true that apartheid has played a key role in the formation and consolidation of these (and other) identities, coloured identities are not simply Apartheid labels imposed by whites. They are made and re-made by coloured people themselves in their attempts to give meaning to their everyday lives.

Third, at the heart of this particular process of creolization was a colonial racial hierarchy which positioned coloured identities as midway between 'white' and 'African'. The legacy of this positioning demands acknowledgement of complicity on the part of those historically classified coloured in the exclusion of and disrespect for black Africans. For many coloured people this complicity has meant a disassociation from all things African. However, with the construction of whiteness having been a colonial project, discriminatory and racist, the ethical imperative – necessary participation in a liberatory project – is that of affiliation with Africa. Coming to terms with these facts is one of the most important and difficult challenges for coloured people. Coloured, black and African ways of being do not have to be mutually exclusive. There are ways of being coloured that allow participation in a liberatory and anti-racist project. The key task is to develop these.

Fourth, in the context of the identity politics of the New South Africa this challenge requires a move away from the tendency to assign moral authenticity or political credibility to 'blackness' or 'Africanness' as such, particularly where these are defined in simplistic or reductionist ways. It requires a new kind of politics founded on values which challenge exclusion based on fixed categories and emphasise reflexive political practice. The latter entails remembering and acknowledging the past – colonialism, slavery, segregation and apartheid – with its wounds and its contradictions, and acknowledging its power in shaping the present.

Conceptualisations of coloured identities

The key problematic of this book arises from the fact that coloured identity has never been seen as an identity 'in its own right'. It has been negatively defined in terms of 'lack' or taint, or in terms of a 'remainder' or excess which does not fit a classificatory scheme. These identities have been spoken about in ways that associate them with immorality, sexual promiscuity, illegitimacy, impurity and untrustworthiness. For coloured people these associations have meant that identifying as coloured is linked to feelings of shame (Wicomb 1998) and discomfort. The complexity and insidiousness of these associations are shown, for example, by Pumla Dineo Gqola's examination, in this collection, of how Rayda Jacobs, in her latest novel, *The Slave Book* (1998), explores the gender inscription of some of these meanings onto the bodies of Cape slaves.

A number of themes recur in ways of speaking about coloured identities. First, pre-apartheid conceptualizations understood coloured identities in terms of 'mixed race'. For example, *God's Stepchildren* (1924), Sarah Gertrude Millin's best remembered novel, represents coloured people in terms of 'race mixture'. 'Miscegenation', a nineteenth century European eugenicist concept referring to 'race mixture' specifically between white masters and black female slaves, was central to her imaginary world.[10] For Millin, 'miscegenation' meant that 'white children [with 'black blood' came] into the world with shame and sorrow in their blood' (1924, 251). In the late 1930s and 1940s context of economic depression, urbanization and the resulting construction of a 'poor white problem', 'miscegenation' was portrayed by Afrikaner Nationalists as a threat to their white identity and to the morality of Afrikaner women in particular. 'Blood mixing' was argued to lead to the degeneration and loss of moral values of poor whites in the cities (Norval 1996, 23, 24). As the Commission on Mixed Marriages (1939) concluded, 'mixed' marriages 'lead [...] to the infiltration of non-European blood into the European population [...] [and produced] risks [...] with regard to racial and social heredity' (Report of the Commission on Mixed Marriages 1939, 33). The proclamation of the Prohibition of Mixed Marriages Act No. 55 of 1949 and the Immorality Amendment Act No. 21 of 1950 soon after the rise of the Apartheid state, were merely the most overt expressions of a deep discomfort with 'race mixture' which formed part of the fabric of (white) society in South Africa. In this collection, the chapter by Cheryl Hendricks, which traces coloured identity formation to the colonial era, illustrates the centrality of the integrally related governance of sexual relations, and the processes of racist representation (underlying the notion of 'miscegenation') in racialising conceptualisations of gender and creating a stigma of shame around those of 'mixed' descent.

Closely linked to 'race mixture' is the conceptualisation of colouredness as a residual identity. An example is the Population Registration Act No. 30 of 1950 which defined a 'Coloured' person as 'not a white person or a native'.[11] The same idea was expressed in the 1980s when Marike de Klerk (F.W. De Klerk's ex-spouse) famously described coloured people as 'a negative group', 'the leftovers', and as 'people that were left after the nations were sorted out'.[12] Similarly, in the late 1990s, Hombi Ntshoko, an African woman from Langa, told a researcher that '[c]oloureds don't know where they come from. We know where we come from. Whites know where they come from. But these coloureds don't know whether they are black or white' (quoted in Caliguire 1996, 11).

This tendency to construct colouredness as a category midway between black and white was given institutional expression in the ambiguous position accorded coloured people in the racial policies of United Party segregation, Verwoerdian apartheid and Botha's tri-cameralism. During the apartheid era coloured people were excluded from full citizenship on the basis of 'race'. At the same time, they were selectively included as partially privileged subjects because they could not fit into the Verwoerdian framework of African black 'peoples'. Apartheid therefore positioned people classified coloured ambiguously between whites as full citizens and Africans as tribalized subjects locked into 'pure' cultural traditions. According to Norval, inconsistencies in apartheid constructions of coloured identity reveal the uneasy interaction between its parallel discourses of white domination and separate development (1996, 116-124). In terms of these discourses coloured identity could not be thought of as an African tribal identity, nor could it be included in white identity. This revealed the 'undecidability' (ibid., 105, 124, 139) within Afrikaner Nationalist ideology – a place at which Verwoerdian apartheid ran into contradictions and inconsistencies. In this volume, Thiven Reddy further explores this theme in his examination of the functions of the category 'coloured' in particular state texts and practices. Shamil Jeppie's work illustrates contested attempts by Nationalists to imagine a 'pure' culture for part of the coloured community.

Politically, coloured people were drawn into compromises and complicity as a result of this ambiguous positioning. This legacy deeply shaped the ways in which coloured identity was seen in terms of servility and collusion with apartheid. Although the Black Consciousness Movement of the 1970s promoted blackness as an inclusive, positive political identity marking the racially oppressed and making visible the unearned privileges of whiteness, the politics of the time prevented this discourse from acknowledging the specificity of coloured experiences or the heterogeneity and locatedness of blackness. The Black Consciousness Movement tended towards a universal and single notion of being black which privileged black African experiences (narrowly defined) and papered over racial hierarchies and differential racialisation[13] among racially oppressed South Africans. Although coloured people could identify with the struggle against apartheid by rejecting coloured identity and identifying as black, they would always still be 'blacks of a special type'.

The same problems were experienced by the United Democratic Front (UDF) in the mid- to late 1980s. While these traditions afforded people classified coloured a place in the struggle, this place still came at the price of renouncing colouredness and forsaking its particularities. As one UDF activist remembers, 'the price that had to be paid to become part of mainstream resistance {was that} there was no place for "Coloureds" as such, but only for "Blacks". In order to be accepted as "Black", Coloured identity had to be forsworn' (De Vries quoted in Van Kessel 1994, 9). The chapter in this collection by Steven Robins and Heidi Grunebaum shows how coloured activists sometimes occupied a precarious place in which their identity as 'comrades of a special type' could be used to withdraw solidarity.

These tendencies persisted in the post-apartheid era. For example, in the mid-1990s progressive coloured activists within the ANC Youth League re-articulated the specificity and marginality of coloured identities in the context of a re-emerging African essentialist lobby within the ANC nationally (Burgess & Dikeni, 1995). This renewed emphasis on the conflation of blackness with Africanness accompanied by a politics of moral and political superiority was referred to as 'African chauvinism'. Struggles about who is 'black' and what it means to be 'black' – 'black' here conflated with an essentialist[14] understanding of both 'black' and 'African' – were further manifested in responses to coloured voting preferences during elections. The political conservatism of working class coloured communities in the Western Cape intensified these struggles. In both the 1994 and 1999 national democratic elections these communities voted for the National Party and later, the New National Party. In the December 2000 local elections they voted for the Democratic Alliance formed by the merging of the Democratic Party and the New National Party. For many South Africans this meant that coloured people did not vote as 'black' and/or 'African' and thus cannot be considered as such. Interestingly, black Africans who aligned themselves with these political parties have not had their blackness and/or Africanness questioned.

Black and white in the rainbow nation

Are these patterns simply the legacy of a past that will soon disappear? Has the end of formal apartheid ushered in possibilities for conceptualizing coloured identities in less constricting ways? I would argue not. The two dominant discourses of national identity in South Africa limit the possibilities for including coloured identities in a positive way.

The first of these is the depoliticizing discourse of rainbow nationalism. Its construction of the nation is encapsulated in the overused South African metaphor of 'unity in diversity'. It reads coloured identities (as all identities) as 'merely different' – simply another aspect of South Africa's cultural 'diversity'. This multi-cultural reading is blind to power relations inherent in cultural formation and representation. It reduces coloured culture to minstrelsy – a dance-music-and-dress understanding of culture. Furthermore, rainbow nationalist discourse does not provide a vocabulary with which to renegotiate and process the racial terrain of South African culture and politics in the interests of transformation. By insisting, simplistically, that we should be blind to 'race', it makes it more difficult to name and recognize the importance of articulating and working through antagonisms and conflict.

Counterpoised to this trivializing vision is the second – an emergent discourse of African essentialism. In its terms blackness is understood in terms of Africanness, and black or African identity is simply associated with authenticity, resistance and subversion, while whiteness is associated with Europe, in-authenticity, domination and collusion. This discourse denies creolization and hybridity as constitutive of African experiences, thus excluding coloured identities from those defined as black and African. It has shaped the ANC's continued inability to successfully articulate a broader black identity able to include and mobilize coloured people, particularly in the western Cape.

This leaves little space for conceptualizing coloured identities and experiences as valid, and even less for imagining progressive articulations of these identities. One option for coloured people is to adopt an identity which alienates them from the New South Africa and thrives on fear of the new government. In the western Cape this is likely to provide much ammunition for the racist and liberal Democratic Alliance in its criticism of the ANC. Second, colouredness can be articulated in apolitical rainbow nationalist terms, relegating it to the decorative presence of 'coons' and/or the entertainment of 'toothless funny people' in the South African cultural landscape. A third option is to deny and pathologize coloured identity. Some progressive intellectuals have advocated this route. In the late 1990s Neville Alexander, for example, denied the reality of coloured identity arguing that it was white-imposed, reactionary and indicative of new forms of racism; an apartheid relic best left behind us in this post-apartheid era.[15] Others have explained it away as an aspect of 'slave mentality'[16] and 'coloured psychology'.[17] A fourth alternative is to retreat into ethno-nationalism along the lines of the *Kleurling Weerstandsbeweging* or, like the Hamcumqua,[18] to ride the wave of fashionable indigeneity, claiming authenticity based on historical links to the Khoi-San.[19] Such claims of purity, argues Wicomb, deny history and prevent 'multiple belongings [from being seen as] an alternative way of viewing culture' (1998, 105).

Neither one of these options is conducive to articulations of coloured identities in progressive ways.

Re-imagining coloured identities in post-Apartheid South Africa

The challenge is to move beyond these limitations and to contest these frames. These identities need to be re-imagined if we are to provide space that allows coloured identities to be part of a liberatory political practice. It is only from such a place that we can begin building new relationships with fellow South Africans and finding ways in which to contribute to processes of democratization and anti-racism in SA.

Colouredness, culture and creolization

In re-imagining coloured identities we need to move beyond the notion that coloured identities are 'mixed race' identities. Rather, we need to see them as cultural identities comprising detailed bodies of knowledge, specific cultural practices, memories, rituals and modes of being. Coloured identities were formed in the colonial encounter between colonists (Dutch and British), slaves from South and East India and from East Africa, and conquered indigenous peoples, the Khoi and San.[20] This encounter and the power relations embedded in it have resulted in processes of cultural dispossession, borrowing and transformation. The result has been a highly specific and instantly recognizable cultural formation – not just 'a mixture' but a very particular 'mixture' comprising elements of Dutch, British, Malaysian, Khoi and other forms of African culture appropriated, translated and articulated in complex and subtle ways. These elements acquire their specific cultural meaning only once fused and translated.

The fact that the hybrid character of coloured identity is so evident[21] has prompted some to question its existence. Norman Duncan recently asserted, for example, that '[i]t's incorrect to speak of "coloured" [...] there's no such thing as a coloured culture, coloured identity. Someone has to show me what it is [...]' [22] But this is to make the mistake that any culture has to have an irreducible 'something' that can be shown to exist as its core. The danger of the argument that coloured people lack a distinct culture is that it tends to reify culture. Underlying the notion that there is no such thing as coloured culture and identity is the assumption that because coloured identity does not have an 'essence', in the sense that African ethnic identities are assumed to have one, it is not a 'real' identity (Erasmus and Pieterse 1999, 179). All cultural formations involve borrowing and hybridity. This is part of the ongoing social construction of cultural identities which makes them 'never completed – always in process' (Hall 1996, 2). This understanding challenges commonsense notions which view identities as natural and based on 'pure' origins or shared experiences.

Colouredness must be understood as a creolised cultural identity. For Glissant, creolization is a process of infinite cultural transformation (1992, 142). Central to his conceptualization of creolization is not the celebration of cross-cultural formations but the disruption of the idea that creolization results from a 'mixed' *category* between two 'pure' categories (ibid., 140). Creole identities do not exist between European and African identities. This questions the notion of 'purity' as such. The value of Glissant's conceptualisation for this work is its emphasis on hidden histories of multiplicity, its disruption of 'coloured' as a fixed category caught between black and white, and its emphasis on cultural creation.

One can identify a wide range of coloured cultural 'possessions' and practices – culinary traditions, forms of language, of dance, of hairstyling (Erasmus, 2000c); the appropriation of black American popular musical forms throughout the twentieth century; religious and literary traditions; street carnivals (Constant-Martin 1999), and so forth. None of these practices are universally shared by coloured people nor is any particular tradition hegemonic. But for all that, there is enough of a family resemblance between all these strands to make colouredness a distinctive cultural form.

However, it is not sufficient to characterize coloured identity only with reference to its content. Much of what is distinctive about coloured identity is the condition of its making and re-making. For although all cultures partake of hybridity, coloured culture has been shaped under very specific conditions. For the purposes of this text, hybridity refers to the condition of all cultural formations. Creolization refers to cultural formations historically shaped by conditions of slavery.

The creolization of colouredness is not simply about cultural fusion, connection and contact. It is about the conditions under which such contact is made and how these shape and position the new cultural formation. Coloured identities have been constructed in contexts of domination which have left little room for cultural autonomy and control over self-representations. This has had certain implications. Coloured cultural production has always been precarious and marginal, making it difficult to claim and mark a space powerfully. Coloured self-representations have been shaped by struggles against dominant representations. Glissant describes this evocatively: 'Where the absence of a pre-existing cultural hinterland does not allow people to take cover in a cultural underground and where an autonomous system of production has no longer been maintained, the tragedy begins [...] This is a case of what I call a "cornered community" ' (1992, 103). Cornered communities have had their cultural histories and institutions eradicated. For example, in distinguishing enslaved from persecuted communities, Glissant notes that 'a population that is transformed elsewhere *into another people* [...] has not brought with it, not collectively continued, the methods of existence and survival [...] which it practised before being uprooted. These methods leave only dim traces or survive in the form of spontaneous impulses' (1992, 42).

Coloured identities were constructed out of fragmented cultural material available in the contexts of slavery, colonialism and cultural dispossession. This leaves their constructed and composite historical nature always evident and their dislocation always present. These are identities produced and re-produced in the place of the margin. In this volume, Desiree Lewis further explores the conditions of coloured identity formation and acts of self-representation as revealed in specific literary works by Richard Rive and Zoë Wicomb. She notes that the positioning of colouredness off the boundaries of both 'black' and 'white' leaves it with no authority to draw on the resources of racial discourses for the re-creation of dignity and respectability. Her work illustrates that the institutional and cultural mechanisms in which coloured identities are produced and re-produced are always fragile.

At the same time, as several authors in this collection illustrate, colouredness is not a passive identity. Although marginal, coloured identities are not caught athwart official and hegemonic frames that attempt to define or erase 'coloured'. Instead, people historically classified coloured appropriated and contested these frames. Processes of creolization involve agency. Coloured identities are productive subjective realities shaped and re-shaped by people under the conditions given them by history. In this volume, Crain Soudien's focus on the reconstruction of District Six illustrates how coloured identity can be created and celebrated through a sense of place. In a similar vein, Adam Haupt highlights the agency involved in the process of creolization. This is shown in what he calls the 'counter-discursive' lyrics of *Prophets of da City* and *Brasse vannie Kaap,* and their attempts to rewrite, in the vernacular, the story line of the historical meanings of being coloured and black.

This creativity and agency is an important theme in *Coloured by History*. Coloured identities cannot be wished or explained away. Nor can they be subsumed under a national identity. We have to recognize that constructions of what it means to be 'coloured' have shaped particular black experiences in South Africa in a very real way and that these identities are meaningful to many. This requires respect for ordinary people and their subjective experiences which should be valued in their own right; such experiences and identities are not simply white-imposed. Cultural, class and regional differences in coloured identity formations challenge the argument that these identities are white-imposed. Instead, coloured people have creatively produced their own identities in the context of their relationships to both whites and Africans, as well as their relationships within different coloured communities. These relationships are marked simultaneously by continuity and change.

Acknowledging complicity and living with entanglements

There is, however, an aspect of coloured identity that is not captured by Glissant's characterization of 'cornered community'. Coloured identities were shaped not only by the need to survive and resist on terms dictated by slave-owners and colonizers, but also by the compromises and opportunities that arose in the context of settlers' encounters with indigenous Africans. These identities were shaped by their position in the middle of the colonial racial hierarchy.

Coloured identities are formed in the context of racialized relations of power and privilege. They are not 'merely different' but are formed in hierarchical relation to both white and black African identities; they are experienced and constructed as less than white and better than black. On the one hand, the meaning of being coloured is shaped by the lived experiences of white domination (Erasmus 2000b). On the other hand, it is shaped by complicity with these racist discourses through its creation of an inferior black African Other as one of its 'constitutive outsides' (Laclau 1990, 9) and complicity with the exclusion and subordination of black Africans. This discourse of racial hierarchy and its association of blackness with inferiority is mobilized by coloureds against coloureds as much as against black Africans. For example, dark skin and kinky hair are the markings of coloureds constructed as 'other coloured', inferior or lower class. These excluding relations are reflections of unresolved internal contradictions at the heart of coloured identity formation. Living with these contradictions is part of the pain of being coloured. In this collection, Sean Field's examination of memory, forgetting and the loss of place highlights the racial Othering of black Africans as part of the process of creating coloured selves. Re-imagining coloured identities requires acknowledgement of this complicity.

Having acknowledged complicity, what do those historically classified coloured do about it? We can either try to wipe coloured out of our skins and memories. Or we can try to live with this complicity and work against repeating it. This is neither easy nor comfortable. Glissant's concept of entanglement captures this difficulty. In exploring the available options, he argues that diversion – turning away from the pain and difficulty of creolised beginnings – needs to be complemented with reversion – a return to the point of entanglement, the point of difficulty (1992, 26). Returning to the moment of entanglement entails an emphasis on hidden histories and on memory, and an acceptance of irreducible difficulty. It comes with an awareness that a return to 'roots' in search of a sense of 'original' blackness or any original identity is impossible. In the case of coloured identities, returning entails reclaiming and living with fragments of origins and entanglements with whiteness, Africanness, East Indianness in the process of creating new cultural forms, practices and identities which do not have to be coherent and/or complete. These entanglements often result in multiple and seemingly contradictory engagements with both the past and the present (Erasmus 2000a, 202). The nature of these engagements and the power and pain of living with entanglements allow one to understand coloured subjectivities as encounters with difficulty – encounters which remain entangled with the political history of being coloured. The essays in this collection point to various ways in which coloured identities are encounters with difficulty.

Against authenticity

The decision to acknowledge the act of living with complicity means that all black South Africans have to forgo certain claims, for example, the moral authority based on blackness, Africanness or indigenous-ness. It calls for a new kind of politics premised not on 'who we are' but on 'what we do' with 'who we are'. This means a shift of focus from 'who you are' in terms of fixed categories, and 'what you look like' in terms of skin colour to 'what you do', more specifically, 'what you do' with your identities, and 'where you're at' (Gilroy 1993, 120-145). It challenges the notion that your politics, your alliances and your right to speak can be read off from 'who you are' and/or 'what you look like'.

The power and pain of living with entanglements demands politics based on remembering and living with the wounds of the past, and acknowledging complicity in the present. It demands living with everything one is. In the case of being coloured this includes living with the racist aspect of coloured identity formation and finding ways of changing it. It demands finding ways in which to relate to others from a place of 'truth' rather than a place of denial.

For me it is a 'truth' which defies the safe prison of the dominant ideology: that I ought to identify only as black and not coloured; that coloured identity is an illusion from which I need to be saved by my black sisters who promise to put me on the right road and confer my 'true' blackness upon me; that the former aspect of my identity is best discarded as a relic of the past. I refuse the safety of identifying only as 'black' because it allows me to forget or deny the 'truth' of racial hierarchies between coloured and African and of present privilege, and their significance in the formation of my own identities. The safety of identifying only as 'black' denies the 'better than black' element of coloured identity formation. It denies complicity. It denies the privileges of being coloured. It places engagement in racial relations of power outside of the coloured self. Identifying only as black further expresses a desire for political authenticity. If, however, black political identities are themselves constructions, they too are multiple and marked by internal contradictions. There is no 'pure' black politics. There are no 'pure' black identities. There is no authentic black self.

Closure

The final and most difficult challenge is a re-evaluation of racial relations of power and their reality in our national life in the present. Such reflexive political practice means an acknowledgement of racism(s) as an everyday reality in South Africa rather than an exception, and of racist sentiments as an integral part of every South African self. It further implies a commitment to doing the work required to transform this everyday reality and sense of self. The discourses of rainbow nationalism and politically authentic blackness allow projections of racist sentiments outwards onto traitorous[23] working class coloureds and/or stalwart Afrikaner right wingers. This pathologizes such sentiments and practices creating a different form of Othering which conveniently absolves the black or liberal self from responsibility for and complicity with racism. The challenge for all South Africans is to begin to recognize racist sentiments and practices as part of our everyday reality and the shaping of all our selves. It is to relinquish the desire to leave the past behind and instead, to start processing the past with due regard to the powerful emotional burden which accompanies it: feelings of anger, guilt, betrayal, shame, pain and humiliation. A progressive, transformative politics cannot be based on a denial of the past. The realization that no one South African can claim a moral high ground, that all of us have been profoundly wounded and shaped by the past, is more likely to provide the ground for creating new identities.

Notes

1 Special thanks to Andries du Toit for long, insightful discussions which enabled me to refine the arguments presented in this introduction, and for editorial assistance with this piece. Many thanks to Gail Smith, Zoë Wicomb and Isabel Balseiro for invaluable comments on the first draft of this introduction. Thanks also to Colleen Crawford-Cousins and Robert Berold for moral and writing support during the writing process. Finally, thanks to Marion Wertheim for facilitating my feeling through what it means for me to be coloured.

2 'Boesman korrels' or 'bushman hair' is a derogatory term used to refer to kinky hair.

3 See, for example, Holiday, A. 'Mastering Slave Politics' in *Cape Times*, 25 August, 1995; Legassick, M. 'Slave Mentality', Nuafrica internet discussion group: debate between Legassick, M. and Du Toit A., June/July, 1996; Williams, B. 'The Power of Propaganda' in James, W., Caliguire, D. & Cullinan, K. (eds), *Now that We are Free: Coloured Communities in a Democratic South Africa* (Cape Town, Idasa, 1996).

4 Ali Rattansi is professor at the City University of London. Françoise Vergès is professor at Goldsmith's College, Oxford University.

5 Lueen Conning now goes by the name of Malika Ndlovu.

6 Not all the papers presented at the conference are included in this collection. Furthermore, the chapters by Cheryl Hendricks, Pumla Dineo Gqola and Thiven Reddy were not presented at the conference. These contributors were invited to join the book project after the conference.

7 The terms 'subjectivity' and 'identity' are often used interchangeably. See Mama

(1995) for a critique of the use of the term 'identity', and on the link between gendered and raced subjectivities.

8 The *Kleurling Weerstandsbeweging* (Coloured Resistance Movement) constructs coloured people as an ethnic group and argues for self-determination of coloured people in post-apartheid South Africa. It sees the new government as hostile towards coloured people. Other movements with similar notions of the place of 'coloured' in the new SA include the Brown Nationalist Front and the Coloured Forum, among others. At this stage these movements are marginal in the politics of the Western Cape.

9 The concept of 'hybridity' is contested. The terms 'hybrid' and 'hybridity' are used here to refer to cultural rather than biological hybridity. See Young, R. *Colonial Desire: Hybridity in Theory, Culture and Race* (1995) and Werbner, P. & Modood, T. *Debating Cultural Hybridity: Multi-Cultural Identities and the Politics of Anti-Racism* (1997) for detailed discussions of these terms.

10 See Coetzee (1988) for a detailed analysis of Millin's works.

11 The term 'native' is defined in the Act as 'a person who in fact is or is generally accepted as a member of any aboriginal race or tribe of Africa'.

12 *Sunday Tribune* , 5 February 1983

13 Differential racialisation refers to the various ways in which different black people have been and continue to be racialised. This conceptualisation is based on an understanding of racisms and racialisation as processes which are not uniform and immutable. Racisms and racialised identities are formed in the context of and so shaped by very specific relations of social power.

14 Essentialism is generally understood as a belief in the unchanging and transhistorical true essence of identities. Diana Fuss (1989) brings our attention to the argument that essentialisms can be used as resources for resistance. Essentialist standpoints are inherently neither progressive nor reactionary. Black essentialisms can be understood as positions which advocate one way of being black, a monolithic blackness. Such positions have a totalising function often erasing gendered, and various other ways of being black.

15 Alexander, *Cape Times,* 28 March 1996; Alexander quoted in Fakier in *Cape Times*, 4 December 1996 & *Cape Times*, 11 December 1996.

16 See, for example, Holiday, A. 'Mastering Slave Politics' in *Cape Times*, 25 August 1995; Legassick, M. 'Slave Mentality', Nuafrica internet discussion group: debate between Legassick, M. and Du Toit A., June/July 1996; Williams, B. 'The Power of Propaganda' in James, W., Caliguire, D. & Cullinan, K. (eds), *Now that We are Free: Coloured Communities in a Democratic South Africa* (Cape Town, Idasa, 1996).

17 Ebrahim Harvey, 'Why it's better if the ANC wins the Western Cape' in *Mail & Guardian*, 1-7 December 2000.

18 In the late 1990s Mr Joe Little proclaimed himself chief of a Khoi grouping, the

Hancumqua. He founded the Cape Cultural Heritage Development Council for the purposes of building pride in origin among coloured people through an emphasis on Khoi lineages.

19 Processes of reclaiming Khoi-San history among coloured people are not always based on claims of authenticity and 'purity'. Such processes are often part of a recognition of the fragments which make up the history of being coloured and an acknowledgement of the violence of the colonial encounter.

20 For Glissant, creolization is 'the contemporary manifestation of contact between peoples' (1992,17).

21 For Glissant, '[c]omposite peoples [are] those who could not deny or mask their hybrid composition nor sublimate it in a mythical pedigree' (1992,141).

22 *Cape Times,* 4 December 1996.

23 Wilmot James notes senior political officials claimed that coloured people who did not vote for the ANC in the 1994 elections were 'traitors' (James, 1996, 42).

Chapter One

'Ominous' Liaisons: Tracing the interface between 'race' and sex at the Cape

Cheryl Hendricks

Coloured identity has been an intensely contested South African identity. Located in the interstice of white and black racialized social identities, coloured identity has largely been dismissed as a social construction of the Apartheid regime. In the run-up to the 1994 national elections the identity gained political salience as its bearers began to increasingly reassert particularity and voiced their rejection of an ANC-governed post-apartheid state. This phenomenon led to a flurry of intellectual activity attempting to elicit the nature of coloured identity and its relationship to post-apartheid nation-building processes[1]. Analysts engaged in this inquiry were predominantly preoccupied with the conjunctural moment they were in, that is, the changed social relations of the 1990s, and consequently neglected to address the historicity of coloured identity.

Coloured identity in this chapter is approached through the analysis of the ways in which 'race' and sex intersected in the Cape, especially during the colonial era. By focusing on the discourses and practices that shaped it this approach provides historical depth to the study of the construction of coloured identity. Constructions of coloured identity are intimately linked to the long-established language of 'race'-fixed identities and owe much to the beliefs that emanated from 'scientific' theories formulated in Europe and the New World during the nineteenth century. To gain insights into present expressions of coloured identity, one needs to unpack the processes through which the identity was constituted. This chapter illuminates one aspect of these processes[2].

The representations of those of 'mixed' descent (which is a signifier for coloured identity[3]) are tied to racial and sexual politics. For, to conceive of people as of 'mixed' descent it is necessary to believe in the existence of separate 'races', 'racial purity' and, concomitantly, that sexual intercourse between 'races' – 'miscegenation' – produces a hybrid group. In this regard, Young (1995), analysing hybridity through the interrogation of colonial desire, emphasises that it is mainly by exploring hybridity that the language of 'race' is fully revealed.

In the historiography of the Cape there is a glaring absence of a focus on 'race', sex, sexuality, and their articulation. The dominant portrayal of the colonial Cape is that of a society in which religion, origin, or class, are seen as the primary cleavages.[4] Liberal historiography, which introduced this conceptualization, attributed racism to the Afrikaner's experiences at the frontier.[5] The Cape is posited as having been above the racial politics which materialized in, and characterized, Afrikaner-governed territories in the nineteenth century.

Racialism (imputing a racial essence into an identity) and racism (attaching differential value to 'race'-based identities and treating them accordingly) have been seen primarily as late nineteenth century phenomena instead of as common social practices from the beginning of the conquest of the Cape.[6] Similarly, late nineteenth and early twentieth century 'scientific racism' – typified through eugenics theories – also has been viewed often as an impetus for the development of the racist practices which evolved in South Africa. The acceptance of these premises, which assumed that racialized distinctions, with their corresponding boundary markers and hierarchical valuations, were not prevalent at the Cape prior to this period, implies a view of the construction of coloured identity exclusively as a twentieth century phenomenon. The Cape's colonial history, engraved by Dutch and British imperialism, with practices of slavery and indentured labour, negates this and points to the early use of phenotype and origin (used as signifiers for 'race' categorization) as markers for hierarchically structured difference. The racism that was common currency in the frontier derived from much earlier social thought, policies, and customs prevalent at the Cape and not vice versa. Conceptualizations of inherent differences between groups of people, including that of a differentiated 'mixed race', were carry-overs of metropolitan ideas, contoured by the specificity of the colony. These were the discourses that informed the structure of social relations at the Cape.

Analysts like Lewis (1989), Goldin (1989), and Freedberg (1987) trace the construction of coloured identity to the turn of the twentieth century. Although they make mention of the periods of slavery and enserfment, they gloss over them. Instead, their focus is on the political expression of the identity through the study of the formation of coloured political parties and their reactions to state-building policies and practices. Goldin (1989), in particular, emphasizes the 1904 government census as the harbinger of the classification of coloureds as a separate group. Absent from these analyses is the foregrounding that the formation of coloured political parties, and government classification of coloureds, could only transpire if the identity had a prior resonance. Supporting this argument is the work of Adhikari who points out how slavery assisted in the creation of an embryonic sense of community amongst previously diverse peoples (1992b, 97).

Sex (the biological categorizations of male and female; and coitus/intercourse) and sexuality (as the social construction of sex, desire, body language, etc) have only recently been incorporated into analyses of colonialism. In studies of the history of the Cape a gendered analysis has sprung forth but this is still largely limited to a few feminist historians.[7] Much of this literature is recuperative, that is, bringing women into the narrative, and the explicit link between 'race' and sex and the power relations which underpin these are seldom focused upon. This link, however, is important for understanding not only the form of colonial rule at the Cape, but also for the representations of those of 'mixed' descent.

Racialized representations of sexuality are ubiquitous and have been theorized about[8], but the interaction between racial and sexual politics in the maintenance of colonial rule has been less of a focus. Ballahachet's (1980) and Stoler's (1991, 1997a, 1997b) work on East Asia explicitly deal with this aspect, whilst McClintock (1995) explores the relationship between 'race', gender and sexuality in the securing and maintenance of the imperial enterprise. Ballahachet and Stoler show how the interactions between indigenous communities and colonialists were regulated through various measures of sexual control. Stoler goes as far as asserting that 'the very categories of "colonizer" and "colonized" were secured through forms of sexual control that defined the domestic arrangements of Europeans and the cultural investments by which they identified themselves' (1991, 52). Sexual encounters between Europeans and the indigenous, Stoler contends, threatened the necessary social boundaries which had to be maintained for colonial rule to be a viable exercise. As such, sex became something which had to be administered. The *metisse* reproduced through these encounters posed a particular problem for the colonialists for they straddled and disrupted the demarcated binary social and racial divides (see Stoler 1997a, 1997b and Ballahachet 1980).

These observations prompted this study, which examines the specificity of the Cape colonial experience in order to tease out the relationship between the representations and practices at the Cape and the formation of what is in the mid-nineteenth century labelled coloured identity. The kinds of questions that have directed this work are: did the 'tolerance' of 'miscegenation' prior to the twentieth century signify, as often touted, an absence of racism or was 'interracial' sex officially tolerated for other reasons? What were the shifts in attitudes towards 'miscegenation' and when and why did they occur? How were the Khoikhoi, slaves and the offspring of 'interracial' liaisons represented and governed? To what extent can we trace the constructions of coloured identity to colonial practices of inclusion and exclusion?

This chapter therefore examines the role of, and shifts in, racial and sexual politics in the Cape. In particular it tries to discern the impact of racial and sexual (predominantly heterosexual) politics on representations of those of 'mixed' descent and notes how these representations fed into the construction(s) of coloured identity(ies).[9] The work highlights the fact that racist representations of the indigenous people were prevalent from the beginning of the encounter between whites and indigenous people in the Cape and that racial politics constituted a central feature of the social and economic relations which materialized. An analysis of the interface between 'race' and sex reveals that circumscribed, gender-specific, 'interracial' sex was permitted, even encouraged, as long as it did not destabilize colonial interests. Shifts in the socio-political structure of the Cape, and perceived threats to white identity and white rule, brought corresponding shifts in the tolerance of 'interracial' sex and the closures of racial boundaries. The classification, treatment, and representations of the offspring of 'interracial' unions are indicative of the racialized practices of creating hierarchy and differentiating in order to maintain colonial boundary markers, and, by extension, white rule.

Many individuals whose identities were conferred to them through this process of differentiation often internalised them. This could not have been simply a top down process. People give meaning and content to their identities through lived experiences and become active participants in defining the group's boundaries. Periods of marked social change are often accompanied by the re-presentation of identities as groups attempt to adapt to the new milieu. In this reconstitutive process the aspects of identity representation which no longer hold appeal or capital are reframed, whilst those which are still contextually relevant persist, thereby endowing identity reconstruction with both change and continuity. This can be seen in the post-1994 attempts to reconstruct coloured identity. Here we note how coloured racialization is played down in favour of more culturally based representations which emphasise the indigeneity of the identity.

Early encounters at the Cape

Representations of the indigenous people by travellers passing through the colonial Cape illustrate that racist stereotypes were present from the onset of the European encounter with Africa[10]. These stereotypes utilized sexuality to describe, define, categorize and symbolize the 'Otherness' of the indigenous inhabitants of the Cape. Strother (1999) analysed sixteenth century pictures of the Khoikhoi and observed that it was primarily the representations of the women that were employed to reconcile savage culture with savage form. The Khoikhoi woman's body was used as evidence that they formed the 'missing link' between humans and animals[11]. These gender-encoded racialized representations were bound to inform the colonizers of the Cape of the position held by the Khoikhoi in the colonial hierarchy. Thus the ways in which the Khoikhoi were incorporated into the colonial economy can partly be explained by their characterisation as inferior anachronistic beings.

Travelogues are not innocuous documents containing the written accounts of the meanderings of impartial observers. They were written by 'explorers', often with official status, with the intent of depicting the land and bodyscapes of the territories they encountered, and these travelogues were the source of knowledge through which an imaginary of, for example, Africa, could be produced.[12] Their descriptions both structured and reinforced the dominant representations which Europeans held about the continent and its inhabitants.

The following entries, which are extracts from journal entries in travelogues of the Cape, all cited in Raven-Hart (1967, 1971), highlight the common stereotype of the Khoikhoi as savage and the use of sexuality to accent representations of the indigenous groups:

> As regards the people of the said Cabo de bon Esperance, they are yellowish in colour, like mulattoes, very ugly of countenance, of middling stature, lean and thin of body, and very fast runners, having a very strange speech, clucking like turkeys (op cit 1967, 28). *Joris van Spilbergen* (1601)

> The people who live along this coast ... are very brutish and savage, as stupid as can be and without intelligence, black and misshapen ... They cover their privy parts with the hairy skins of beasts ... (op cit, 47).
> *Pyrard de Laval* (1610)

> The sex organs of the men are large. Yet, they have, it is said, one testicle only ... It is said that by this cutting off of the right testicle they are made more agile and better runners. The women have long breasts, especially the married ones: these they have hanging loose and uncovered, and from them give suck to the child hanging on their back. The lining of their private parts seems to be loose and to hang somewhat. The Hottentots often squat on their heels (op cit 1971,19). *Johan Nieuhof* (1654)

> All the women of the Kaffers ... are so hot-blooded that when they have their menses and make water, if a European pass over it he at once gets a headache and fever, and even sometimes the plague (op cit, 71).
> *Jean-Baptiste Tavernier* (1660)

> ... but I swear to you, that he who could not keep his hands off these anointed ones must have a murderous knife [penis] (op cit, 109).
> *Arnout van Overbeke* (1668)

> It is also noteworthy that the men have a member surprisingly longer than that of Europeans, so that it resembles the organ of a young bull than that of a man. So also the females are something exceptional in this respect, and by many are taken for hermaphrodites, because of a supra membrum genital [apron] a hanging flap a quarter ell long, like a wattle of a turkey's beak.

> The reader must not take it amiss that I reveal such secrets of nature, nor ask how I could examine them so closely, since this is contrary to polite usage. [...] Since also they are extreme lovers of the noble weed nicotine or tobacco, these charming females will show an inquisitive and salacious amateur everything that he may ask for, for a pipeful of tobacco (op cit, 204). [13]
>
> *George Meister* (1677)

Within these citations we note the varied ways through which an essence is attributed to the Khoikhoi, i.e., beast-like, disease-ridden, lascivious, and so forth. Inherent difference is constructed through a focus on language, the body, and perceptions of cultural practice. The 'clucking like turkeys' conveys a 'state of nature' associated with animals for, as Strother notes, language 'marked the frontier separating humanity from beasts' (1999, 3). The use of the turkey as comparison comes up frequently within the seventeenth century Cape travelogues and is not innocent or happenstance. The turkey was exported into the rest of Europe and North America in the mid-sixteenth century, from Turkey, and therefore represented a new, exotic yet simultaneously grotesque, bird. The word turkey was also used to describe someone as stupid or inept. Thus the metaphor is employed to convey the image of the Khoikhoi as abhorrent and asinine.

In these Eurocentric gazes there is a fascination with the body of the Khoikhoi. Pratt, analysing the work of Barrow, noted his description of the 'body as seen/scene' and that in the text the genitals became the 'crucial site/sight in the "bodyscape"' (1985, 139). Gilman (1985) and Sharpley-Whiting (1999) also powerfully illustrate the ways in which sexuality became a salient marker for racial difference. The body was, and still is, a text for Othering both racially and sexually. In the above extracts the focus is on the 'abnormalities' of the genitals of the Khoikhoi and this, together with depictions of perverse sexuality, is meant to confirm their racial difference. In Tavernier's account we see how it is particularly Khoikhoi women who are perceived as disease-ridden and able to contaminate Europeans. These are early signs of the development of the discourse on black women's sexuality as infectious that gained widespread currency in the mid-eighteenth and nineteenth centuries. McClintock (1995) has detailed the long tradition of the use of gendered metaphors by explorers and the 'gendered erotics of knowledge' produced, with Africa and the Americas becoming the 'porno-tropics' for the European imagination. Hence, by the nineteenth century when the 'scientific' discourse on 'race' ensued, there was already a well-established body of thought, with concomitant practices, on what was seen as the inherent differences between groups of people.

The 'scientific' discourse on 'race' was therefore influenced and reinforced by the representations of difference emanating from the colonial encounters, especially in the Cape. Dubow notes that the 'position and status of the "Hottentot" figured prominently in the great classificatory schemes of eighteenth-century science' (1995, 22).

Many of the classificatory scientists had worked in South Africa and the 'Great Chain of Being' was premised on their self-referential representations of the Khoikhoi as situated at the nadir of the chain. The exhibition of Sara Baartman, in London and France, in the early nineteenth century, was to bring 'home' and display the 'proof' of centuries of othering and confirmation of the superiority of European body, culture and intellect.

A central concern of those studying and classifying 'races' from the eighteenth century into the early twentieth century was the question of 'interracial' fertility, cast in the debate between polygenesis versus monogenesis theories. The fertility of 'interracial' unions became abundantly evident in the colonies, and polygenesists (Long, Nott, Gobineau, Spencer, and so forth) contended that the hybrid product was a new species ('race') with inherently degenerate qualities. Within these conjectures it is also the mulatto woman's sexuality which is registered as deviant and used to confirm difference.[14]

'Interracial' sex, and those born from these liaisons, have a long history of denial. The silences on sexual encounters between Europeans and the Khoikhoi in the travelogues point to the repugnance associated with 'interracial' sex. Young (1995) elaborated on the ambiguity between colonial desire and repulsion and how this impacted upon representations of the Other. Given the negative imagery with which travellers invested the sexuality of the Khoikhoi, it would have been damning to admit to any sexual liaisons. These liaisons, however, did take place and after colonization the sexual interactions became more frequent not only with the Khoikhoi but also with the slaves brought to the Cape. Those of 'mixed' descent born in the Cape, both prior to colonization and during it, were therefore representative of the encounter between Europe and Africa. The visibility of their body-politic would carry the shame which Europeans bestowed on the relationships. People of 'mixed' descent were differentially situated in the racial hierarchy occupying an interstitial space which was valued for its conferred advantages – gained because of an approximation to whiteness, yet despised for its association with 'bastardization/hybridity' in a world that came to privilege 'authenticity/purity'. This shame, with varied and shifting dimensions, is one which has undergirded the social fabric of coloured identity and accounts for the ambivalence associated with it.[15]

'Race', sex and slavery

The Dutch East Indian Company (DEIC) settled at the Cape in 1652 with the aim of establishing a refreshment station for ships en route to the East. From the 1670s a free burgher population began to occupy land granted to them by the DEIC, creating a settler class: a situation which simultaneously led to Khoisan land dispossession.

From the beginning of colonization of the Cape slavery became the chief source of labour. Slaves were shipped in from Madagascar, Mozambique, Angola, the Indonesian Archipelago, Bengal, South India and Sri Lanka. The mix of indigenous Khoisan, slaves from different continents, Europeans (from France and the Netherlands), together with the constant stream of European sailors passing by, made the Cape, in the seventeenth and eighteenth centuries, a racially and culturally diverse colony. Contrary to other slave-based colonies the slave population in the Cape was heterogeneous, differing in origin, religion, culture, and phenotypical features. These differences mutated through the centuries, but they left their mark on present Cape society.

The literature on slavery in the Cape[16] indicates that in the colony slaves from East Asia were readily distinguished from those coming from the rest of the African continent, and locally born slaves (creoles) were differentiated from those who were imported. A further subdivision took place within the creole category as those with European ancestry were set apart from those who had none. Colonialists, especially the slave owners, stereotyped slaves according to their origin, a distinction which largely overlapped with racialized features: East Asian slaves shared physical traits associated with whiteness (lighter complexion and hair being dominant signifiers), the features of slaves from the African continent largely corresponded with those commonly and stereotypically associated with the black body while the body of slaves of 'mixed' descent marked their hybridity. There was a discernible colour-based continuum of physical features amongst slaves, differences which were further culturally encoded. East Asian slaves were simultaneously valued as skilled artisans and seen as thievish, dangerous, and insubordinate . Many of the women of this group were employed in the household and engaged in cooking and needlework. Slaves from the African continent (i.e. beyond South Africa) were relegated to doing the menial task of working the fields. Creole-born slaves were stereotyped as being more dependable (no problems with runaways) and those of 'mixed' descent (which commonly only denoted a white and black admixture) were especially sought after: they were purchased at higher premiums and given the more supervisory-oriented jobs whilst the women were incorporated as domestics into the settler households.

Shell suggests five reasons why creoles were the most expensive and most preferred slaves: (1) for epidemiological reasons they lived longer than imported slaves; (2) they included the mulatto slaves whose high values pushed up all other creole prices; (3) the creole slaves, whose first language tended to be patois, were viewed as natural overseers; (4) they were viewed as the least likely to run away, commit crimes or rebel; and, (5) the owners of a creole slave had to bear the costs of rearing the child. Shell further notes that Cape slave owners were willing to pay a premium as high as 43% for creole slaves of possible European descent (as opposed to up to 7% for other slaves, depending on origin). The value of creole slaves also increased after the ban on the importation of slaves in 1808 (Shell 1994b, 25).

From the inception of the Cape's colonization there were racialized vertical differences – whites as colonialist/settlers/slave owners, that is, constituting the ruling class, and blacks as slaves[17]/enserfed. Within the black category, as mentioned, there were further distinctions – providing for the heterogeneity of black experiences which continues to the present day. 'Race' constituted a primary cleavage within the slave period, differentiating master and slave, colonialist and subjugated, while origin, which overlapped with phenotypical features (a key component for racial distinctions), differentiated the slave population internally.

Colonialist logic operated on the basis of inclusion and exclusion which further necessitated the policing of racial boundaries through the maximization of social, and especially sexual, distances between groups. However, conditions in the Cape made the social transgressing of racial boundaries a necessary inconvenience for the settlers. Nevertheless, this situation was not as free flowing as is often presumed in the literature. On the contrary, various restrictions, both normative and administrative, were implemented to negate the blurring of the racial boundaries. The rest of this section deals with one particular type of boundary crossings – sexual liaisons; it analyzes why they occurred and the attempts by colonialists to regulate them.

There was a gender discrepancy in the settlement patterns of the Dutch-occupied Cape. Shell notes that only a few hundred white women were imported by the DEIC compared to the several thousand male employees of the company and the even more numerous male settlers. Also, between 1652 and 1808, more than 15 000 slave women were imported into the Cape (1994a, 290). This variance meant that white men had to seek other avenues to satisfy their libidos. Black slave women were used for this purpose – with all the associated power differentials this alludes to. Stoler makes a similar observation for East Asia, noting how the DEIC restricted European women from immigrating to the East by

> selecting bachelors as their European recruits and by promoting both extra-marital relations and legal unions between low-ranking employees and imported slave women. Although there were Euro-Asian marriages, government regulations made concubinage a more attractive option by prohibiting European men with native wives and children from returning to Holland. (1991, 58)

The DEIC appeared to encourage sexual liaisons between white men and black women, among lower class employees, as long as this did not impinge upon its rule. In Cape Town, up until the eighteenth century, the slave lodge served as a brothel where white males, both resident and transient, could satisfy their urges.

The company introduced half-hearted measures to maintain social distance between the 'races'. In 1678 they issued a proclamation forbidding all kinds of concubinage and, in 1681, forbade Europeans to attend parties with slave women or to enter the company's slave lodge. These measures were seldom strictly enforced (see Elphick and Shell 1989, 194). This situation echoes Ballahachet's observation that, in colonial India, the provision of facilities for sexual intercourse between British soldiers and indigenous women and the simultaneous discouragement of these relations were both geared to the preservation of the colonial power structure (1980, 9).

Officials turned a blind eye to 'miscegenation' at the Cape, not because they were non-discriminatory, but because it suited their interests. It created an outlet for the sexual desires and loneliness of their lower class employees, without adding the financial burden of having to import and support European women, and at the same time reproduced the labour supply needed at the Cape. The free burghers were also keen on 'miscegenation', especially after 1808 when the importation of slaves was prohibited – making the self-reproduction of slaves the only legal way of acquiring new labour. Many slave owners actively went about reproducing their own labour force by copulating with their female slaves or hiring male studs. Female settlers were not innocent bystanders to this process. Shell (1994a, 295) notes the practice, dating to before 1770, of having courtesan slaves, as settler women allowed their female slaves to live with European males. Their form of tribute was the ownership of the children begot from such liaisons. Shell also notes how female slaves were thrust upon casual visitors to the Cape by their female owners. 'Race' and class therefore mediated the sexual subordination of women in the Cape and 'interracial' sex became part of a business venture, propping up the colonial economy.

Whilst tolerating 'miscegenation' the colonists had to be careful to maintain the social boundaries between black and white. The hybrid offspring of the sexual exchanges between white men and black women (whether forced or free-willed) – and note the gender and 'race' specificity, for the same set of practices/standards did not apply to sex between black men and white women – would present a problem in that they held the potential to straddle racialized social boundaries. The uterine descent rule was used to limit this possibility as it posited that the children of slave women inherited the legal status of their mothers – thereby maintaining the social distance between colonialist and slave. Those children born to Khoikhoi mothers, although not considered to be slaves, lived in virtual slavery for they were bonded to the employer of their parents for a period of service in lieu of the supposed costs of bringing up the child. The uterine descent rule was a form of control designed to retain the slave population and to relinquish the white father's parental responsibility. This is similar to slavery in the United States where the status of the mother became the determining factor for the fate of the mulatto child. This was a departure from traditional English law which stipulated that a child's status was determined by the father.[18]

Another form of sexual control was the prohibition of slave marriages. Only free persons could marry, hence if a white man wished to marry his black lover, and/or assume parental responsibility for his children, he would have to purchase their freedom. Here the likelihood would have been that mostly lower class DEIC employees would have considered the possibilities of marriage but their financial ability to do so would have been limited. Heese estimates that between 1660 and 1705, 191 Germans married or lived with women who were not 'pure-blood' Europeans; of the 191, 114 were Cape-born, 29 Bengali, 43 were from other Asian regions and only five were Madagascans or Africans (cited in Elphick and Shell 1989, 197). Ross (1979, 429) estimates that between 1657 and 1807, 480 women of apparently black descent married into the white population. Apparently only six marriages occurred, during this time-frame, between black men and white women. This statistic is not surprising as black men in all slave societies were severely punished for any presumed liaison with white women. White women were also usually viewed as mentally insane if they fraternized with black men. Two things are striking about these statistics: firstly, there were very few marriages which took place, and, secondly, approximation to whiteness seemed to be an important component of the marriages. Women of 'mixed' descent and women from East Asia were preferred as marriage partners.

Social norms also played their part in restricting the number of marriages. It is most likely that black spouses were frowned upon and thus not easily accepted into the white social milieu. Shell (1994a, 323-324) cites how Cape settler women were embarrassed by these marriages and, quoting Lady Anne Barnard, illustrates the ostracism experienced by black women who married white men (a class component would have been present here). The preference for lighter skinned blacks could partly be attributed to this for it was easier for them to pass as white. Women of 'mixed' descent may have had preference for marrying white men as this was one of the few means for social mobility and/or escape from slavery.

The Cape in the seventeenth and eighteenth centuries was therefore a profoundly 'race'-based society. Sex intersected with 'race' to produce what was labelled a person of 'mixed' descent – or more colloquially – a bastard or *van die Kaap* – denoting their creole status. Colonial society preferred the crossing of social boundaries to be temporary and sought to exclude the products of those unions from entering the white social stratum. Colonialists seemed to have a schizophrenic attitude towards those of 'mixed' descent – not accepting them as white, yet reluctant to have them simply become part of the broader black populace (the indigenous Khoisan and other black slaves). Hence the constant differing of those of 'mixed' descent, positing them as 'in-betweeners'. People of 'mixed' descent therefore occupied an ambiguous position right from the inception of colonial formation. Their interstitial space, materializing because of the contexts into which they were born and bolstered by the discourses which legitimized the social relations and gave a fixity to racial categorizations, persisted into twentieth century attempts to define who was/is coloured. However, the social space of the Cape in the twentieth century had been radically altered and coloured became a marker of difference between Cape blacks and those of the interior.

Proletarians, prostitutes, and degenerates

The British briefly occupied the Cape from 1795 to 1803 and then returned in 1806. Under British rule the Cape saw the ushering in of Ordinance 50 of 1828, which abolished the restrictions placed on Khoikhoi labour mobility, and the emancipation of slaves in 1834 (actualized in 1838). The idea of the liberal Cape is partly due to these Acts for they, along with the colour blind, though gendered, qualificatory franchise measures of 1856 and 1872, introduced the conception of equality before the law. By the time of emancipation the Khoikhoi were a landless displaced group, in a similarly impoverished structural position as the ex-slaves. Given the qualificatory nature of the franchise very few blacks were able to exercise their newly granted civil liberties: they were 'free to be poor' as Van Der Ross (1986) remarked. Hence, much the same set of structural relations between white and black persisted[19].

Ordinance 50 and the Abolition Act exacerbated the existing tensions between the British and Boers and partly contributed to the Afrikaners' Great Trek into the interior in the mid-nineteenth century. An often made assertion is that the harsh experiences of the Boers during the Great Trek – their wars with the Africans, the hostile physical environment they had to conquer, their isolation from the 'modernist' forces in the centres of Cape Town and Grahamstown – together with their Calvinist beliefs and their sense of the natural superiority of Christianity, were the basis for the racist ideologies and practices which emerged in the republics they established. 'Race' based practices, however, emerged at the onset of colonial rule and certainly did not disappear with the arrival of the British. The distinctions between the 'liberal Cape' and the 'oppressive Afrikaner republics' is often overdrawn; though there were undoubtedly differences in policies and practices the overarching aim, and end result, was the maintenance of white supremacy.

Racial discrimination and de facto segregation were defining features of Cape society from the early years of colonialism. The formal institutionalization of racial segregation in the Cape in the early twentieth century was partly introduced to control the large-scale urbanization of blacks which was taking place at the time. Swanson (1977) shows how the imagery of infectious disease was utilized to campaign for residential segregation in the Cape in the early twentieth century, resettling Africans (who had been coming to the Cape in large numbers since the 1870s) into townships located on the outskirts. The image of blacks in general as diseased/contagious is one that emerged from Europe's initial encounters with Africa and which persisted in South Africa in mutated forms during the nineteenth and twentieth centuries. The regulation of prostitution was symptomatic of this way of thinking.

Similar to that which Ballahachet (1980) describes in the case of India, prostitution was institutionalized, and thereby regularized, through the Contagious Disease Act of 1868. The Act, primarily used as a device to provide clean prostitutes for British soldiers (in the context of the fear of the decimation of British soldiers through the spread of venereal disease), was a means of policing sex for it required all prostitutes, who were predominantly women of 'mixed' descent, to register themselves. Prostitution was viewed as a necessary evil and a 'safeguard to our public morals, while a protection to the chastity of our matrons and virgins' (see Van Heyningen 1984, 173). It was only with the influx of continental prostitutes (white women) into the Cape that measures were taken to limit prostitution. It was not just the sight of white women prostituting themselves that caused alarm, but the idea that they were being used by black men. In 1901 the Attorney-General, T.L. Graham, stated in the House of Assembly that,

> There were certain houses in Cape Town which any Kaffir could frequent, and as long as he was able to pay the sum demanded, he could have illicit intercourse with these white European women. This was a matter of the gravest importance, for once the barriers were broken down between the European and native 'race's in this country, there was no limit to the terrible dangers to which white women would be submitted, particularly in isolated places. (cited in Van Heyningen 1984, 192)

The discourse no longer centred on prostitutes as a source of contamination, but on the abuse of, and dangers to, white women. The prohibitions on prostitution were implemented to protect the racial boundaries. Black men sleeping with white women were viewed as a potential threat to the status quo, but the use of black women by white men was viewed as an evil necessity which could be managed.

Eugenics theories also placed the spotlight on 'miscegenation', utilizing the symbolism of contamination. These theories pointed not only to the existence of separate 'races', but, more significantly, to the degeneration of the white 'race' which occurs with 'miscegenation'. 'Miscegenation' was not only seen as morally despicable but as endangering the very survival of the white 'race'. Poor whites were viewed as the visible symptom of the decay of whites in general (see Dubow, 1995). Dubow states that '"interracial" sex was indeed held to sap the fibre of white civilization at its most susceptible point by undermining race "pride" and "purity"' (1995, 180).

Eugenics theories reinforced pre-existing notions that the products of 'interracial' sexual unions were qualitatively different from either of their parents, i.e. that they were inferior hybrids. People of 'mixed' descent were envisioned as being degenerate in both physical stature and social calibre. There was a pervasive belief that one's moral and physical attributes were inscribed in one's blood and passed on intergenerationally. As highlighted by Coetzee, one's social make-up was seen as derivative of one's biological make-up and blood was seen as defining 'the inherited social status of the individual by flowing supratemporally through him [her] and all his [her] blood-ascendants and descendants [...] In this perspective, the individual is simply a carrier of the life of the family or caste or race' (1988, 146). These ideas can be seen in the then popular literary works of Millin (1924, 1951), Plomer (1926, 1984), etc. Millin's work is filled with the imagery of the flaw in the blood of those of 'mixed' descent. People of 'mixed' descent are deemed almost pathological and can never transcend their flaw.

These portrayals of coloureds have had a deep resonance in society and have contributed not only to their Othering, but also to the shame associated with the identity. It also accounts for the obsession by middle class coloureds, especially in the first half of the twentieth century, to act civilized (which usually meant imitating white norms, values and conduct); they were engaged in a constant battle to prove to whites that they were capable of living up to white standards and that, by virtue of this, they should receive the same kinds of rights and privileges.[20] They became, in Bhabha's (1994, 86) conception, the 'reformed, recognisable Other [...] that is almost the same but not quite', inhabiting a space and identity embedded in ambivalence.

The acculturation of coloureds along with their racialized difference was used by the state to distance them from Africans rather than to posit similarity with whites. The consolidation of the nation state in the aftermath of the Anglo-Boer War, as Marx (1998) has outlined, was achieved among other things through a racially bounded citizenship. It became politically imperative to demarcate clearly and maintain the boundary between white and other identities. It is in this context that laws were introduced to prohibit 'interracial' sex: the Immorality Act in 1928, and Mixed Marriages Act in 1948. These Acts formed key components in the 'purification,' unification and consolidation of white identity in South Africa. Unlike in the United States where the 'one drop rule' fixed the classification of who was black, in South Africa, coloureds were officially treated as a separate category. Demographics would largely account for the difference. In South Africa Africans constituted a majority and whites therefore needed to reinforce a buffered identity between a largely 'bi-racially' envisaged conflictual socio-landscape.

This coloured identity could be imagined because of centuries of differential 'race'-based discourses and practices and could be fixed through the control of 'interracial' sex (of all groups), racial distribution of resources, and a congruence between 'race' and space.

Conclusion

This chapter has highlighted the interface of 'race' and sex in the Cape and the kinds of representations and politics this engendered. It has asserted that from the inception of colonialism social relations in the Cape were racially differentiated and that the control of sex had been an important part in the maintenance of a racial hierarchy. 'Interracial' sex produced a large group of people constructed as being of 'mixed' descent and racist discourses defined them and delineated the spaces they would occupy. The alterity of those of 'mixed' descent, as inferior to whites and superior to Africans (though the latter is ambiguous for a tension always existed between the proclaimed superiority which the taint of white blood conferred on 'mixed' descent peoples versus the 'purity' of descent/blood ascribed to Africans), has a long history and it is the resonance of 'difference' which enabled the political mobilisation and realisation of an ethnic consciousness in the twentieth century. Though racism accounts for the initial impetus in constructing coloured identity, the shared historical and lived experiences of coloureds have shaped coloured identity into one which transcends the mere sharing of phenotypical features and which will not simply fade with the removal of 'race'-based policies and practices.

Notes

– I wish to thank Desiree Lewis for earlier comments on this chapter.

1 See, for example, the collection of papers in *Now That We Are Free: Coloured Communities in a Democratic South Africa*, Wilmot James (ed.), et al (1996); William Finnegan, *The Election Mandela Lost* (1994); Simon Bekker *Rainbow nation dream or nightmare?* (1997); Y. Fakier, *A debate coloured by 'race'* (1996); M. Ozinsky and E. Rasool, *Developing a Strategic Perspective for the Coloured Areas in the Western Cape* (1993); Robert Mattes, *The Election Book* (1995) and numerous surveys conducted by, for example, the Human Science Research Council, Institute for Democracy in South Africa, Marketing and Media Research, and so forth.

2 See Hendricks (2000) for an analysis of these processes.

3 The term 'coloured' was introduced into the Cape's official lexicon in the mid nineteenth century as an embracing term for the colony's black populace, many of whom were of 'mixed' descent. In the twentieth century, 'in-breeding', rather than 'interracial' sex became the dominant form through which the group reproduced itself.

4 A notion carried through in more recent writing, for example, Marx (1998) as well as a more subtle variant of this line of thinking in Shell (1994). Keegan, T (1996) and Reddy (1995) are notable exceptions, highlighting 'race' as a marker of difference in the colonial formation. Scully (1995 and 1997) is one of a few scholars analyzing the intersection of 'race' and sexuality in the Cape colony.

5 Macmillan (1927), De Kiewiet (1942), Macrone (1937) were the forerunners of this liberal historiography. Marxist historians also ignored 'race', seeing class as the explanatory variable for the persistence of racial practices.

6 Appiah (1992) provides a useful distinction between the two concepts.

7 See, *Kronos* No. 23, November 1996 for examples of feminist attempts to incorporate gender into colonial historiography. Scully (1997) is also a good example. Shell (1994), a male writing on slavery at the Cape, includes gender into his analysis but this is mainly quantitative.

8 See, Sander Gilman (1985), Anne-McClintock (1995), T. Denean Sharpley-Whiting (1999), and so forth.

9 Multiple constructions of coloured identity have simultaneously co-existed. This chapter focuses on the constructions by the metropolis/colonialists.

10 See, Pratt (1985) for an instructive account of the 'othering' which transpired in the early travelogues on Southern Africa.

11 The exhibition of Sara Baartman centuries later produces the same imaginary.

12 See, Bratlinger and JanMohamed (1985). Pieterse (1990) is useful for an elaboration of images of blacks in western popular culture.

13 I am aware of the critique against reproducing these negative colonial images. However, I still feel that in order to decode the discourse of the day, one has to provide the reader examples of the texts one is alluding to. It is not the mere reproduction thereof which is problematic, but how one uses or analyzes the particular texts.

14 See, Brathwaite's (1971) citations of Long.

15 Wicomb's work, 1987 and 1996, eloquently deals with the aspect of shame.

16 Shell, Ross, Elphick and Giliomee, Eldredge and Morton, and so forth.

17 There were a few free, largely impoverished blacks. But, their existence does not negate the overall structure.

18 See, Russell et al, *The Color Complex*.

19 Bickford-Smith notes that in 1875 there were 2 988 whites considered to constitute the bourgeoisie and only 316 blacks. If one looks more closely at the latter category then 'the socially successful become even paler' (1995, 23).

20 The African Political Organization, a coloured political organization formed in 1902, became an instrument through which the middle class dictated how coloureds should behave thereby shaping coloured culture at least a part thereof, mediated by class.

Chapter Two

'Slaves don't have opinions': Inscriptions of slave bodies and the denial of agency in Rayda Jacob's 'The Slave Book'[1]

Pumla Dineo Gqola

> Whiteness, like blackness, is neither pure nor monolithic. It must be seen as a racialised identity, if only in terms of the advantage that being white brings to it.
> *Marie Helene Laforest*

> Writing entails many areas: control of the word, control of the image [...], control of information, and, perhaps as important, control in the production of the final product.
> *Marlene Nourbese Philip*

Rayda Jacobs named her second novel *The Slave Book* (1998) after the legal document that registered the ownership, and any changes thereof, of slaves. This text positioned slave identities solely according to whose property they were. Drawing extensively on recent historical writings on slavery in South Africa[2], her project is an attempt to explore the terrain of slave experience and subjectivity. She posits this novel as 'a scratch at the surface' since representations are always constructed and therefore partial.

Jacobs's novel can be read in the context of the project of (re-)memory that has been increasingly embraced by creative writers in attempts to imagine the lives about which there is little historical record. These writers engage in the project of (re-)memory to supplement dominant interpretations of history. Recording history has been predominantly the preserve of the conqueror and it is this condition which has been conventionally sanctioned as paramount and universal. Through the process of reduction and distortion, a partial history has been disseminated so that significant European moments and experiences retain 'a potent grip on our imagination' and thus remain readily available.[3] These well-documented moments are presented in the dominant historiography as the most generally applicable and significant times in human history. Attempts to locate the corresponding evaluations from the perspective of the Other within History[4] pose a challenge since 'racism is especially rampant in places and people that produce knowledge'. This racism manifests through 'the narrow spectrum of reality that [the dominant] select or choose to perceive and/or what their culture "selects" for them to "see"'.[5]

In the case of colonial slavery the faces of the oppressed are 'blanked out' and the masters' history is posited as the definitive history of humanity while the Other registers as either absent or objectified.[6] Representations of enslaved peoples in traditional history mirror their physical treatment in colonial slavocratic[7] societies. Slaves were configured as wanting in culture and therefore in humanity or subjectivity. Their objectification followed directly from their dehumanisation and these processes jointly ensured the stereotype became the dominant way through which slave reality is read and interpreted by the Oppressor.[8]

One of the most pervasive ways in which slaves were objectified in the discourses which supported and maintained this insidious institution is through a representation of slaves as a singular undifferentiated mass. Elleke Boehmer observes that representations of the Other within colonial slavery

> offered important self-justifications. For what is body and instinctual is by definition dumb and inarticulate. As it does not itself signify, or signify coherently, it may be freely occupied, scrutinized, analyzed, resignified. This representation carries complete authority; the Other cannot gainsay it. The body of the Other can represent only its own physicality, its own strangeness.[9]

In this sense it is important to stress that the pride of place accorded to the objectification of the racial Other in European imperialist culture is inherent to the intellectual traditions of that culture. History is a fiction which requires constant re-interpretation and revision in order to free the events of the past from 'the veil of prejudice and illusion that shroud them'.[10] Destined to supplant the experience of the Other, this History necessitates an alternate view attentive to the multiple vantage points through which events are recognised.

Reliant on Levi-Strauss's approach of H/history as simultaneously concerned with content, audience and ideology, Hayden White centres the processes of reduction and distortion in the practice of H/history-making:

> The fact is presented where and how it is in the discourse in order to sanction the interpretation to which it is meant to contribute. And the interpretation derives its force of plausibility from the order and manner in which the facts are presented in the discourse. The discourse itself is the actual combination of facts and meanings which gives to it the aspect of a *specific* structure of meaning that permits us to identify it as a product of one kind of historical consciousness rather than another[11] [emphasis in original].

The slave experience has been obliterated from History through writing and in that sense it is the pen that re-presents slave life. This writing, which is a function and expression of memory and reconstruction, symbolically frees these enslaved people from the oppressive ideological controls forced upon them. This use of memory contributes to a social history where the slave is re-humanised and invested with subjectivity.[12]

The creative writer's project of memory, however, remains a work of the imagination. It presents possibilities and makes no absolutist claims since the writer is not attempting to record factual data in the same manner that historians purport to. The project of memory is influenced extensively by historic events and indeed draws extensively from historical accounts. However, it seeks to present possibilities as they could have been played out in various lives at an identified historical juncture. As creative texts they offer the writer the ability to imagine and invent aspects of a life which was possible at the given moment in history (Durix 1998).

The challenge to represent slaves imaginatively is one that needs to be sensitively confronted since these writers do not wish to cast their slave characters in ways which reshackle them. What is necessary if writers are to invent credible and artistic literature is an 'attempt at a sincere imaginative perception that sees [the life being portrayed] as having a certain human validity'[13], in order for the characters to transcend the denial of complexity in flat characterisation which is the 'dialectical equivalent of the anonymity to which the oppressive systems consign millions of oppressed Africans'.[14]

Interpretations of history and re-imaginings of that past are not without ideological influence. In what follows re-membering is interpreted as 'a constructive process as opposed to a retrieval process'[15], underlining the writer's *active* participation in the construction of a historical memory.

According to Njabulo Ndebele, writers involved in this project should direct themselves to the challenge of 'rediscovering the ordinary' since this focus on individual lives is more important in creative ventures than a focus on the larger events and how these impact on people at various historical junctures. For Ndebele (1994) then, creative writing which focuses on the lives of those written out of traditional history should provide the reader with insight into the multiplicity of ways through which people live and the circumstances under which they make meaning of their lives. When writers focus on the nuances of the everyday their characterisation is engaging to the reader because it avoids stereotypical and simplistic portrayals. It necessarily explores various possible eventualities.

From Ndebele's argument above, it therefore follows that the projects of memory and rediscovering the ordinary are well suited to creative representations of slave lives, because it moves away from 'an epistemology [...] conceived purely in terms of a total polarity of absolutes'.[16] The project of memory unsettles the representation of slaves as a single undifferentiated mass by naming individual slaves and exploring their various experiences.

In *The Slave Book* Rayda Jacobs has 'searched for the humanity in history and found it'. She believes her stories have given a voice to the voiceless, to the indigenous people 'almost pushed off the end of the earth'.[17] It is clear then that Jacobs partakes in the project of (re-) memory, a project increasingly embraced by creative writers in attempts to imagine the lives about which there is little historical record. Toni Morrison argues that (re-)memory necessitates a *willed* creation, in which 'the point is to dwell on the way it appeared and why it appeared in that particular way'.[18] This is echoed by Homi Bhabha who has written of re-membering as an arduous putting together of historic fragments self-reflexively to better grasp the influence of the past on present hierarchies and their resultant traumas (Bhabha 1993).

This chapter seeks to examine ways in which Jacobs's narrative engages with the objectification of slave bodies pervasive throughout Dutch colonialist writings in the Cape. I examine how Jacobs's language of characterisation configures the slave body, centring more specifically on the representation of the 'coloured' slave, Somiela. Focusing on narratorial inscriptions of the body, I analyse the variety of ways in which slave bodies are presented, paying particular attention to the configuration and explorations of 'miscegenation' amidst discourses of 'racial purity' and geography. I probe Jacobs's treatment of bodies and use of stereotype attentive to literary representations of the 'coloured' body in literature. Finally I ask whether her usage of stereotype is in accordance with Trinh T. Minh-ha's hypothesis that 'to use stereotypes in order to attack stereotypes is [...] an effective strategy, for irony here needs no lengthy explanations or rationalisations',[19] in her treatment of both 'mixed race' and 'black' slave bodies.[20]

Jacobs's novel details the lives of several slaves in the nineteenth century Cape. It focuses specifically on a romantic relationship which develops between a slave woman, Somiela, and a free man, Harman. Somiela's mother was raped by her previous owner and as a result of this we are informed that Somiela is fair enough to be mistaken for a white woman at least once. Harman lives as the white son of an Afrikaner farmer. However, he is revealed to have been born of a Sonqua woman and therefore to have been labelled the Dutch Sonqua. That both Somiela and Harman look white even though each has a Black mother is central to the development of their relationship.

Centring on the dynamics of slave relationships and community, the novel examines the positions which slaves occupy in relation to slaveowners and one another. While their relationship to slaveowners is mediated by the gradations of skin tone, geographical origin and religious background, the effect of these factors on the relationships between the slaves themselves is portrayed as minimal.[21] Jacobs's slave characters are drawn from the entire slave spectrum which made up the slave communities in the Cape on the eve of abolition.

Slaves on each farm were often drawn from diverse geographical origins.[22] According to Andries de Villiers, the man who buys Somiela and her stepfather, Sangora, 'to have [slaves] all from the same part of the world, speaking the same language, was asking for trouble. You mixed up the races to avoid mutiny.'[23] The slaves on Andries de Villiers' farm are Khoi, South Asian and East African. This variety was essential to the policing and regulation of slave life.

Objectification is a form of representation and 'stereotypes function as a means of social control and repression'.[24] Attitudes to 'mixed race' slaves were recorded by historians such as G. M. Theal, on the eve of manumission, who argued that these were 'deserving of freedom, but the change was not beneficial to "pure blacks"'.[25] While all slaves and Black people were seen as inferior, it is interesting to note that the writings of the nineteenth century demonstrate quite clearly the existence of a hierarchy based on pigmentation. Given that freedom was synonymous with whiteness, attitudes to the offspring of Black and white people were often contradictory. Whereas attitudes such as the one articulated by Theal did circulate, it was not uncommon for 'mixed race' bodies to be a source of resentment because they were clear evidence of 'miscegenation'.

If the body of the Other is silenced and cannot be told, in colonialism, outside colonial signification, it holds true that for the postcolonial narrative, 'technique [...] is inseparable from the exploration of human perception'.[26] Additionally, Stuart Hall suggests that identity is constantly under construction and therefore contested and in flux. Corporeal inscription is central to the constitution of identity in colonial slave societies. In Jacobs's text the body of the Other receives extensive attention and this necessitates an exposition of the ways in which this body configures stereotypically in colonialist discourse. Social hierarchies are stamped on the bodies of the Other to identify and define them and their position in the ordained social order. Reading the manner in which bodies are constructed, therefore, especially in a novel which places so much emphasis on the appearance and relevance of the Other's body, reveals some of the ways in which these hierarchies are constituted, particularly with reference to the 'coloured' *body*.[27] This chapter is mindful that corporeality has social significance, since bodies are inscribed and re-inscribed, and is an examination of how Rayda Jacobs's chooses to inscribe Somiela's body.

Vernon February identifies the stereotype of the lazy, weak 'Hottentot, who was wiped out by the smallpox epidemic in the eighteenth century, or who drank himself to death'[28] as a pervasive trope extensively articulated in literary representations of 'coloured' South Africans. The Khoi are represented in colonialist discourse as noble savages prone to fighting, South East Asian slaves as aspiring to whiteness, adept at witchcraft, and West African slaves feature conspicuously as promiscuous, violent and threatening.

Jacobs explores current knowledge about the slaves' natures, linked in colonialist thinking in the eighteenth and nineteenth century Cape to their respective places of origin. In *The Slave Book* the central characters, Somiela and Harman, are located as 'coloured' and this becomes crucial to Jacobs's narrative where responses to 'miscegenation' are explored and whiteness as a 'pure' racial category is deconstructed. This is a concern to which Jacobs returns repeatedly in her literature and which forms the central thread of her first two published works, *Eyes of the Sky* (1996) and *The Middle Children* (1994).

We encounter Somiela for the first time as she, her mother Noria and stepfather Sangora are to be placed on the selling block under the slave tree in Cape Town. Noria pleads with Andries de Villiers, a wine farmer, to buy her entire family as the narratorial frame shifts to focus on each of the bodies to be sold. Sangora is described as 'tall and husky' with 'wild hair' scarred ankles from chains and 'an intense face, defiant' (13). Somiela is described as 'too handsome' because she is not 'the same hue as her mother, and has a tawny complexion, with green eyes and brown hair; a half-breed. The half-breeds were the favoured slaves, and the price for both mother and daughter would be high' (16). Noria, whose 'colourful dress and shoes spoke of respectability, and although she was black as any Madagascan, the smoothness of her hair and features told him that she was also Malay' (15-16), is bought by a doctor since Andries does not heed her plea.

As we glimpse the horror and sadness experienced by the three family members upon their separation, we are also invited to view Andries' reading of Somiela's body primarily for her potential childbearing abilities. From the onset, she is interpreted by him as 'a beauty that surely shouts to be tamed, who could help in the kitchen with his children and perhaps [...] increase the slave population on the farm'.[29] Andries further surmises that his wife, Marieta, will disapprove of the purchase of a white-looking slave. When Marieta meets Somiela, Andries' suspicions are confirmed. Marieta imagines Somiela's body as sexually promiscuous. Martinus Kloot, their daughter Elspeth's fiancé, is unable to stop himself remarking: 'A fine looking thing' (25). It is in response to this fascination from both Martinus and Andries that Marieta calls Somiela a *naaimandje*, a slut (25). Somiela's light skin gesticulates to her position as the offspring of Noria and the man who, as Somiela recollects from her mother's words, 'had brutally taken her against her will' (115). However, she is stamped with the blame for 'miscegenation' and held responsible for the repercussions of white male abuse of power. While for Marieta all slave women 'come easy' (104), Somiela's fair skin sees her labelled as more promiscuous than the 'black' female slave. Thus fair-skinned slaves, who bear the mark of 'miscegenation', exist contradictorily as both the most prized and the most reviled. Under these circumstances, Somiela is at times described and celebrated by those characters viewing her precisely because of her fair skin. For instance, when Andries de Villiers considers whether to buy Somiela as she, her mother Noria and stepfather Sangora stand on the auctioning block, his thoughts pertaining to Somiela are presented as follows:

> The girl wasn't of the same hue as her mother, and had a tawny complexion, with green eyes and brown hair; a half-breed. The half-breeds were the favoured slaves, and the price for both mother and daughter [Somiela] would be high (16).

Even Rachel, the slave who works in the kitchen at the de Villiers household and acts as a surrogate mother for Somiela, is not immune to the association of whiteness with beauty. This is clear when she thinks to herself, after observing Somiela for a while, and warning her about the possibility of abuse that slave women face at the hands of white masters, 'The girl was too attractive for her own good' (114).

The projection of promiscuity onto the Black female body is well documented since 'one of racism's salient features has always been the assumption that the white man – especially those who wield economic power – possess an incontestable right of access to black women's bodies'.[30]

Indeed Jacobs's novel is filled with references to the regularity of the rape of slave women and some of the ways in which this is justified in the racist discourses of the early nineteenth century.[31] Upon her arrival at Zoetewater, Andries de Villiers' wine farm, Marieta de Villiers asks her husband: 'What good will she be except to cause havoc amongst the males?' (25). Somiela is assumed to be even more sexually accessible than darker-skinned slave women are. Later on in the same conversation Marieta remarks: 'We can see all right what she is. A *naai-mandje*' (25).

Marieta, who is complicit in the white supremacist patriarchy, which inscribes the Black female body in this manner, punishes Somiela in accordance with the myth of promiscuous slave sexuality, even when faced with obvious evidence to the contrary. Returning from a visit to a neighbouring farm, Marieta arrives in time to witness Somiela's humiliation by Andries who demands that she wash him. As she stumbles upon the scene, Marieta notes that her husband registers clear enjoyment of this act. Marieta's decision to burn Somiela reads as an attempt to alter the inscriptions on Somiela's skin, which she reads as threatening. If '[t]he sexual dimension of slavery has been well documented by historians, and it is an undercurrent lurking beneath the surface of the novel',[32] it becomes important to *name* this undercurrent. Somiela's approximation of whiteness positions her as one who is in competition with white women for the attention of white men. Marieta's perception of Somiela's body is unsurprising since,

> [s]ystems of racial oppression depend upon the notion that one can distinguish between the empowered and disempowered populations. Those boundaries that demarcate racial difference are best policed by monitoring the congress between members of opposite sexes of opposite races. Yet the bodies of mixed-race characters defy the binaries upon which constructions of racial identity depend. Signs of the inescapable fact of miscegenation, they testify to the illicit or exploitative relations between black women and white men or to the historically unspeakable relations between white women and black men. The light-skinned black body thus both invokes and transgresses the boundaries between the races and the sexes that structure [colonialist] social hierarchy.[33]

Somiela embodies a transgression that could not be taken lightly if the socially rigid distinctions between free and unfree were to be maintained. Consequently, Somiela is violated twice: sexually by the slaveowner Andries and then scalded by his wife Marieta. Her body becomes the terrain upon which the tensions between white women (represented here by Marieta and Elspeth) and white men are played out: a battleground. These tensions showed the contradictions between the anxiety created by 'miscegenation' and its actual pervasiveness in the nineteenth century Cape.[34] The imagined marker of sexual permissiveness on the body of Somiela is indicative of the stereotyping of ('coloured') slave women's bodies as a means of justifying their repeated violation as a form of control. It stems from an unwillingness to recognise the subjectivity and humanity of the slaves. The regulation of the slave body was essential to the success of slavery and through its policing it was 'marked, scarred, transformed, and written upon or constructed by the various regimes of institutional, discursive, and non-discursive power as a particular kind of body'.[35]

The inscriptions seek to establish a controllable, malleable body which is a constantly violated body as,

> [s]lavery relied as much on routine sexual abuse as it relied on the whip and lash. Excessive sex urges, whether they existed among white men or not, have nothing to do with this virtual institutionalization of rape. Sexual coercion was, rather, an essential dimension of the social relations between slavemaster and slave. In other words, the right claimed by slaveowners and their agents over the bodies of female slaves was a direct expression of their presumed property rights over Black people as a whole. The licence to rape emanated from and facilitated the ruthless economic domination that was the gruesome hallmark of slavery.[36]

Jacobs's novel underlines the threat posed by Somiela's light skin and its possibility to blur the distinction between Black/slave and white/free in the scene where

> [s]he realised, walking in the street with these shoes, that they affected the way in which passers-by regarded her. Some people even greeted her. Then she realised something else. Some of these people thought she was white. White! Why else would they greet her? Almost unconsciously, she straightened her shoulders, and kept her head more erect as she continued up Wale to Long Street, where she turned left, walking slowly to browse, scan, and look into all the windows (251).

Somiela, whose body allows for her being mistaken for white, is read as such when she is seen wearing shoes. This is particularly so when the 'right' to wear shoes belonged to the free only and slaves were barred from this attire. Jacobs draws constant attention to the ways in which Somiela is viewed by those around her, and the narrative is peppered with their comments on her looks. Her beauty approximates to that which is held as the white ideal in the nineteenth century, the period of the novel. Consequently, the novel conflates her skin tone with an evaluation of her beauty.[37] Of white hostility to Somiela's light skin, Rachel, the slave who works in the kitchen, notes,

> Don't you see? You're a threat to her. You're a slave and you dare to look white, dare to have straight hair, green eyes, and then have the cheek to open your mouth. Slaves don't have opinions. They stand with their mouths shut and take it.[38]

The threat to which Rachel alludes concerns Somiela's ability to transgress boundaries of colour which distinguish between free and enslaved. The ability to approximate whiteness is a '*potentially* subversive activity'[39] [emphasis added]. The only other characters described in a similar manner are Arend, himself the child of Rachel and a French man, and Harman, the Dutch Sonqua.[40] In Jacobs's novel, the aesthetically pleasing character is characterised by 'mixed' parentage and is labelled by Harman as 'not one, not the other. In the middle somewhere' (142/3). It is this *perceived* unbelonging which makes such characters dangerous and attractive because they are seen to embody traits associated with both the coloniser/slaveowner and the colonized/slave.

For instance, about Somiela, we are told: 'The girl was too attractive for her own good' (114) and 'She's handsome for a slave' (136). Similarly when Harman announces to his brother Martinus his desire to marry Somiela, the latter responds,

> [t]hat girl is something to look at, don't think I haven't noticed. *One would never say what she was.* But what will it bring you? Grief. Rejection by your own people. No one will accept you. In the end you're alone with a house full of unbaptised children. You've just been here a few months. This is the first girl you've seen. There're others. Of the same ilk, language, and God. Don't be unequally yoked (188) [emphasis added].

Not even Harman is immune to the fact of her parentage. Declaring his love for her, he locates himself too within this paradigm of difference, arguing that he is attracted to her because she is not 'common' like the other slaves; that she is 'different from the others', 'mixed race' like him. This category of inbetweenness is evoked repeatedly in the novel and it is through this discourse of desirable hybridity thanks to its 'proximity to the "norm" of whiteness'[41] that Somiela is primarily defined. It is also the bond which she shares with Harman even as she chooses to refute it when she says, 'perhaps if you didn't know, you wouldn't waste your time with me. Perhaps you think you are tainted' (142).

However, he asserts his pride in his genealogy and again stresses their similarity. This assertion is nonsensical because his body is read as white and free, while hers gestures (in the main) Black slave. The scene where Somiela accidentally 'passes' for white can be seen as questioning the meaning of whiteness as a 'racially pure' category in the same manner that Harman and later their daughter do. It reveals the arbitrary discursive construction of the rules which inscribe the bodies of slaves. While Somiela, Salie and Harman are all 'coloured', in Jacobs's novel the implications of their racial origins are different. The assumption of heightened sexual desire and availability is gendered, so that although racially Somiela and Harman (as well as Salie and Arend) are inscribed similarly, the sexual associations attach themselves only to Somiela, the female slave. Her decision to challenge this through the cutting of her hair is circumscribed by this dynamic. However, even when he chooses to resist the connections between 'race' and social positioning, Harman's ability to 'cross cultural boundaries and expose [...] the reactionary ethics of De Villiers'[42] is protected; his 'ancestory does not doom him to social rejection, it is not suspected by those who would object'.[43]

Harman's resistance, initiated by his defence of the Koi-na,[44] distances him from white privilege and he is forced to leave the Karoo for the coastal Cape. It is an exercise of choice of the same kind which sees him marrying Somiela and converting to Islam. Forewarned by various people, he is aware that his actions may lead to his complete alienation from the privileges granted to him in white society as a member of the Kloot family. It is ultimately because he refuses to inhabit the proscribed privilege of white normality that he is killed a year after his marriage to Somiela when he imagines it is safe to return home to his family's farm in the Karoo. He assumes that he has been forgiven for his defence of the Koi-na against the African(d)ers a few years earlier. This return proves to be a miscalculation as he is killed as punishment for siding against his 'own' people. After Harman's death, Somiela returns since she is no longer at home in the Karoo. Back at the Cape, Somiela marries Salie. She loses contact with her and Harman's daughter, who integrates into white society. Somiela's and Harman's realities remain divergent for Harman remains socially a white man, free to act in ways which please him, while, as a slave, Somiela's body is constantly under control. Even when one considers that Harman is ultimately killed for acting as he pleases, there is still room for him to choose to act in a variety of ways prior to this incident. Therefore, although ultimately the consequence of *one* of Harman choices is death, as a free man he is entitled to choices and therefore their consequences. For Somiela, as a slave, any evidence of the existence of a will is heavily policed in a slavocratic society. For, as Rachel repeatedly announces, 'slaves don't have opinions' and are therefore not permitted to express agency. Somiela's own interactions with the de Villiers family bear testimony to this.

In Jacobs's narrative Harman points to the widespread existence of 'Black blood' in 'white Afrikan(d)er blood', even as this community defines itself by notions of 'racial purity' and supremacy in distinction from Others. The shame around 'miscegenation' is explored repeatedly in relation to the Kloot family, whether it is through the suppression of the 'coloured blood' in the family, outright denial, or some children passing for white and cutting family ties. The fear of visible traces of Blackness, however, remains prominent as even Harman's father warns of the consequences of marrying a slave woman because 'Black blood's a funny thing. You never know when it will surface' (137). The implication is that its presence is best hidden, repressed and unacknowledged like the 'Black blood' in the Kloot family tree which remains shrouded. In his steadfast desire to inhabit marginal spaces, Harman seems to identify marginality as

> much more than a site of deprivation [...] is also a site of radical possibility, a space of resistance. [It is a] central location for the production of a counter-hegemonic discourse that is not just found in words but in habits of being and the way one lives.[45]

While Somiela in her enslavement is not free to act it is important to avoid reading her purely as a blank text inscribed wholly by the discourses of the slavemaster class. For there are ways in which she reflects, responds to and deflects some of these attempts to define her. When Marieta and Elspeth attempt to erase her beauty, by confiscating her clothes, covering her in unflattering attire and cutting her hair, it is an attempt to make her less desirable. As Rachel remarks, 'Elspeth felt threatened. The slave had a beauty you had to be born with. Elspeth wanted to shame her, make her look ugly, take away the little that she had' (32).

Somiela continues to speak where a slave should not, challenging the language in which she is represented, as well as the meanings attached to her life. In an indeterminate move she cuts her own hair shorter to look like a boy (102) and there is speculation on the farm about whether she had done it to make herself look ugly. This unresolved ambiguity simultaneously suggests the contradictory possibilities of resistance and self-hatred. The act foregrounds her agency even as it motions to internalised self-hatred finding expression through self-mutilation.

Somiela's body is not the only one which is described in detail. Andries's thoughts on the various places of origin of his slaves betray his confidence in his ability to inscribe them with characteristics which he can then utilise.

> He had slaves from Malabar and Ceylon, and to have them all from the same part of the world, speaking the same language, was asking for trouble. You mixed up the races to avoid mutiny. And the Malays were a sly lot, taking

> every opportunity to rebel. They were not as suited for field work as the Mozambiquans and Madagascans. His prize negro, Kananga, captured by a Portuguese slaver off the coast of Mozambique, was an excellent *mandoor* (14).

Because he is able to catalogue these meanings onto their bodies, since as objects they are deemed his property, his interpretation of their bodies carries complete authority, backed by the institutional power of slavery. In her exploration of hybridity within whiteness and Blackness, Jacobs unsettles the binaries upon which colonial representation is premised, and thus appears to be making the point that 'racial purity, like language purity, is a fallacy'.[46]

However, as the brief analysis which follows reveals, it is only her characters of 'mixed race' parentage who are endowed with the ability to subvert and resist colonial inscriptions. Elleke Boehmer has argued that:

> In colonial representation, exclusion or suppression can often literally be seen as 'embodied'. From the point of view of the coloniser specifically, fears and curiosities, sublimated fascinations with the strange or the 'primitive' are expressed in concrete physical anatomical images. The seductive and/or repulsive qualities of the wild or Other, and the punishment of the same, are figured on the body, and as body. To rehearse some of the well-known binary tropes of postcolonial discourse, opposed to the colonizer (white man, West, centre of intellection, of control), the Other is cast as corporeal, carnal, untamed, instinctual, raw, and therefore also open to mastery, available for use, for husbandry, for numbering, branding, cataloguing, description or possession.[47]

In Jacobs's *The Slave Book* representations of 'coloured' characters challenge, albeit in very limited ways, the manner in which colonial inscriptions have structured these bodies. This is particularly seen in Somiela and Harman, who both offer subversive readings of their bodies by challenging the ways in which they have been located and defined in colonial slavery. However, the representations of other Black bodies in her narrative echo colonial representations of the body of the Other.

The body of Kananga, the Mozambican slave, is marked with animal sexuality which is framed as bordering on animal behaviour. Indeed, the narrator and the other slaves repeatedly refer to him as an animal, as unfeeling, and so forth. What is perhaps most troubling for the narrator and the community of the novel is that Kananga is attracted to younger male slaves whom he rapes repeatedly. He is responsible for sexual assaults on young male slaves, a fact to which the other slaves are privy. Thus although 'Hannibal had fought against it and cried out for help, [...] everyone shut their eyes and ears to his pleas. To interfere was to find themselves face down in the mandoor's mattress' (53). Whilst the slaves are willing to challenge the slaveowner periodically, they are too frightened of the overseer, Kananga, to come to the aid of Hannibal while Kananga rapes him. Kananga appears throughout the narrative 'with his hand down the front of Petroos's pants', as one who 'hardly ever washed himself or his clothes, and [consequently he] gave off a powerful odour of rotting onions' (55), and his abusive pursuits are seen as random.

Having been inscribed as the brutal overseer, described often as animalistic, perpetrating random violence and controlling the other slaves with his penis and whip in equal measure, his body bears the burden of being characterised in the manner in which slaveowners usually exert their control. Because he assaults young men, however, it is unclear whether the condoned behaviour is the violence, his sexual orientation, or both. This is precisely where the character of Petroos, the slave perceived as 'corrupted' by Kananga into homosexuality – of whom we are disapprovingly told, 'he'd never had these inclinations when he first arrived at the farm five years ago, Arend said, but now he acted just like a woman, as Sangora could see from that silly laugh he had, and the way he waived his arms when he talked' (53) – complicates the narrative.

It becomes clearer that Kananga's influence on Petroos is 'corrupting' and that while Petroos is the 'victim', he nonetheless is inscribed with some of the blame. The manner in which he inhabits his body is read as inappropriate by the other slaves because he inscribes himself 'feminine' in their readings of femininity and masculinity as fixed and diametrically opposed positions. The binaries of male/female and slave/free are unsettled through Somiela and Harman only to be reintroduced in Kananga and Petroos. The latter pair is framed primarily sexually, where Kananga is additionally inscribed with 'savage' disregard for the other slaves. These inscriptions of 'black' male slave bodies as bursting with sexuality regurgitate colonial emblems of the Black male body. Kananga further uses his B/'black' penis as a means of control and is therefore firmly and comfortably able to inhabit colonial markers of his body. Framed like this, '[h]e is turned into a penis. He is a penis.'[48] He is caught in Jacobs's narrative in a manner which ensures that for the reader '[c]onsciousness of the body is solely a negating activity'.[49] This is especially the case seeing as Jacobs reinscribes the bodies of his slaves in a manner which closely resembles colonial inscriptions of the Other's corporeality.

The narrator pays minute attention to the physique of 'black' male slaves in a manner resonant of colonial travel writing, which dwelt on parts of the body of the Other in an attempt to catalogue the various 'species' in southern Africa, but also in the rest of the 'new' world. For instance, of Tromp we are told that he was 'a thin, dark-skinned slave with tight, wiry hair, grey at the temples' (97). Geduld, the Khoi slave, is willing to be enslaved at Zoetewater since he repeatedly asserts, 'I can leave anytime I want' (58). He is 'a little hunter, a pleasant little fellow' (58), 'the little hunter [...] the warm brown eyes, the small, round head with tight balls of hair' (83).

These paternalistic descriptions perpetuate the stereotype of the Khoi as willing slave, represented here in the figure of Geduld, who, like his name, patiently endures slavery even though he 'can' flee. This character undermines the severity of enslavement because he implies that he is not forced into slavery, but can flee whenever he chooses to. One of the most central tenets of slavery is the denial of freedom (choice) and the humanity of the enslaved. Geduld's implying that he *allows* himself to be enslaved gives fuel to the assertions of slaveowners about the minor suffering in slavery, since, as Harman announces in response to Andries' conflation of the identities of 'slave' and 'worker', '[n]o slave is ever content' (106).[50] Perhaps the most illuminating of Jacobs's corporeal descriptions is the detailed description of Gumtsa, the *bosjeman*, as,

> the apricot-skinned hunter. Gumtsa didn't walk like most men. Dressed in his little leather flap, the quiver with the six arrows on his back, a digging stick in his right hand, his sturdy little buttocks lifted left, right, left, right, as he trotted at a half run, his small feet hardly touching the sand. That's how they did it through the desert, he said, covering long distances. A bosjeman learned to walk very fast when the sun burned down on his head and water was two days away. Silence preserved the last juices left in his body (199).

These descriptions, found in Jacobs's novel, duplicate those used to inscribe the body of the Khoi in much eighteenth- and nineteenth-century travel writing in the era of scientific racism. Careful focus on the body and colour, and the paying of particular attention to whether the Khoi could be classified as human at all, became the order of the day, and genitals became the loci of the colonial gaze. This preoccupation with the Other's body became a discursive weapon and when Jacobs reiterates and uses the words and techniques of this era to name the bodies of her characters she is reinscribing the colonial power and foregrounding this as the primary and sole manner in which these bodies can be inscribed.

Thus, testifying to the wide range of sources she has consulted and on which she bases her creative text and her imagination of slave society on the eve of manumission, she colludes with the representations of the 'black' body as savage and uses some of the tools which engendered its mutilation and control. Jacobs admits that her novel is her attempt to 'recreate and inform', but in leaving some colonial inscriptions unproblematised she allows them entry into a potentially subversive space where re-membering slave subjectivity is explored. For while Jacobs frees the 'coloured' character from racist inscription in South African literature as 'God's step-children' doomed to social rejection, this unshackling remains flawed and incomplete. If the novel and recent historical writings reveal that 'almost all coloureds in SA are descended from slaves',[51] then, as February eloquently demonstrates, various stereotypes of the Other at the Cape combined to form contemporary (literary) 'coloured' stereotypes.

Even if Jacobs's claim of merely scratching the surface is to be used in her defence, her fixed characterisation of 'black' bodies considerably undermines the laudable manner in which her work unsettles and undermines the socially rigid constructions of whiteness and opens up 'coloured' bodies in literature for complex signification.

Notes

1 Some of the findings in this chapter were presented as part of 'Reading Slave Bodies: Memory and Representation of Slave Subjectivity in Selected Twentieth Century Literature', MA Dissertation, University of Warwick, 1999.

2 She acknowledges several sources in her preface, among them Robert C.H. Shell. 1994. *A Social History of the Slave Society at the Cape of Good Hope, 1652-1838.* Johannesburg: Witwatersrand University Press; Robert Ross. 1983. *Cape of Torments: Slavery and Resistance in South Africa.* London: Routledge & Kegan Paul; several articles by John Edwin Mason, Susan Newton-King, Christopher Saunders and, Wayne Dooling.

3 Wilson, James. 1998. *The Earth Shall Weep: A History of Native America.* London and Basingstoke: Picador. p. 17.

4 Hayden White distinguishes between officially sanctioned history (History) which details the exploits of the powerful, and a more inclusive record of events (history).

5 Anzaldua, Gloria. 1990. 'Haciendo Caras, Una Entrada: An Introduction', in her (ed.). *Making Face, Making Soul, Hacienda Caras.* San Francisco: Aunt Lute. pp. xv-xxv (p. xix, and xxi).

6 See Saunders, Christopher. 1988. *The Making of the South African Past: Major Historians on Race and Class.* Cape Town and Johannesburg: David Phillip; and February, Vernon. 1981. *Mind Your Colour: The 'Coloured' Stereotype in South African Literature.* London and Boston: Kegan Paul.

7 I use 'slavocratic' here in accordance with its extensive usage by scholars of Caribbean, South African, North and South American chattel slavery. In this body of scholarly work, where it has acquired general usage, it refers to the power system which defined slave societies with the European masters/slave owners at the top of the hierarchy and African and South Asian peoples at the bottom rung as slaves/property. The control and regulation of these societies is invested in/with the slaveowners who are able to maintain their lives and profits from the labour and exploitation of the chattel slave population.

8 Or, in the emphatic words of Michele Cliff. 1990. 'Object into Subject: Some Thoughts on the Work of Black Women Artists', in Anzaldua, Gloria (ed.). *op cit.* pp. 271-90 (p. 272).

[t]hrough objectification – the process by which people are dehumanized,

made ghostlike, given the status of Other – an image created by the Oppressor replaces the actual being. The actual being is then denied speech; denied self-definition, self-realization; and overall this, denied self-hood – which is after all the point of objectification. A group of human beings – a people – are denied their history, their language, their music. Their cultural values are ignored. This history, this language, this music, these values exist in the subculture, but in the dominant culture only certain elements are chosen, recast, co-opted and made available to the definition of these people. And these elements presented by the dominant culture tend to serve the purpose of objectification and, therefore oppression.

See also hooks, bell. 1992. 'Representing Whiteness in the Black Imagination', in Grossberg, Lawrence, Cary Nelson and Paula Treichler (eds). *Cultural Studies*. New York & London: Routledge. pp. 338-346; and Hambidge, Joan. 1998. 'Roman Gee 'n Stem aan die Geskiedenis se Stilgemaaktes', *Rapport,* 6 December. p. 18.

9 Boehmer, Elleke. 1992. 'Transfiguring: Colonial Body into Postcolonial Narrative'. *Novel: A Forum for Fiction* 26 (1). Fall. pp. 268-277 (p. 270).

10 Dubois, Dominique. 1998. 'Wilson Harris's "Infinite Rehearsal" '. *Commonwealth* 21(1). Autumn pp. 37-46 (p. 38). This is a similar task to that which Gyan Prakash in his, 'Writing Post-Orientalist Histories of the Third World: Perspectives from Indian Historiography', in *Contemporary Studies in Society and History.* pp. 383-408 (p. 407), posits as the challenge of 'post-foundational' historiography, since, '[t]he power attributed to the knowledge about the past makes historical writing into a political practice and turns the recent post-Orientalist historical accounts into contestatory acts'.

11 White, Hayden. 1978. 'Historicism, History and the Figurative Imagination'. *Tropics of Discourse: Essays in Cultural Criticism.* Baltimore: John Hopkins University Press. pp. 101-119 (p.107).

12 See George Lamming's 'Concepts of the Caribbean' and Dionne Brand's 'No Language is Neutral', both in Frank Birbalsingh (ed.). 1996. *op cit.* pp. 1-14 and pp. 120-137.

13 Ndebele, Njabulo. 1994. *South African Literature and Culture: Rediscovery of the Ordinary.* Manchester: Manchester University Press. p. 25.

14 Ndebele. 1994. p. 28.

15 Halbwachs, Maurice. 1992. *On Collective Memory.* ed. and trans. by Lewis A. Coser. Chicago and London: Chicago University Press, p. 30. See also Van Vuuren, Helize. 1999. 'Puik Roman oor Slawe Tref met Uitbeelding'. *Die Burger* , 7 April p. 9.

16 Ndebele, 1994, 60. See also Figueroa, John J. 1986. 'The Relevance of West Indian Literature to Caribbean People Living in Britain'. *The Caribbean Europe: Aspects of the West Indian Experience in Britain, France and the Netherlands.* ed. by Colin Black. London: Frank Cass.

17 Crocker, Jen. 1999. 'A Look into the Metaphorical Fire: The Interview', *Cape Times*. 22 January, p. 14. See also Hambidge, Joan. 1999. 'Roman Gee 'n Stem aan die Geskiedenis se Stilgemaaktes', *Rapport*. 06 December, p. 18; and Van Vuuren, Helize. 1999. 'Puik Roman oor Slawe Tref Met Uitbeelding', *Die Burger*. 07 April, p. 9.

18 Rushdy, Ashraf . 1998. 'Daughters Signifyin(g) History: The Case of *Beloved*', in *Toni Morrison*. ed. by Linden Peach. London: Macmillan. pp. 140-153 (p. 140).

19 Trinh, Minh-ha T. and Annamaria Morelli. 1996. 'The Undone Interval', in Iaian Chambers and Lidia Curti. eds *op cit.* pp. 3-16 (p. 13).

20 Throughout this chapter I use *Black* inclusively. My usage of 'coloured', 'mixed-race' and 'black' are strategic in order to discuss intra-Black differences. I am mindful of the ideological problematics attached to each usage and my usage of quotation marks for each draws attention to the danger of fixing these categories and even of referring to them in the precise labels I resort to. The label 'black' as put to use in this chapter refers to people who are not assumed socio-historically to be of 'mixed' ancestry, 'coloured' and 'mixed-race' refer to those who socio-historically have been assumed to be of 'mixed racial origin'.

21 The Mozambiquean slave, Kananga, is one exception to this. His relationships with other slaves will receive attention later in the chapter.

22 The Dutch slaves were captured variously from South East Asia, India and East Africa. These were first brought to the Cape to work on wine farms in 1658, after the enslavement of the Khoi between 1652 and 1658, and continued to be abducted from the same areas headed for the Cape until the eve of manumission.

23 Jacobs, Rayda. 1998. *The Slave Book.* Cape Town: Kwela. p. 14.

24 February, Vernon. 1981. *Mind Your Colour: The 'Coloured' Stereotype in South African Literature.* London & Boston: Kegan Paul. p. vi.

25 Quoted in Saunders, Christopher. 1988. *The Making of the South African Past: Major Historians on Race and Class.* Cape Town and Johannesburg: David Philip. p. 27.

26 Ndebele, Njabulo. 1994. *South African Literature and Culture: Rediscovery of the Ordinary.* Manchester: Manchester University Press, p. 73.

27 Or, in the words of Anzaldua, Gloria. 1990. 'Hacienda Caras, Una Entrada: An Introduction', in *Making Face, Making Soul, Hacienda Caras: Creative and critical Perspectives by Feminists of Color.* ed. by Gloria Anzaldua. San Francisco: Aunt Lute, p. xv:

> 'Face' is the surface of the body that is the most noticeably inscribed by social structures [...] we have different surfaces for each aspect of identity, each inscribed by a particular subculture. We are 'written' all over, or should I say, carved and tattooed with the sharp needles of experience.

28 February, Vernon. 1981. *Mind Your Colour: The 'Coloured' Stereotype in South African Literature.* London & Boston: Kegan Paul, p. 19. Since the Khoi and the San were randomly labelled 'Hottentot' and 'Bushman' and there exists no collective term

indigenous to these nations, to distinguish them from the other indigenous nations which have been labelled the 'Bantu'. Hence postcolonial references to them are plagued with problems of naming.

29 Eichenberger, Beryl. 1999. 'The Review: *The Slave Book*', *Cape Times*. 22 January, p. 6.

30 Davis, Angela Y. 1982. *Women, Race and Class*. London: Women's Press, p. 175.

31 For example, Marieta asserts, 'Slave women, they come easy' (104). For other expressions of this, see p. 115, 103, 114, 115, 122, 135, 142, 144, 146, 160, 178, and so forth.

32 Robert Plummer. 1999. 'Fascinating and Unexplored Slice of our History', *The Sunday Independent*. 07 March, p. 17.

33 Smith, Valerie. 1998. 'Class and Gender in narratives of Passing', *Not Just Race, Not Just Class*. New York and London: Routledge, pp. 35-62 (p. 40).

34 See February, Vernon. 1981. *Mind Your Colour: The 'Coloured' Stereotype in South African Literature*. London and Boston: Kegan Paul; Saunders, Christopher. 1988. *The Making of the South African Past: Major Historians on Race and Class*. Cape Town and Johannesburg: David Phillip; and Elphick, Richard. 1985. *Khoikhoi and the Founding of White South Africa. Johannesburg: Ravan.*

35 *Grosz*, Elizabeth. 1995. *Space, Time and Perversion: Essays on the Politics of Bodies* (New York and London: Routledge, p. 33.

36 Davis, 1982, p. 175. In *The Slave Book*, several characters, both enslaved and free refer to the regularity with which slave women are raped by masters. There are also few references to consensual sexual relations between slaves and white men such as in the case of Rachel. However, incidents of the latter are cited far fewer times than those of the former.

37 In the novel, the aesthetic value of characters is explicitly mentioned as tied to and only after a lengthy description of the fairness of the character being described. Descriptions which conflate fairness with beauty are used repeatedly in reference to Arend, Somiela, Salie and Noria. For examples see, among others, pp. 25, p. 33, 59, 90, 104, 114, and so forth.

38 Rachel says this to Somiela after repeated warnings and advice on how to stay out of trouble with the de Villiers family. Somiela responds, 'I won't take it, I won't!' (33)

39 Smith, 1998, p. 36.

40 Harman, who eventually converts to Islam, is the son of a Dutch farmer, Roeloff Kloot, and a Sonqua woman, Zokho. He successfully lives as a white person with all the accompanying benefits until he and Somiela choose to pursue a relationship, whereupon he declares his racial status.

41 agarwala, shelly. 1999. 'A Literary Politics of Reinscription: Embodying and Transforming the Subject in Toni Morrison's *Paradise*', Unpublished Paper, p. 5.

42 Jones, Tim Trengrove. 1999. 'From the Outside Looking Back to the Present, *Sunday Times*. 25 April, p. 20.

43 Plummer, 1999, p. 17..

44 Harman comes across a scene where several Afrikan(d)er farmers from the Karoo are laying a trap which will enable them to ambush some Koi-na: 'It was an old ploy, killing game and leaving it for the hunters to find, only to attack them while they were eating' (41). Harman chooses to fight on the side of the Koi-na, injuring a farmer and a horse. Shortly after this he flees from the Karoo, where his family lives.

45 hooks, bell. 1991. *Yearning: Race, Gender, and Cultural Politics*. London: Turnaround, p. 149

46 Anzaldua, Gloria. 1990. 'En rapport, In Opposition: Cobrando cuentas a las nuestras', in her. ed. *Making Face, Making Soul, Haciendo Caras: Creative and Critical Perspectives by Feminists of Color*. San Francisco: Aunt Lute, pp. 142-150 (p. 146).

47 Boehmer, Elleke. 1992. 'Transfiguring: Colonial Body into Postcolonial Narrative', *Novel: A Forum for Fiction*. 26.1. Fall, pp. 268-277 (p. 269).

48 Fanon, Frantz. 1986. *Black Skin, White Masks*. London: Pluto, p. 170.

49 Ibid, p. 110-11.

50 For an overview of some of these arguments about the severity of slavery or lack thereof in the Cape, see Thomas Pringle's introduction to *The History of Mary Prince: A West Indian Slave*. London: Westley & Davis and Edenburgh: Waugh & Innes (1831). Thomas Pringle, active in the abolition movements in the Cape and England, details some of the ways in which slavery in the Cape and the Caribbean could not be characterised as anything less than dehumanising and brutal. He uses, in particular references to slaves being sold in the Cape in the nineteenth century. Prince's narrative and with Pringle's introduction and commentary is readily available in Henry Louis Gates' Schlomberg Collection of slave narratives, Moira Fergusson's edited version (Michigan Press, 1997) and Sarah Salih's Penguin edition (2000).

51 Podbrey, 1999, 10.

Chapter Three

The politics of naming: The constitution of coloured subjects in South Africa

Thiven Reddy

The importance of racial and ethnic identities in the interpretation of social and political behaviour in South Africa's history cannot be exaggerated. The fact that racial and ethnic identities are felt strongly and perceived six years into a new democratic dispensation invites one to reflect on the discursive power of these collective identities. Neither the composition and electoral campaigns of the main political parties during the first and second national and local government democratic elections, nor the quality of parliamentary debate and the public transcript in general, nor, for that matter, the content of private discussion, suggest that old racial and ethnic divisions are dying in the post-Apartheid South Africa.

After the first democratic elections there was much debate over why overwhelming numbers of those historically classified as 'Coloured' and 'Indian' voted for the Nationalist Party, the party of Apartheid racism. In the second democratic elections, held in June 1999, voting statistics showed the beginnings of more cross-ethnic support for the ANC, a trend which was reversed in the local government elections of December 2000. Despite the nuanced relationship between identity and election results, the dominant trend has been comfortably to interpret election outcomes along racial and ethnic lines. The South African state has democratized but racial and ethnic understandings associated with the old racist order remain.

This chapter provides one way of comprehending the persisting salience of 'old' ethnic attachments in South Africa. It proposes to approach our understanding of collective identities by locating these within discourses of classification and their constitution of subjects. To consider collective identities as part of discourses of classification, where each category of classification has its meaning in relation to other categories and the system of classification as a whole, allows one to see the category denoting the group from a non-essentialist perspective. This approach makes it possible to see and to argue that the category 'Coloured' functions to hold the whole system of classification in South Africa together. The stability of the main racial categories, by which I mean that these categories assume an unquestioned and taken-for-granted status, rely on some notion of a category denoting 'mixed' and Other. In South Africa, the category 'Coloured' functions in this role.

A discourse of racial and ethnic classification plays a large part in producing certain types of identities – making them 'real' by providing them with everyday meanings – for those captured within the category and those excluded from it. These everyday, taken-for-granted meanings provide the commonsense understandings within which social relations in the society are approached, comprehended, spoken, written and thought about. This discourse of classification has a long history in South Africa and has had a particular impact on the way the state and civil society have been organized. In this sense, from the perspective of a discourse on classification, the state and civil society in South Africa may have slightly different configurations during the periods historians have labelled colonial and Apartheid. Despite these differences the key features of these configurations display striking continuity between both periods in the reliance on notions of ethnic and racial division.

To understand collective identity as part of discourses of classification, and in relation to the organization of power such that we can identify dominant or hegemonic and subaltern discourses, offers a different perspective from those once influential in South African studies. Two views on collective identity can be traced in the English-speaking literature on 'race' and ethnic relations and both have been extensively relied upon to understand social relations in South Africa. Traditional views on collective identity in South Africa assume that the words (signifiers) used to denote collectivities of people, like 'Coloured', 'African', 'White', and 'Indian', are unproblematic (Davenport 1977; Elphick and Giliomee 1979). According to these perspectives these labels do not pose a problem if they are accepted as commonsense for the people designated by the label and/or the broader society within which they form a part. These collective names are assumed to convey positive ethnic markers. These could be either physical or cultural attributes differentiating a given group of people from others. Another more Marxist and instrumentalist-oriented view suggests that these collective names derive their stability because they resonate with political or social interests. As such they serve as symbolic containers within which material interests assume their expressions.

I want to challenge both views on the following grounds. First, physical and cultural markers do not 'speak' in themselves, their meanings only resonate and take on social significance in an already existing system of signs and practices, which Foucault has called discourses. Second, instrumental interests of groups also assume their various forms in a pre-existing system of signification. In short, group interests cannot be isolated from the politics of meaning. I want to take the example of the category 'Coloured' because among all classificatory categories in South Africa it has received the most attention as a 'problem identity' – both for the discourses associated with the previous racialized system and those associated with resistance. I want to suggest that all labelling categories are equally unstable or arbitrary, and, following Derrida, accept that the relationship between the word and the thing (signifier and signified of the sign) is purely arbitrary. In South Africa, the stability of the 'non-Coloured' categories, their unquestioned status and the empirical political terrain which makes them uncontestable, is a function of the word and sign 'Coloured'.

By looking at specific key state texts/practices dealing with racial classification we can see the arbitrariness between labelling categories (signifiers) and the conceptualization of the people these categories were supposed to capture (signifieds). By focusing on the category 'Coloured' I deconstruct the meaning, function and role of this signifier in two state texts/practices: the South African Native Affairs Commission (Sanac) Report (1903-1905) and the Population Registration Act (1950). It is obvious that these are not the only texts one could use. There are countless other expressions of the dominant discourse on classification to show the arbitrariness of racial and ethnic categorization. I choose these two documents because both dedicate large sections to classification and give the reader access to the ideas about collective identity as reflected in dominant discourse. As documents produced close to or within the state's institutional ambit, they also indicate how the state acted upon such notions to constitute the social relations of civil society on the basis of these understandings. In this sense categories of classification assume a material basis in the organization of social relations. Lastly, the different points in time and context allow us to see differences and continuity in the manner with which dominant discourse approached its conception of subaltern classification. The Sanac report was produced during the period leading up to the formation of the modern South African state and the Population Registration Act was enacted when the racialised state assumed a developed form with its politics of racial terror. Involving extensive debate, the labelling of colonised subjects was an important issue for the 1903-1905 commission, which in the end adopted an ambiguously uncertain position towards 'Coloured' classification. It is illuminating to contrast this rather ambiguous 1905 position, concluded at the time around the formation of the South African colonial state and describing its first systematic effort to classify scientifically the subaltern population, with the more confidently strident, more certain position articulated in the Population Registration document of the Apartheid state.

Towards a discursive understanding of identity

It has become commonplace in contemporary studies of 'race' and ethnicity to acknowledge and emphasise the constructiveness of collective identities. Some scholars still insist on arguing that without some set of constraining social conditions, group identities are primordially grounded in biological characteristics, or, alternatively, are exclusively instrumental mechanisms dependent on some more rationally defensible set of values. The former position views ethnic identity as independent of other values, while the latter considers it as dependent on some other more significant set of values (Rex and Mason 1987; van den Berghe 1987). The debate between these two positions once dominated the social science ethnic studies literature. However the 'linguistic turn' in philosophy (Foucault 1977a, 1977b, 1978, 1980; Derrida 1974), history, and literary and cultural studies (Said 1979; Bhabha 1985; Spivak 1988) has helped the debate move beyond its earlier contours to posit the idea that all values, including that of identity, can have no foundation other than its meaning/s in various discursive systems (Hall 1996; Bhabha 1994). It is this last perspective which guides the analysis to follow.

Colonial and Apartheid discourses of state and civil society located themselves firmly within the tradition that saw identity based on biology. Such a move allowed for the rigorous, far-reaching, and bureaucratic organization of South African state and civil society in conformity with the notion of naturalized boundaries between subjects. It should be noted that I explicitly do not advance a theoretical framework that draws upon a separation between discourses of state and civil society and discourses of identity and then concludes that each type of state-society arrangement was different – one for the colonial period and another for the Apartheid period, where each constitutes a different and separate social formation. That would be a misinterpretation because it is precisely this demarcation between colonialism and Apartheid that I want to challenge. I propose that discourses of classification set the context, the parameters, within which politics get enacted and in both 'periods' (to use a more crude historical periodisation), the notion of the naturalised, biological divisions between subjects is a crucial element of dominant discourse. Once the terrain establishing key notions of racial and ethnic classification becomes the taken-for-granted context, a situation where, how and what constitutes political subjects outside racial markers becomes beyond contestation. In this context the conflicts are over the mechanics of organizing state and society within the parameters of a discourse on racial and ethnic classification.

The political organization of the social space conformed to the idea of the natural division between racialised subjects. The opposition discourses to colonial and Apartheid practices, somewhat in contrast to hegemonic practice, organized its subjects of resistance such that the idea of group identity was considered instrumentally, either benefiting dominating or resisting practices. Ethnic divisions were not natural, but social and political devices. In other words ethnicity was either strategically useful for resistance practices or an ideological obstacle to more politically radical social categories such as 'black', 'working class', or 'African'.

An important consequence of these competing discourses – and their multiple combinations of dominant and resisting discourses – was that colonised and Apartheid subjects expressed themselves in daily practice in terms of contradictory pressures or motivations. At times essentialised identities were pronounced (such as 'Coloured', 'Indian', 'White'), at other times, alternative, more political categories assumed precedence (such as 'progressives', 'non-racialists', 'black working class'), and still other times, various combinations and mixtures of both positions become evident. The point I hope to make is that ethnic or racial collective identity, discursively, opens up the possibility of assuming both essentialised and constructivist expressions as meaningful tactical stories. The story chosen depends on the struggle over systems of signification and its various constitutive terrains.

This approach, locating colonised (and colonising) subjects between dominating and resisting discourses, sometimes essentialised and sometimes fluid and malleable, offers an innovative way of understanding subject formation in South Africa. It accounts for the emotional appeal addressed by primordial positions and, according to instrumentalist readings, the political and social utility that ethnic markers make available to political agents. Additionally, and far more importantly, it allows us to see how, contradictorily, the very notion of 'impure', 'mixed', 'the borderline', 'the unclassifiable', 'the doubtful' people/category, represented by 'Coloured', functions as both the extreme Other of dominant racial discourse in South Africa, and also as its very ambivalent core. Without it the remaining discursive categories, 'white' and even 'aboriginal native' and 'Indian' categories, lose their central grounding. In a rigidly, hierarchically structured racial classificatory system, there will and must be a category for the 'unclassifiable' – the Other – which resists the discourse but also functions to give the classificatory system its very meaning. 'Coloured' has been the home for this function in South Africa.

Sanac and the definition of 'Coloured'

A striking feature about the Sanac commission report is its rather unsure, ambiguous definition of the meaning of 'Coloured'. The commission sat in 1903, a few years before the formal formation of a centralized South African state. One interpretation of the setting up of a commission at the turn of the century to investigate all aspects of the African life and world was to see it in relation to shortages facing the labour-thirsty mining sector. The Sanac commission was to formulate general principles of subaltern governance and in so doing provide a long-term solution to the demands facing modernist development. According to Ashforth (1990) the commission made three distinctive influential contributions to official discourse. First, it prepared a language for the state 'to talk about, for, and on behalf of "natives" '. Second, it systematised and summarised leading intellectual thinking on the most 'rational' and 'scientific' practices for the governing of the lives of the subaltern majority. Finally, to it we can trace the two major pieces of state legislation that left an unmistakable imprint on South African society: the 1913 Land Act and the Hertzog Bills of 1936.

For the purposes of understanding how the colonial state went about organizing its relations with its subaltern subjects, the Sanac commission report also expresses the dilemmas confronting official discourse in its quest to define and name colonised subjects scientifically. Of interest is the unique way dominant discourse attempts to classify subjects by endorsing two epistemological moves: to generalize characteristics for all colonised subjects and to specify particularities for colonised sub-groups. In this sense the definitions of the category 'Coloured' offered by the commission refer to generalized 'native' subjects and also to subjects with certain special and unique features, thus contributing, in comparison to other ethnic identity categories, towards the ambiguity and ambivalence of this category in official and resistance discourses in South Africa.

Defining the 'native'

The Sanac report (1905) has two sections relevant to a discussion on the construction of subaltern identity. The first presents an historical overview of each region and its inhabitants from the moment of the presence of the European settlers and from their perspective. The second part discusses the various definitions of 'natives' in the statutes of the different colonies.

The report merely states the numbers of 'Coloured' inhabitants in the Transvaal and Natal. In the Transvaal it gives a number for 'coloured people [small letter] and Asiatics [capitalised]', whereas in Natal the numbers are given separately for 'Indians' and 'coloured people'. More detail, suggesting relations with other ethnic signifiers, emerges in the discussion of the Cape Colony and the Orange River Colony. In the Orange River Colony the report mentions the 'Griquas' and describes them as a 'people of mixed Hottentot and slave descent with an infusion of European blood'. In the Cape colony the earliest known inhabitants were referred to as the 'Hottentots' and 'Bushmen', more recently referred to as the Khoi and San. The report presents these as separable 'races' which did not exist any more in 'pure types', but whose 'characteristics are preserved in the coloured people'. The report draws sharp distinctions between the 'Bushmen' and 'Hottentots'. The former are described as a 'race' of hunters without government, socially inferior to the 'Hottentots' and without any potential for 'adopting the habits of European civilization'. The latter are comparatively described as displaying rudimentary forms of government, showing themselves to be socially superior to the 'Bushmen' and as 'able to adapt themselves to Europeans modes of life'. However, when appearance was the only criterion of classification, it was difficult to tell the difference between the 'Bushmen' and 'Hottentots' (3-5).

In the section subtitled 'The Definition of Native', the report laments the fact of different definitions between colonies and within the same colony. A 'native', according to the Cape definition, was 'any Kafir, Fingo, Zulu, Mosuto, Damara, Hottentot, Bushman, Bechuana, Koranna, or any aboriginal native of South or Central Africa, but shall not include any native while serving in any of His Majesty's Ships and while in uniform' (11). It includes 'Hottentot' and 'Bushman' but excludes the category 'Coloured'. The Natal definition emphasises the indigenous characteristic of 'native', yet leaves out 'Hottentot' and 'Griqua'. It however includes these categories in the definition of 'native' when prohibiting the sale of liquor to 'natives'. The Liquor Act of 1896 in Natal includes in its definition 'aboriginal races', 'Griquas', 'Hottentots' and the children of parents classified 'native' but does not mention 'Coloureds' and 'Asiatics' although the act applied to these groups.

In the Transvaal, very importantly, most definitions of 'natives' focus on the category 'Coloured'. One definition on the statutes states: 'The word "native" shall apply to the males of all coloured people and coloured races in South Africa' (12). Another, encompassing an extremely broad view, even includes women. It states: 'The term "coloured person" shall signify any African or Asiatic native or coloured Americans or St Helena person, Coolie or Chinamen, whether male or female.' Here 'native' appears to be a sub-category of 'Coloured', which included all people of colour (to use a phrase of recent currency in the US). The act dealing with the pass laws applied to those where 'both parents must belong to an aboriginal race,' thus excluding 'Coloureds' and 'Asiatics'. The definition in the Orange River colony, like the Transvaal which relies on the emphasis on colour difference, adds the criteria of custom, law and dominant political discourse. It states: 'The expression "coloured person" [...] to apply to [...] any of the native tribes in South Africa, and also all coloured persons, and all who, in accordance with law or custom, are called coloured persons, or are treated as such, of whatever race or nationality they may be' (13). The Rhodesian definition is the most blatantly discursive, defining 'natives' as all those 'not of European descent' (13).

The commission faced the enormously difficult task of choosing a definition with a scientific basis. It decided to accept all the existing definitions in use but also proposed a new definition sufficiently broad to serve as a classificatory device for the unionizing colonial state. A 'native', it decided, 'means an aboriginal inhabitant of Africa, South of the Equator, and to include half-castes and their descendants by Natives'. This definition adopted the position of the Afrikaner republics rather than that of the Cape, which differentiated between 'Coloured' and 'native'. The commission admitted that this decision was arrived at hesitantly because: 'It is notorious that a great deal of racial intermixture has taken place, and many of the so-called coloured people have, by their industry, intelligence and self-respect, raised themselves to a high standard' (13). After acknowledging the 'industry, intelligence and self-respect' of 'this class' the commission decided that it was more important to create a language medium in which the colonies could address each other on equal terms and with similar meanings concerning subaltern subjects.

The politics of naming the Other: some thoughts on the Sanac report

The manner in which the commission went about trying to name subalterns in South Africa and to demarcate who belonged under what category, provides insight into the discourse of racial classification in South Africa and its different manifestations over time. The search for appropriate signifiers associated with the signified 'indigenous inhabitants' or people of 'mixed races' suggests the desire by experts to find a suitable definition for an objective, homogenous social group. There is no acknowledgement that such a naming process of the Other, by experts representing and articulating dominant interests, was open to question. All the possible 'names' come from the dominant discourse. Characteristic of processes of silencing of the Other, nowhere do we get a sense of what the people call themselves or whether they in fact saw themselves as a group or even wanted to be treated as a group. Why is this naming so important in the first place? Is it because the subjects of state administration must always be clearly delineated? This makes sense when we consider that the goal of the commission is to develop a common plan to administer all 'natives', and that this administration requires the neat demarcation of the targeted group from the body politic as a whole. The state, Ashcroft (1990, 25) emphasises, has to know upon whom it can and should act. But like the notion of citizenship, this negotiation and demarcation of rights between the state and its subjects also have the effect of constituting itself and the identity of the subjects.

An aspect of the functioning of the master narrative becomes visible in relation to the category 'native', under which 'Coloureds' were uncertainly included. The choice of the category 'native' as the all-embracing concept to refer to the subaltern classes demarcates (and consequently accentuates) the arrival of Europeans as marking the fundamental moment in South African history, to the extent of determining the identity of the colonised subjects. The European arrival demarcates the before and the after or, in other words, gives meaning to the word 'native'. European colonization makes 'nativeness' and 'mixed race' categories possible.

Based on the way the commission report describes the inhabitants in the colonies it is possible to conclude that the report depends on a foundational assumption. It assumes a distinction between some categories representing static, fixed and neatly bounded groups, groups with 'racial essences', and 'mixed groups', whose 'racial essence' is the 'mixing of blood'. Europeans, 'Bantus' and perhaps 'Asiatics' are considered examples of 'pure races' and 'Coloureds' as the counter example of 'mixed race'. The 'Coloured' signifier functions as the residual category representing the 'mixing of races', peoples, and ethnicities. The enormous emphasis placed on 'pure blood' pervades the dominant discourse as well as the all-important assumption that 'pure bloodlines' actually did exist in certain 'races'. In keeping with Gobineau (1967), the assumption was that 'pure blood' of whites ranked the highest, in that it was responsible for the greatest civilizations. The 'mixing of blood' (or 'miscegenation') was a horrific prospect that led to 'race degeneration' (Young 1994; Evans 1911; Loram 1917).

The notion of 'racial purity' assumes a special place among European discourses from the eighteenth century onwards (Gilroy 2000). It acquires further importance and wretchedness, Dubow (1989) points out, when connected with 'scientific' discourses in the nineteenth century. In the colonies the idea plays itself out on the political terrain – combining with administrative practices and relations of production and exchange. The fear of 'miscegenation' acquired in the colonies, especially where ideas of 'racial purity' were highly pronounced, a privileged meaning. The dominant discourse therefore generates this fear. It is evident in the Sanac report but its importance needs to be appreciated as a social practice within South African society. Between the 1920s and 1940s it becomes a crucial factor in white political party campaign agendas. During the height of the segregationist period, in the 1920s, 'interracial' sex activity was prohibited. During the 1940s, with the emergence of 'multiracial' inner cities, this fear, naturally became a dominating theme within white politics.[1] When this idea of 'race degeneration' was coupled with the notion that it would involve black and white workers, Dubow points out, the idea of a 'mixed blood proletariat' was abominable. For segregationists, a 'mixed blood proletariat' in a rapidly developing capitalist economy and in the conditions of an urban environment that under 'normal' conditions brought out the worst in people (as for example among 'poor whites') was to be avoided at all costs. Even though the 'mixing of blood' was, according to Young (1994, 150-58), absolutely taboo, it was also quite ironically, in colonial discourse, a central white male desire, reflecting the ambiguity between sexual desire, sexism and racism.

This reliance on notions of natural biological difference sits uneasily with the political and social criteria that also constitute the dominant discourse. The signifier denoting Europeans remains whole, without further division. By contrast, the indigenous 'natives' are further broken down into 'tribes'. The 'Coloured' and 'Asiatic' categories are sometimes put together (Transvaal) or separated (Natal). Even though it recognised that the 'natives' were divided into 'tribes' the report did not expand on this division beyond an emphasis on the role of 'tribalism' and the function of 'tribal reserves'. This marks a contrast to the Apartheid era. There is a definite tension in the dominant discourse between the desire for an all-embracing demarcation of the Other as 'non-European' or 'savage' or 'native' or 'Bantu', and the political imperative to further sub-divide its subaltern subjects.

The inclusion of the 'Coloured' category within the definition of 'native' had important political implications[2]. It meant that the commission decided to generalise the situation of the Transvaal, Orange River Colony and Natal (where 'Coloured' men did not have qualified voting rights) as the proposed policy after the formation of the Union of South Africa in 1910. Rather than extending the qualified voting rights of the 'Cape Coloured' propertied class - which was the main demand of the African Peoples Organization to 'civilised' 'Coloured' men in other colonies, it was planning to extend to the Cape the situation prevailing in the conservative colonies (van der Ross 1986; Lewis 1987). The commission concluded that this voting group posed long-term threats to the colonial status quo and suggested adopting a new code of separate representation which did not threaten European interests, a position which was implemented by the Nationalists during the post-war period.

Apartheid and the Population Registration Act

In this section I discuss the classificatory system of the Apartheid state, which offers striking contrasts to the ambiguous place of the 'Coloured' category in colonial discourse. Once subaltern subjects were categorized according to the Population Registration Act under certain signifiers, the state treated its own categories as real – i.e. unproblematically linked to an 'essence' – and went about organizing civil society in terms of these categories. This operation and implementation of its strategies led to an expanded state and, more importantly, contributed towards establishing a material basis for its own categories of subject identity. Soon enough the Apartheid social formation made it difficult to separate world from text. It is important to realize that this interaction between discourse, state and civil society results in social relations, expressed as divided 'races' and ethnicities having a material basis in the institutional structure and everyday practices of the society.

Very little under the Apartheid system could have made any legislative and administrative sense without a framework of racial and ethnic classification inscribed in the legal order. It is from such a starting point that all other state legal measures and practices follow. Apartheid made the 'racial group' the determinant of all social interaction. How else could it have been possible to restrict 'racial groups' to particular places of residence, to develop racially defined public services, to allow for the unequal access and provision of public goods, and to limit the possibilities of human interactions to racially confined groups? In dominant discourse the 'racial category' was everything; individual persons did not exist outside the group categorization. The group defined and determined where and with whom the individual person could live, work, own land, worship, have sex, attend school, obtain health services, play sport, enjoy entertainment or marry. Those few spheres of interaction that legislation could not prescribe (like interactions on public roads, walkways and unplanned social gatherings) were satisfactorily racially secured by social and individual prejudice. An essential component and starting point to operate such a strategy of division was a state imposed 'racial classification' system. In 1950 the Nationalist Party legislated into law a Population Registration Act.

The Population Registration Act of 1950, a striking example of the power/knowledge nexus, allowed the state to classify every person along the lines of colour, 'race' and ethnicity. The 'Coloured' and 'native' 'racial groups' were further classified in certain instances according to residence and ethnicity. According to the Act:

> Every person whose name is included in the register shall be classified by the Director as a white person, a coloured person or a native, as the case may be, and every coloured person and every native whose name is so included shall be classified by the Director according to the ethnic or other group to which he belongs. (Statutes 1950, 279)

The state identified each person in this register with the following information – racial/ethnic classification, name, sex, age, address, marital status – and entered this information in the register which was verified by an identity card containing the person's recent photograph, identity number and fingerprints. Minister of the Interior Dr. T.E. Donges, who initiated the Bill, described the basic principle behind a population register. He saw it as a somewhat grand dictionary of state

> containing the life-story of every individual [...] All those important facts regarding the life of every individual will be combined in this book and recorded under the name of a specific person, who can never change his identity. It is only when the last page in that book of life is written by an entry recording the death of such a person that the book is closed and taken out of the gallery of the living and placed in the gallery of the dead. (Brookes 1968, 21)

The state would henceforth compose the life story of every subject while ensuring that his/her identity remained politically unchanged. The individual is in a way chained to her/his classification. One notices the movement from real life to the life of signs that characterizes Donges' understanding of this state register i.e. the person is only 'truly' dead when his name is removed from the register.

Unlike the prevailing ambiguity and quest for science that characterizes the Sanac document, the Population Registration text places certainty in the arena of the political. In the opening section it offers relational definitions of racial subjects. A 'coloured person', it says, 'means a person who is not a white person or a native' (Statutes, 277). A 'native' 'means a person who in fact is or is generally accepted as a member of any aboriginal race or tribe of Africa'. And a 'white person means a person who in appearance obviously is, or who is generally accepted as, a white person, but does not include a person who, although in appearance obviously a white person, is generally accepted as a coloured person' (Statutes 277). Subject classification relies on 'general acceptance', the existing social and political discourse constituting civil relations, instead of exclusive reliance on physical appearances despite the 'obvious' conclusions between colour and 'race'. This is quite different to the detailed efforts to create fine gradations within the 'mixed race' category that characterizes colonial discourse in the nineteenth century especially in the colonial discourse of the Americas.

The experience of living within the Apartheid racial grid and the institutionalization of its divisions contributed towards its naturalizing. To perfect its classificatory system so that it corresponded more fittingly with 'reality', the state resorted to a series of amendments; many of which aimed to tighten the loopholes against people making appeals for 're-classification'. The government proclaimed in 1959 that the 'Coloured' category be further sub-divided into 'Cape Coloured, Cape Malay, Griqua, Indian, Chinese, "other Asiatic", and "Other Coloured" '. The aim of this sub-division was to enhance the 'meaning' of the larger category, 'Coloured', by making it more encompassing (Horrel 1978, 16). In 1962 an amendment placed 'acceptance by the affected community' on an equal footing with 'physical appearance' – the criterion which until then constituted the main test of 'race classification'. A 1969 amendment made it harder to obtain a 're-classification' by placing the burden of proof on the person challenging his or her 'racial categorization'. Strangely, the same amendment fell back on the previous emphasis on appearance by making it possible for a person to be 'classified as Bantu [indigenous African] if he appeared to be an African, even if he had white or Coloured blood, and even if he was generally accepted as being Coloured' (Horrel, 16). Another example of the ludicrous ruling on racial boundaries and its patriarchal emphasis was an amendment declaring that a person would take the categorization of his or her natural father in cases where the father was classified into one of the 'Coloured' sub-groups. An Appeals Board was established as the highest and only legal authority to which a person could take a disputed case.

It is quite revealing that despite the primacy of 'race' in the organization of the social structure, the criteria used to determine 'racial characteristics' moves from the space of the biological to the social and the political. The first and last determinations were made by state officials. They applied a series of 'tests' to reveal the 'essence' that described the 'race' of the person. The most important of these tests included some combination of physical appearance, descent, and 'general community acceptance'. Once a record of parents existed, the process of classification became less arduous because this bit of data served as the main source of information. In the typical case, a child, is 'racially classified' on his/her birth certificate. At the birth of any citizen The Births, Marriages and Deaths Registration Amendment Act, no 18 of 1968 required that hospital staff perform this process of classification. This certificate constituted the first record, and (unless challenged) became the original source for the 'true racial identity' of the person. Challenges to classification could come from any person provided they paid a small fee and provided 'proof' that the official classification was incorrect.

The Population Registration Act required all citizens to obtain a 'race' identity card. Public resources (because they were allocated by 'race') became inaccessible without any authorized 'racial identification'. In May 1955, for example, the Transvaal Provincial Administration ruled students without identification cards would not be admitted into the 'Coloured' Teacher Training College. In that same year the Minister of the Interior announced that his department encountered 90 000 'borderline' cases. As some might expect, the state and its various agencies went on daily raids searching out violators of its law – persons who were legally in the 'wrong place'. A case heard by the Johannesburg Magistrates Court in 1956, cited by Brookes (1968, 24-25), is typical of state practices and the torment experienced because of 'racial classification', affecting the 'Coloured' signifier more than any other 'racial category'. After a family moved into a white area some neighbours raised doubts about the family's 'race group' to the Group Areas Board. Upon visiting the family, a Group Areas Board inspector declared that the family was white and therefore entitled to live in the area. The local school principal insisted that the family was 'Coloured'; and they were forced to move into a 'Coloured' group area. At a court hearing it was pointed out that the father had lived all his life as a white person (he had two brothers serving in the Navy), that the mother considered herself a white, that the father's sister was living as a 'Coloured', that one of their children was attending a white school, and that two others (who were darker skinned) were attending a 'Coloured' school (Brookes, 25). This is yet another example displaying the arbitrariness of the sign and the state's role in organizing civil society according to 'real divisions' based on the dominant discourse.

The dominant discourse of racial/ethnic classification, the state and civil society

Horrel (1978, 16) suggests that the intention of the 1950 Act was to prevent the 'passing' from one group to another. She notes that before the Apartheid classificatory system 'definitions of various racial groups were incorporated in numbers of laws passed from 1911'. These definitions were made for the purposes of particular pieces of legislation. However when taken as a whole, as a system, it contained loopholes through which a few individuals could 'pass' for white to avoid the harsher discriminatory conditions facing 'non-whites'. Van den Berghe (1965, 55) disputes the degree to which 'passing' constituted a problem and thinks it served to legally entrench the racial-caste hierarchy of South African society.

There are, however, two other factors that need to be taken into account to help explain why the Nationalists decided to legislate individual identity along racial and ethnic lines and to make legal what appeared to pervade the society socially.[3] The first deals with the already mentioned fear of 'miscegenation' that the discourse on the subaltern Other necessarily produces. The second relates to the structural imperatives of the state's expansion into what is traditionally defined as civil society (Migdal 1988; Migdal et al 1994).

The South African state expanded the terrain of its authority with the Population Registration Act. It entitled itself to despotically impose racial identities on its citizens and acted as final judge when these classifications were appealed against. We can recognise the tyrannical effects of such power by remembering that racial identity determined the 'lifeworld' of the Apartheid subject. All other identities were subordinate to the racial/ethnic political categorization of the person. Such enormous jurisdiction promised substantial benefits to the state. It extended its jurisdiction into what is 'traditionally' designated as the domain of individual consciousness and into the sphere of private individual activity – civil society.

Individual consciousness and civil society are, however, not equally private spheres. The Apartheid state, like all racist states, by imposing a certain racial signifier onto the signified – the individual – breaks down the traditional separations between the categories state, individual and civil society. The racial signifier permeates all three categories. How is this possible? The state, through its practices of 'racial assignment' to individual consciousness, moulded the terrain (civil society) in which supposedly private individuals act out their desires. The political division between state and civil society is therefore sacrificed because identity, which is supposedly a part of the private realm, is, in the Apartheid case, the determinant of social relations in the public sphere.

Apartheid South Africa politicized collective identity. When state praxis has the effect of making an area of personal identity open to public debate and personal contestation, personal identity becomes politicized. When the body determines, in Marx's words, his or her 'species activity', then the person easily draws the connection between personal constraints and political forces. In this situation the distinction between personal and public space becomes blurred. The subaltern Other immediately realises that struggles over the distribution of public goods cannot be separated from personal identity; and simultaneously, that personal desires express political desires. The personal is the political. When the political superstructure (in Gramsci's nuanced sense of this category) fails to draw this distinction, at least ideologically, subject identities consist of something like a double-edged sword – they produce the potential for stable domination and extreme resistance.

A consequence of expanding the range of state activity (in our case into civil society) is an expanded state. The state was re-designed to organize civil society along the lines of 'race' and ethnicity. A system of state-imposed classification, especially one that works against the majority of the citizenry, requires a large, repressive police force. The repressive apparatus of the state, consequently, was expanded and centralized by taking over many of the local policing responsibilities from the municipalities. A few years into Nationalist Party rule the size of the South African Police (SAP) rose from

14 743 in 1946 to 23 016 in 1955 (the number of police per 1 000 persons rose by 25%) (Posel 1991).

Apartheid social engineering translated into an administrative practice where each social service for each ethnic group required its own department, thus creating a massive administrative and policing bureaucracy. In a system where almost everything depended on each 'race' having its own administrative organ, the state had an excuse to reproduce itself endlessly. There were departments of 'Native', 'Indian', and 'Coloured' Affairs. Each of these established departments and sub-departments to deal with education, health, welfare and other services. In addition, the Bantustans (which were really adjunct organs of the central state) established their own bureaucratic network to dominate and monitor the population within their territories.

To conclude, the Population Register, that giant state record of every subject and a key manifestation of the discourse of 'racial classification', accomplished textually that which escaped biology – certainty. This political certainty was, in any case, the ultimate objective. Naturalist, scientific, and moral discourses, no doubt, do make important contributions to the constitution of the Other but it is the political objectives that matter. The text accomplished political certainty by using the racial signifier as if the words conveyed an unambiguous, unproblematic reference to a real, existing 'thing' with a real 'essence'.

In the case of the 'Coloured' category, it is the opposite of the typical 'racial categories' – the 'essence' denotes not 'pure racial blood' but 'mixed racial blood'; the 'essence' signifies the unclassifiable, the doubtful and the borderline. A set of characteristics which is the norm for all people becomes the abnormal, the dangerous, the Other. Unless *all* these stable, racialised categories are problematised, located in discourses, and made the focus of countless attacks and contests, the dominant discourse of racial classification and its material expressions in everyday social relations, will remain in the formidable position it sadly won for itself in South Africa.

Notes

1 The frailty of an 'autonomous', sovereign collective identity is evident in any discussion on the fear of 'miscegenation'. It suggests that identity is always constructed and relational to Others — that white identity and its political ideology of white supremacy could be rendered obsolete by the simple fact of 'blood mixing'. The fear of 'blood-mixing' has many functions beneficial for a discourse on 'racial purity'. It stabilizes the belief in 'pure blood', biology, and nature as values in themselves; and it secures the 'insiders' from the 'outsiders', — the Otherness of the Other becomes not only a matter of difference but more importantly, the survival of the 'insiders'. We see this fear manifesting itself in all elections since 1910.

2 People of South East Asian 'descent', it was hoped, would be removed from the society altogether by shipping them back to India and the strategies of this relocation were the main issue of debate in dominant discourse.

3 These two may be viewed as 'justifiable reasons' for introducing a classificatory system; but it should be noted that in its operation as an administrative system there was also the need to combat what was felt to be the inefficiency and flexibility of the existing system monitoring and policing 'race relations'.

Chapter Four

Re-classifications: Coloured, Malay, Muslim

Shamil Jeppie

The question of identity for the Muslims of the western Cape has a long and complex history. For a long time in dominant discourse – such as the press and government reports – they were referred to as Malays, then as *slamse* (a corrupted form of 'Islam' and a wholly negative term), and also as coloured Moslems. Because poor and politically powerless peoples' voices are seldom heard it is hard to say for sure what they called themselves between the arrival of the first Muslims in the latter part of the seventeenth century and the late nineteenth-century proliferation of names for them. By the mid-twentieth century being Muslim was endowed with a singular ethnic marker – Malay – most often separate and distinct from the larger community of people termed coloured. This trajectory presents rich opportunities to look at how multiple subject positions or identities are constituted, negotiated and articulated. This chapter looks at work done by Izak David Du Plessis, an influential Afrikaans-speaking intellectual, to articulate a Malay identity for the Muslims of the western Cape.

In this chapter I want to look at the means and methods by which, and the purposes for which, a Malay ethnic identity was constituted in the period after World War One. Here I must introduce an entirely new set of issues. The constructions of 'Afrikanerness', the growth of Afrikaner *volkekunde*, and the biography of Du Plessis are essential in an explanation of the projects to constitute a bounded Malay community.

From the 1920s on the 'Malay' was constructed as a distinctive Afrikaans-speaking community close to, though not part of, the politically dominant white population of the country. Here I want to look at the ways in which an originally non-African, but at the same time non-white, community was constituted as an ethnic group in modern South Africa. Du Plessis was the most energetic proponent of a distinctive past and separate culture for these people.

Official diasporic discourse

In November 1997 the then president of Indonesia, Muhammad Suharto, came to South Africa on an official state visit. He was given all the respect due to a visiting statesman and was awarded the highest state honour the country can bestow, the Order of Good Hope. President Mandela had been on a state visit to Indonesia earlier in the year and was treated in similar fashion. The governments of Indonesia and South Africa, as represented in this exchange of visits, obviously established a special relationship very quickly.

However, spokespersons for a section of the South African population, representatives of the Muslim community in Cape Town, make claims to even closer and deeper ties to Indonesia than the formal connections between the administrations of the two countries. The late Achmat Davids was a researcher and public figure from the Bo-Kaap, also known as the Malay quarter, in Cape Town, who spent a lot of his energies examining the historical connections between the Indonesian archipelago and the Muslims of the city. He wrote of Indonesia as the 'ancestral homeland' of the 'greater majority' of the Muslims of the western Cape, who 'can trace their roots to one or other island of the Indonesian archipelago'.[1]

The Muslims of the western Cape have been constructed as members of a larger Malay diaspora. The Malaysian government and Malay cultural foundations have promoted the idea of a Malay diaspora and have funded numerous international conferences and other events to reconnect Malays throughout the world to their purported region of origin. The Muslims of the western Cape have been made part of this diasporic community and the Malaysian sponsors of this idea encountered local proponents, such as Davids, who supported it. In this way the Muslims of the Cape are given cultural roots that are not local at all, nor 'creole', as I have elsewhere argued about the nature of Islam at the Cape (Jeppie 1996). Instead they are wholly foreign, in the (until recently) flourishing economies and modern nation states of Malaysia and Indonesia. In this context they should therefore be reconnected to their origins. This appeal to the putative roots of the Muslims of the western Cape is highly contentious but it is certainly not new.

In April 1994, a festival, 'Three hundred years of Islam in South Africa', was celebrated. Just as Islam and Cape Malay identity came to have a very strong affiliation throughout most of this commemoration so, not surprisingly, Cape Town and South Africa were conflated (Jeppie 1996). All the festivities were held in the 'mother city' and Islam was made to appear as the religion only of the Malays of the city. The Malay character and ethnic links to Southeast Asia of South African Islam were stressed, elaborated upon and celebrated. Davids, a vocal proponent of this approach, said: 'When we rediscovered each other there was total amazement on both sides that the culture had been so well preserved in South Africa.'[2]

The 1990s have seen the proliferation of claims to a separate and unique Malay identity. According to Davids: 'Xhosas were looking for their Xhosa distinctiveness; Zulus openly expounded their culture; and the Cape Muslims were looking for their niche.' Davids expresses a truth there. The 'new South Africa' has seen the proliferation of claims to actual and symbolic property based on ethnicity. New and contending interpretations of the past have been central to such demands. The re-interpretation of the Muslims' past in the light of new political realities influenced at the outset the decision to hold the tercentenary celebrations of Islam in Cape Town in 1994. Davids was the chairperson of the organizing committee.

These frank assertions of Malay ethnic identity by a section of the Muslim community surpass all the previous claims to Indonesian or Malay ancestry in the entire post-World War Two period.[3] During this period the representation of the specific ethnic origins and culture of Cape Town's Muslims was articulated by secular organizations such as the Cape Malay Choir Board and its white, Afrikaans-speaking founder, Du Plessis. The religious and political leadership of the Muslim community was rather ambiguous about the Malay classification given to them.

For instance, in 1961 the Prime Minister of Malaysia, Tunku Abdul Rahman, had, according to *The Cape Times*, made a call on 'Malay settlers who were being oppressed in South Africa' to 'return to Malaysia permanently'.[4] Instead of a gracious acknowledgement of the invitation there was a muted response to this call. The leading community organizations of the local Muslims simply ignored the invitation, and young political radicals rejected it outright. 'There are apparently no Malays in Cape Town interested in the offer,' commented *The Argus* laconically.[5]

The question of identity can be rephrased as the question of subjectivity. Both terms are always about issues that can only be productively addressed in the plural. Thus we are looking at identities and subjectivities (or subject positions) even in approaching an apparently singular object of analysis. Identity or subjectivity refers always to an aspect or moment or position in a much more complex ensemble of subject positions or identities.

We now think of various or multiple or layered identities. An ethnic term or marker of ethnic self-identification – coloured, Malay or Muslim, in our case – should be seen as one among a number of identities which an individual can or will articulate depending on the circumstances. However, it is not a matter of simply choosing which of a range of identities or positions to articulate at a freely chosen or appropriate moment. It is not merely a matter of personal choice, nor of social context simply determining what is expressed. A subject emerges both as an effect of a prior power and the condition of possibility for a substantially conditioned form of agency (Butler 1997, 14).

Religious identity is particularly powerful. It is often very visibly expressed in the western Cape among people named, or who call themselves, coloured. Small suburban churches and their lay preachers and the legacy of mission station religion have given shape to a form of Christianity closely linked to 'being' coloured in some way.

Terms for classification

Muslim slaves and free blacks in the Cape colony came mainly from South and Southeast Asia (Shell 1994). The popular religious practices of slaves and exiles from the Indonesian archipelago emerged as the dominant theme in local Muslim culture but this by no means indicates that they were the only Muslim slaves. African slaves, and converts from among both the free and unfree population, brought to the Muslim community an ethnic variety that both confused and impressed visitors and locals outside the community. They were variously, and often interchangeably, labelled Malay, Mohammedan, Mussulman and coloured Moslem in Dutch and British colonial records, and in traveller's accounts, from the eighteenth century through to the early twentieth century. An English visitor, Lady Duff-Gordon, expressed the interchangeable use of Malay and Muslim clearly when she said that, 'Malay here means Mohammedan. They *were* Malays, but now they embrace every shade, from the blackest nigger to the blooming English woman' (Duff-Gordon 1927 [1820], 37). John S. Mayson also commented that the Malays were actually synonymous with a religious group that included 'Arabs, Mozambique prize Negroes, Hottentots and Christian perverts' *(sic)*. Mayson also added that 'the most ignorant Malays', when questioned about their identity, would simply reply: *Ik ben Islamisch* ('I am Islamic/Muslim') (Mayson 1861, 15 & 21). In the late nineteenth century the eminent Dutch Orientalist, Snouck Hurgronje, describing Cape Town's Muslim pilgrims, whom he had met in Mecca, concluded that 'the Capelanders have almost no intercourse with the Jawah' who were also present in the holy city (Hurgronje 1931, 217). In other words, according to Hurgronje, the Cape Muslims and their fellow pilgrims from Java had little in common.

There was a great deal of confusion over how to classify the various groups in the colony. Particularly disconcerting was the way in which a whole range of people who professed Islam should be classified. Was the Khoisan convert from the countryside a Malay or a Muslim? The first census of the colony expresses this confusion.

The Muslim-as-Malay came to be constructed against the Christian-as-coloured in official and dominant discourses in the nineteenth century. By the end of the century the arrival of new immigrants from South Asia (and Mauritius) in South Africa added another element to Cape Town's population. Among these migrants were many Muslims. Distinctions emerged between the newly arrived Indian Muslims and the long-settled Muslims of the city, many of whom themselves had distant South Asian backgrounds.

The first so-called Passenger Indians arrived in Cape Town in the 1880s – compatriots from the Natal colony joined them after 1897. Their total numbers increased in the early 1900s and by 1906 there were about 8 500 of them, according to the local municipal census. They never grew to become significant in number. The majority of them were Muslim and many became traders in the city. They settled in areas inhabited by the existing community of Muslims and interacted with the established Islamic institutions in the city (Bhana & Brain 1990, 121-127). Distinctions and controversies developed between the locally established Muslim community – the so-called Malays – and the newly arrived Indians around questions of ritual practice and language. In 1892 Cape Town got its first Indian mosque (Davids 1980, 186). The newly-arrived Indians' role as traders, who stuck closely to their own group, partly for linguistic reasons, and built their own institutions, contributed to the distinctions among the city's Muslim population. Difference was expressed through a language of ethnicity; the Malay Muslim was different to the Indian or Asiatic Muslim. Threats of 'Asiatic repatriation' and other hardships placed on them by the government made 'Malay' a preferable term of identification. In 1925, for instance, a newly established Cape Malay Association's main task was to make it clear to the government that South African Malays should be given full rights of citizenship for they were neither 'natives' nor 'Asiatics'.[6]

Re-classifications: the poet and the Malay

The construction of a Malay subject had its proponents among the Muslims themselves and its champions among members of the white elite. The Cape Malay Association and its small membership, for instance, insisted on speaking on behalf of the Muslims-as-Malays. But this organization quickly disappeared from Cape Town politics; it did not displace the appeal of Dr Abdullah Abdurahman's African Peoples Organization to middle-class coloureds and Muslims.

Du Plessis and fellow folklorists attempted to represent the Malays and make them conform to an imaginary model of the 'original' Malays, like the 'real Jawah' whom Snouck Hurgronje met in Mecca. 'Original' here has the dual meaning of, firstly, the geographically 'genuine' Malay of the Orient, and, secondly, the displaced ones or earlier exiles who were sent to the Cape by the Dutch East India Company in the seventeenth century. In this project all the evidence of creolization, ethnic interaction, cultural exchange between the slaves, and newly-forged identities in the setting of the slave society of urban Cape Town was rejected.

In 1925 the South African Minister of Interior and Education, Dr D.F. Malan, in a speech in Cape Town, elaborated on the intimacy of the Malay and Afrikaner. He said:

> The Malay community earned themselves a definite status in South Africa, a status of which they can be proud. In the first instance, they formed one of the oldest elements of the South African nation. They came virtually at the same time that the white man came here and experienced the same history with the white man. The history of South Africa is also their history. The white man did not come here to give the Malays civilization. They were always civilized, and came here after they had adopted the white man's civilization. Afrikaans is not only their language but together with the Dutch-speaking white man they developed that language. It is their language in the fullest sense of the word.[7]

Malan's speech was delivered at a time when the Afrikaner nationalist project was still very much in the making and while the Cape coloured vote had importance in a few of the western Cape constituencies. It was only in that year that Afrikaans became one of the two official languages of the country. A totally Afrikaans-dominated government was yet to become a reality, and electoral alliances were a necessary part of achieving parliamentary power.

Malan's view, however, was not simply a momentary ploy to gain allies in Anglophile Cape Town in a critical period of the Afrikaner nationalist movement, though, to be sure, it was that as well. What is significant, however, is that it was possible at all to conceive 'the Malay' and Malan's 'white man' so closely linked, sharing a common language and civilization. Du Plessis is the one intellectual who attempts to give academic substance to that conception. His doctoral dissertation at the University of Cape Town was entitled '*Die bydrae van die Kaapse Maleier tot die Afrikaanse volkslied*' ('The contribution of the Cape Malay to the Afrikaans folksong'), wherein he does more than simply produce texts to establish the historical ties. He exerts himself to preserve artefacts and even the living practices of an imagined pure Malay civilization in Cape Town. In terms of the segregationist discourse of the time, their separate identity meant a different politics for them. As will be clearer later, in order for political claims and social demands to have some legitimacy increasingly they had to be put in Malay ethnic terms by community leaders. Furthermore, a patronage relationship would develop whereby favours to 'the Malay community' would be dispensed by the State via persons endowed with an 'intimate' knowledge of Malay affairs, like Du Plessis himself, or to self-professed Malay leaders such as certain Imams.

Du Plessis's ventures on behalf of 'the Malays' occurred during a period of social crisis and political turmoil in Cape Town and South Africa. His innovation and reinvention of Malay tradition was viewed as politically innocuous by many in the Muslim community. Black political, and later Islamic youth, organizations in Cape Town, however, voiced some opposition to him when the full political implications of his undertaking were more clearly seen. Who was he, where did he come from, and how did he go about 'capturing' aspects of subaltern cultural life?

Du Plessis started studying literature – Latin, English and Dutch – at the University of Cape Town (then still known as the South African College) in 1918. It was the start of a long and varied involvement with the university. Before he completed his doctorate in the early 1930s he was already engaged in teaching *Afrikaans en Nederlands* there; a vocation which he continued, with periodic interruption, until the mid-1950s. UCT was decidedly English and liberal and 'Afrikaans students had to fight to maintain their identity' during those years, Du Plessis recalled. But this was precisely the environment that would thrust Du Plessis into close affiliation with the burgeoning Afrikaans literary world.

He would become involved with the *Dertigers*, a literary movement that was distinguished by its resemblance to nineteenth-century Romanticism, its concern with the exotic, and the psyche. He was prolific as a poet and short-story writer. The Karoo – where he spent his childhood – and the Muslims of the city were the raw material for his literary output (Du Plessis 1975).

Romanticism and Du Plessis's obsession with the local, and in his mind pre-modern, Malays reinforced each other. He expected to see an exotic oriental presence in the city; he wanted to live in intimate involvement with an 'other' world. The countryside – *die land*, such a central element in *volk* imagery – of his childhood was the subject of his 'patriotic' poetry, while the Muslims were imaginatively appropriated for his more fantastical inventions. For instance, he wrote numerous stories and poems in which 'Malay magic' featured prominently.

Du Plessis would write of that 'exotic part of Cape Town' which stimulated his interest in the real Orient and which was strengthened by a journey among the *ur*-Malays in the Dutch Indies in 1933. His own native Malays, however, also functioned in the narrative of Afrikaner *volk* history. In a certain sense the very existence of Malay culture, which shared a language with the Afrikaans-speaking *volk*, added to the veracity of the Afrikaner nation. The function of the Other was to affirm the self. Studying the Malays enabled more reflection on the *volk* itself. In reviewing Du Plessis's first monograph on Malay-Afrikaans music S. J. du Toit – a senior figure in Afrikaans folklore studies – saw the work as an inspiration to study the development of Afrikaner *volkskunde* since the momentous Voortrekker movement of the 1830s.[8]

While Du Plessis's creative writing was consistently fed by a romantic impulse his attempts at ethnographic representation of the Malay were produced in the period of the establishment of Afrikaner anthropology in South Africa. This *volkekunde* was nourished by nineteenth-century German Romantic thought. *Volkekunde* ideology rested on the centrality of an ethnic essence (ethnos) in all human groups (Sharp 1981). Its proponents were generally involved with bureaucracies such as the Native Affairs Department as an expression of *volkdiens* (Gordon 1988). The academic centres for Afrikaner anthropology since the 1920s were the Universities of Stellenbosch and Pretoria.

The University of Cape Town had a different tradition of ethnographic endeavour, which also addressed the 'native problem'. In 1921 A. R. Radcliffe-Brown was appointed to the first chair in the new Department of African Life and Languages at UCT. It is more likely that Du Plessis conferred with anthropologists there, since he was virtually sharing office space with them, rather than with the Afrikaans-speaking professors at the other institutions. For instance, he drew on unpublished research of A. J. Goodwin, a one-time student and colleague of Radcliffe-Brown, for evidence on 'the Malay strain' in a racially 'mixed' community about eighty kilometres outside Cape Town, while he nowhere refers to the *volkekundiges* (Du Plessis 1944).

But Du Plessis was by no means a professional ethnographer with any commitment to one or other school of ethnography. His works were largely based on his own 'fieldwork' for which there is no record of field notes or published secondary sources. Often his writing would consist of long extracts of nineteenth-century accounts of Cape Town; he collected the oral tradition and folklore reproduced in his work. Du Plessis quite plausibly belonged to that late nineteenth-century class of 'fieldworkers' in southern Africa who were both the 'generators of raw materials and the manufacturers of ethnology' at the same time (Thornton 1983). His ethnographic knowledge also had little real administrative value such as for disciplining the 'natives'. For, unlike the Bantu-speaking majority, the Malays were a minority in the western Cape where there were few Africans in any case.

The western Cape was a region that had been reserved for coloureds since the late nineteenth-century. The emerging African proletariat of the country was located in regions such as the Witwatersrand where Native Administration had to apply itself with particular thoroughness. 'Native administrators' would first take courses on 'Bantu life' offered by Afrikaner *volkekundiges*; then they would work in the offices of the Native Affairs Department. The Malays were not the object of the type of disciplinary discourse and practice that affected the African working class. The Malays lived in a 'coloured labour preference area' and were for a long time viewed as the 'respectable working-class' and even a sort of labour aristocracy in urban Cape Town.

While the same measure of surveillance was not imposed on the coloured working-class as on the African it was nevertheless necessary to fragment the development of autonomous political movements among the coloureds. Part of this strategy was to emphasize and deepen differences among the coloureds of the western Cape. This coincided with the radicalization of extra-parliamentary politics. During the Second World War and thereafter there was a proliferation of left-wing organizations in Cape Town. These political groups contrasted dramatically with the earlier coloured, liberal and somewhat accomodationist African People's Organization of Dr. Abdullah Abdurahman. The National Liberation League, New Era Fellowship, Non-European Unity Movement, and Communist Party were the leading and potentially dangerous forces in the poor constituencies of Cape Town (Lewis 1986). In fact, the leadership of these groups was largely drawn from the coloured petty bourgeoisie (especially teachers) and they had little regard for the popular culture or ethnic peculiarities of the common people. Popular culture had to be reformed and ethnic identity repressed so that a nation could be born (Jeppie 1990). Du Plessis involved himself with the 'folk' and popular culture of the inner city but that culture had already been dismissed as 'reactionary' by the radicals. It was through these very practices that Du Plessis would contribute to the political fragmentation of the poor people of the city.

In a context of intensifying popular urban struggles the boundaries of 'Malay' identity were therefore constituted against the coloured identity. Malay, as a metaphor for Islam, was constructed as different from the Christian and the secularized coloured. In his 1925 speech in Cape Town the Minister of the Interior, D.F. Malan, represented the Malays as different from the 'Asiatic' Indians.[9] This Malay-Asian opposition is, however, not present in Du Plessis's work at all.

The Malay in Du Plessis's work

Du Plessis's project consisted of knowledge (texts), expertise (institutions), the associational life (social clubs) and geographical space (residential segregation).

His position as authority on the Malays was established by his book, *The Cape Malays*, which was first published in 1944 and re-issued numerous times until 1972. It is a slim and lavishly illustrated volume of less than 100 pages. His first work was *The contribution of the Cape Malay to the Afrikaans folksong*, a more substantial and academic study but with a smaller circulation. In both works, however, the Malay is characterized in similar terms. The author's starting point is the body: the gestures and mind of the original Malays of the Cape. Their social norms and religion are treated next, followed by folklore and music. In describing the Malays Du Plessis was essentially recapitulating earlier writers on the Malays in South Africa and Indonesia. These writers portrayed the Malay as generally passive and feminine, but someone who could easily lose control and run amok under certain circumstances. 'He is introspective, kind towards women, children and animals; inclined to speak slowly, to be passive and insolent. When aroused he may lose all self-control and run amok,' writes Du Plessis (Du Plessis 1944, 3). 'Running amok' by slaves was a recurring theme in colonial texts on the slave population and can be found in the colonial literature on the Dutch Indies. The notion that it was in essence a Malay trait has since then been hard to unlearn.[10]

'Race', history and language. These were the essentials in Du Plessis's narrative on the Malays. 'Race', history and language were also the key elements in Afrikaner anthropological thought at the time. Between 1935, when his first work appeared, and 1950, two years before he became Commissioner of Coloured Affairs, hardly anything changed in Du Plessis's discourse and construction of the Malay ethnic subject.

According to Du Plessis the contemporary Malays shared only in some of the qualities of the original Malays because of changes due to a *vermeningsproses* (process of mixing). This 'mixing' affected mainly facial features, blood and size. This concern with blood and the body was, as J. M. Coetzee has remarked, 'viable intellectual currency for a long time' among South African writers and, we may add, the Afrikaner anthropologists (Coetzee 1980 & 1988). It is notable that Du Plessis begins with ethnic essence: body and mind, and then moves to narrate a history of the Malay in the Cape. This is a highly abbreviated history: a story of the early leaders of the 'race' at the Cape. Shaykh Yusuf, who was sent to the Cape in 1694 for his role in fighting against the Dutch in Macassar, and the other 'great figures' who were exiled to the Cape are given credit for contributing to the existence of the 'Malay race' in the Cape colony. Du Plessis mentions slavery very briefly but never discusses its significance in the shaping of Cape Town's history and cultures. He wanted to make the colonial past appear as the age of tranquillity (a Golden Age) for the Malays, by concentrating on the political exiles instead of the hard life of the slaves. Moreover, Du Plessis never explores the reasons for exile. Afrikaner historians have, of course, never written about slavery, except as a benign system of making slothful groups do something worthwhile.[11]

He also considers the language of the earliest Malays at the Cape. When Malayu became mixed with Portuguese and Dutch at the Cape the Malays were again hindered in the maintenance of their 'national identity', according to Du Plessis. But the fact that a variety of people, including 'his' Malays, spoke Afrikaans did not make them automatically available for incorporation into the Afrikaner nation. For Du Plessis there was '*Malay*-Afrikaans', '*coolie*-Afrikaans', '*kafir*-Afrikaans', and '*coloured*-Afrikaans' (Du Plessis 1939). Everybody spoke a version of Afrikaans but only a specific, white, group was capable of contributing to the formation of the language. Thus the role of Malayu vocabulary in Afrikaans was not taken into account.

'The things to look at are style, figures of speech, setting, narrative, not the correctness of the representation nor its fidelity to some great original,' argues Edward Said in *Orientalism*. In Du Plessis's orientalism it is not difficult to point out the language and style in which the Malay is represented, but neither is it hard to point to the real lives and communities that he wanted to freeze and fix in otherness.

Du Plessis's most popular work of prose, *The Cape Malays*, became a standard work on a South African community mainly resident in the urban western Cape. Public libraries bought and circulated it. Likewise private, presumably white, citizens and tourists purchased and read the slim volume. The text and illustrations gave the Malays a visibility and presence; perhaps it even contributed to placing them, in Timothy Mitchell's phrase, 'on exhibition', by isolating them and representing them in a marketable commodity form, the modern book (Mitchell 1986). However, more explicit means of exhibiting this rediscovered ethnic group were devised. The attempts to preserve a residential 'group area' and reserve a 'homeland' for Malays, in addition to the institutionalization of a Malay studies programme at the University of Cape Town, were additional ways of exhibiting the Malays as a specific ethnic entity. Another means was found in popular culture: the appropriation of informal singing and folk music as a symbol of Malayness.

Du Plessis's research on folk music had practical consequences. He initiated the formation of choral clubs and was responsible for the creation of an organizational structure for that which he called 'Malay choirs'. In 1939 Du Plessis founded the Cape Malay Choir Board (CMCB) as a forum for the promotion of Malay music and the co-ordination of Malay choir activities. This music had a long history among the slave population and the ex-slave working class coloured communities. This secular music was composed using locally produced instruments and included local versions of antiquated Dutch songs *(Nederlandseliedtjies)*, bawdy ditties (*moppies*), and adaptations of contemporary popular songs. Music skills were learned casually, and the lyrics of all genres were orally transferred from one generation to the next, and were usually transformed in the process (Kirby 1939; Winberg 1992). Du Plessis developed ties with old Malays who taught him the songs, which he transcribed for his dissertation. He relied on these informants to bring together the first troupes of Malay singers. Where such groups existed at all before 1939 they would usually gather informally at weddings or picnics. Now there was an organization stipulating rules and procedures, specifying a dress code, ordering the manner in which songs could be performed, and hosting an annual competition. The casual singing in households and at social gatherings of course continued but the CMCB was an innovation; one which was used as a signifier of Malay leisure and community.

Choir members, who were all male, were made to wear tailor-made dress suits. Each troupe would have special outfits for public performances, and a 'best dressed' prize was awarded for the most impressively attired troupe. In addition, a red Turkish fez was made part of the troupe uniform. The fez had not been a part of Malay headgear for almost the whole of the nineteenth century. It could only have been introduced to South Africa in the late 1860s when an Islamic scholar was sent by Istanbul to bring the Muslims of Cape Town closer to 'orthodoxy'.[12] Istanbul had only recently decreed the fez as the headgear of the reformed Ottoman army (Lewis 1961 & Quataert 1997).

These respectable working class Malay troupes contrasted sharply with the 'coon troupes' of the city. The latter wore cheap, loosely-fitted, colourful satin outfits and sported black faces in American minstrel fashion. Their songs were strikingly similar to the repertoire of Malay music but their performances less controlled. For instance, all coon troupes had male transvestites (*moffies*) at the head of their parades. The coons became a regular feature of New Year celebrations in the city. From 1906 various inner-city clubs organized the coon carnival. These clubs drew on Malay, Coloured, African and even a few white participants. Likewise, the Malay choirs had a mixed membership, even though they were presented as inherently and exclusively Malay by

Du Plessis. From 1939 the Malay choirs also became a part of the city's New Year celebrations, and from that time Du Plessis was the life president of the board of control of the Malay choirs.[13] If the Malays constituted a tribe then Du Plessis was self-appointed chief of the music-making clan.

The re-constitution of Malay music through the Cape Malay Choir Board was the re-invention of an imagined Malay tradition. As Eric Hobsbawm has noted about the 'invention of tradition' in general (Hobsbawm & Ranger 1986), it was 'essentially a formalization and ritualization, characterized by reference to the past, if only by imposing repetition'. Du Plessis had his own unarticulated agenda for promoting Malay choirs but the participants themselves gave their own cultural meaning to the music, performances and dress. Muslim tailors and fez manufacturers and the city's, largely white, fabric merchants certainly benefited from the introduction of Choir Board. An essential item of choir 'tradition' became a new source of income for tailors and fabric wholesalers. In whatever cultural or ethnic terms Muslim tailors thought of themselves they certainly profited economically from this innovation. Du Plessis was successful with this popular institution but at the University of Cape Town his attempts at getting an Institute of Malay Studies established were less successful.

In 1944 Du Plessis started protracted correspondence with the Council and Senate of the University of Cape Town regarding the establishment of an Institute of Malay Studies. He was then a senior lecturer in the Department of *Afrikaans en Nederlands*. In his memorandum to the university administration he stressed the utility of an institute, which he also referred to as a Department of Oriental Studies, for the 'Moslem community'. The Department would teach 'Cape Malay Studies' and Arabic. The former would comprise courses in the history of the Malay 'race', the origin and history of the Cape Malay, folklore, current language, reading Malay texts, and the westernization of the Cape Malay.[14] Again, 'race', history and language. But now also change, in the form of westernization of the Malay – the source of the loss of their original nature and essence. This loss of innocence and the corruption of the Malay appears elsewhere in Du Plessis's work as well. He, of course, was the one in a position to initiate measures to preserve and protect the Malay from the destructive modern world. The idea of an institute devoted to the study and research of the Malay population did not convince the university authorities. In 1944, four years after his initial correspondence, all that the Senate approved was an 'honorary organizer in Malay studies' with a grant of 550 pounds.[15] By this time Du Plessis's perception of the programme in Malay studies had expanded to include the training of 'professional fieldworkers in History, Afrikaans, Social Anthropology, Social Science, Human Biology, and Music'.[16] I have been unable to trace what happened to the idea of Malay studies after 1948. (In the early 1990s it reappeared, with the Malaysian government's initiatives to establish such a programme at the University of the Western Cape. By 1999 there was no such programme in place.) At that time Du Plessis, however, was not alone in arguing on behalf of Malay and oriental studies. In 1949 David Lewis wrote in the influential *Handbook of Race Relations in South Africa* that:

> Whereas all the great institutions of Europe, Britain, and American support departments of Oriental study, there is no such department in any of the South African universities. The inclusion of Oriental studies in the curriculum offered to students is urgently needed, not only to promote the education of Malays. The fact that material for study is so readily available is a further incentive. (Lewis 1959, 597)

Between the time of the successful formation of the Choir Board in 1939 and the failed initiative in Malay studies in 1944 Du Plessis had started to canvass for the 'preservation of the Malay Quarter' and for the establishment of a Malay museum. In 1943 Du Plessis founded the 'group working for the preservation of the Malay quarter' and had such 'prominent South Africans as the governor-general, the artist Ruth Prowse, and Chief Justice Watermeyer' as members of the lobby. The Malay quarter was a section of the city where the earliest urban slaves and their masters lived. Located at the foot of Signal Hill, and part of the Bo-Kaap residential area, it was close to the port and business district, and, because of the quaint Dutch architecture and size of the dwellings, it was a favourite place, especially among tourists, for capturing a vanished colonial past. But in the early 1930s and 1940s there was alarm in the press, and among the public generally, about the situation in the so-called Malay quarter. David Lewis expressed a South African liberal view of the problem:

> The responsibility for these conditions cannot be ascribed to the Cape Malay himself. The number of Malay-owned properties is negligible. In fact, it is safe to say that the whole area is privately owned by speculators, who collect the rents and are concerned with the condition of the houses on their properties. (Lewis 1949, 597)

Living conditions there were certainly demeaning but Du Plessis was not so much concerned with deteriorating material conditions as the crumbling architecture. Aesthetic preservation was an important impulse motivating Du Plessis and his group. More significant, however, in terms of an imagined Malay ethnic identity, the area was a space with a quintessential ambience of Malayness. The champion of the Malay cause said: 'These houses, single-storied and with backyards, were eminently suitable for the Malay way of living – until overcrowding set in' (Du Plessis 1944, 22). This description seems to be suitable for anyone in an urban setting but Du Plessis here again hopes to promote a particular cause. In Du Plessis's view, overcrowding was the problem, not the parsimonious landlords, as David Lewis had suggested. However, it was not the Malays who were to blame for overcrowding. The natives and others were responsible for the loss of beauty and order in the area. '(T)he destruction of this area is due mainly to the influx of natives and others who are not Malays,' said a brochure issued by Du Plessis's group.[17]

He wanted a specific space which Malays should identify as historically theirs. Moreover, he wanted a place where they could be permanently on exhibition as 'that semi-eastern colony'. His group continued to push the case for the Malay quarter as an 'historical monument'. They succeeded in the early 1950s when the National Party passed its notorious Group Areas Act and started forcibly removing millions of black South Africans from land that the state had declared white areas. The Malay quarter was declared a Malay Group Area, so that non-Malays could not take up legal residence there, although the white landlords lost nothing. In 1953 Du Plessis spoke of Macassar, some fifty kilometres outside Cape Town – where the great Shaykh Yusuf lived in exile, and was buried – as another Malay Group Area. Even though Du Plessis admitted that Macassar was 'sandy, bushy, partly waterlogged' he nonetheless thought it necessary that Malays lived near the tomb of their first ancestor and the 'founder of Islam in South Africa' (Du Plessis 1975, 57).

Disavowal and dissent

Texts and troupes, a research unit and a residential area: Du Plessis's project covered many fields of discourse and practice. Neither the popular classes nor the elites were left untested by his attempts to define and specify a distinct Malay ethnic subject in South Africa. In certain respects he was successful, in other interventions he failed. Despite his efforts he also failed in getting Malay re-inscribed on the list of ethnic categories in the South African censuses.

Malay had last been used, even though vaguely defined, in the late nineteenth century in the Cape colonial censuses but never after that. Subsequently Malay was included under, although not completely subsumed by, the equally nebulous 'coloured'. Du Plessis was unsuccessful mainly in the constituencies where emergent left-wing and nascent Islamic youth groups had most impact. In the regular mouthpiece of the Non-European Unity Movement, when Du Plessis failed to get unanimous support from his Malay choirs for the Van Riebeeck festival of 1952, the paper's editors wrote:

> Du Plessis believe(s) the Muslims are a docile, servile lot. The growing spirit of non-collaboration among the Muslims, their solidarity with other Non-Europeans – as shown in their break with Du Plessis's Choir Board, and their boycott of the Festival Stadium – these facts show that there are hundreds

> of Toussaint L'Overtures among the Muslims, as there are likewise among the rest of the Non-Europeans.[18]

This rhetoric was rooted in fact but it was also an attempt to mobilize support. Du Plessis had his own allies. They came especially from among the senior Muslim clergy. All his books on the Malays were apparently previewed by what the press called the 'chief priest' of Islam in the western Cape, Shaykh Ahmad Behardien, lest Du Plessis offend the religious sensibilities of Muslims by misrepresenting their faith and festivals. But a few months after his book, *The Malay quarter and its people* (written with C. J. Luckhoof), appeared in 1954, a 'small study group' organized a huge protest meeting.[19] The meeting condemned the book and resolved that 'the book propagates Islam as a Malay religion whereas Islam is a universal religion'.[20] The book was a rallying point for anti-Apartheid Muslim groups. However, it did not offend the powerful Imams because it had nothing offensive on theological grounds.

Conclusion

This chapter has looked at the context for the emergence, and the details, of a project to constitute a distinctive Malay Muslim ethnic subject in twentieth-century South Africa. While Du Plessis was the focus of the chapter, it should not be thought that he was working single-handedly. In the official Coloured Affairs Department from 1951 Du Plessis had a small bureaucracy to assist him; and before this he had other colleagues and supporters, and informants, in Bo-Kaap. Also, the customary press coverage – feature articles, letters to the editor, and book reviews – of matters related to Du Plessis and 'the Malay' contributed in many subtle and inconspicuous ways to the construction of his Malay community. I do not want to convey the impression that it was all simply a personally motivated effort. There was a discourse of 'the Malay', primarily one based in nineteenth-century colonial conditions, and Du Plessis draws on this store of travel and ethnographic writing and reworks it. He is very much a subject in a moment of a developing white, Afrikaans-speaking nationalism and an expanding Afrikaner anthropological and folklore endeavour. He employs the methods of these disciplines to craft his own terrain of expertise.

His diverse efforts to represent, literally and figuratively, the Malays were not uniformly successful, but neither were they all manifest failures. This chapter has not explored the 'internal' or 'interior' voices and processes through which the Muslims imagined and constructed their own sense of community. These activities were the fertile grounds for Du Plessis's specific project. My concern has been to explore the constitutive force of power, of representatives of authority, of the 'colonizing' function of a white intellectual over the other. Furthermore, the consequences of his project would enable the Malays to begin to see their world and identity in a very particular way.

But Du Plessis's Malays were negotiating numerous cultural and political identities at the same time. Apart from the inherent attributes he gives them he has to define them against the white Afrikaans-speakers, then against the coloured, then against the natives; D. F. Malan constituted them against 'the Asiatics'. Du Plessis would at one point simply refer to them as different to all others.

Yet, he left a legacy, which in the 1990s took on a different shape, in a new world and a new South Africa as I indicated at the beginning of the chapter. The very distinctive characteristics that he attributed to the Muslims of Cape Town were used by some of them to lay claims to membership of a Malay diaspora from which they could benefit. This image of the *fin-de-siècle* Malay of Cape Town finding his soul brother in Kuala Lumpur would have made Du Plessis proud of his efforts, which stretched over nearly five decades.

However, just as it seemed that the Malays were progressing well in the resurrection of their identity, a series of local and international events marginalized their project. The political and economic woes of Malaysia and Indonesia on the one hand and the militant struggle, in the name of Islam, against gangsters, drug-dealers, and the African National Congress government on the other, displaced the small world of Malay identity politics in the western Cape. Identities and the attendant politics are fluid.

Notes

1 *Cape Argus,* 21 November 1997.
2 *Mail and Guardian*, 25-31 August 1995.
3 For details see S. Jeppie, 'Historical process and the constitution of subjects: I.D. Du Plessis and the re-invention of the 'Malay' (Hons. Thesis, University of Cape Town, 1986).
4 *The Cape Times*, 11 January 1961.
5 *The Argus,* 11 January 1961.
6 *Moslem Outlook,* 27 June 1925
7 Cited in UG 20/1954. Dr Malan was speaking at the first Cape Malay Association conference. For a report on the conference see *Moslem Outlook*, 27 June 1925
8 *Die Huisgenoot,* 28 February 1939.
9 'Dr Malan showed how the Malays were peaceful and industrious and helped to build up the Afrikaans language. The government had not classified them as Asiatics but as South Africans.' *Moslem Outlook,* 27 June 1925
10 See entry on 'amok' in the *Encyclopaedie van Nederlandsch-Indie* (1917) vol.1 (Leiden,

E.J. Brill,); see also Edna Bradlow, 'Running amok and its historical significance,' *CABO* (1990) 5 (1).

11 Exemplary here is Victor de Kock's *Those in Bondage* . 1950. Cape Town.

12 The teacher was Abu Bakr Effendi. The fez itself was introduced in the Ottoman Empire in the mid-nineteenth-century. Depictions of Malays in the nineteenth-century art show men wearing the *tudong* (conical straw hat) over a turban.

13 By the start of 1945 the CMCB had a membership of twenty-six choirs. See *Cape Standard*, 30 January 1945. By 1952 it had an even larger number of choirs. But because Du Plessis forced troupes to participate in the Van Riebeeck festival – a celebration of the white founding of South Africa – a group of troupes left the Board and formed a new choral union. The disaffection of certain troupes and the loss of individual members from other choirs were partly due to the mobilization against the festival of political organizations such as the Non-European Unity Movement.

14 University of Cape Town. *Council minutes*, 31 January 1944. Appendix.

15 *UCT Senate minutes*, 18 April 1948.

16 *Senate minutes,* 1 March 1948.

17 *The Malay quarter: the case for preservation* (no date; issued by the 'Group for the preservation of the Malay quarter.').

18 *The Torch*, 4 March 1952.

19 Du Plessis, *Aantekeninge*, 57.

20 *Cape Times*, 21 April 1954.

Chapter Five

Fragile identities: Memory, emotion and coloured residents of Windermere

Sean Field

People are not only social beings, they are also fundamentally emotional beings. There has been a tendency amongst academic authors to erase the traces of feeling and emotion from the analysis of coloured identities[1]. I will argue that as all identities are by definition hybrid and impure (Bhabha 1994), all identities are emotional and fragile. The fragility of all identities is ambiguously constructed through weakness and strength, continuity and discontinuity, difference and sameness, clarity and confusion (Field 1996). The analysis of hybrid identities is directly relevant to the contestation and understanding(s) of coloured identities in Cape Town. As important as they are in this context, the hurtful effects of the labeling and stereotyping of coloured communities (Western 1981), using terms such as 'mixed masala', 'emotional', 'childlike' and 'confused',[2] will not be explored in this chapter. Instead I will focus on particular emotional experiences and patterns of popular memory amongst coloured residents of a Cape Flats community.

This chapter is drawn from 23 oral history interviews with former (and current) residents of the Windermere community. These interviews formed part of a social history study of Windermere from the 1920s to the 1990s. The area was originally a partly squatter community with most residents being classified either coloured or African. The community is located between the Cape Town suburbs of Maitland and Goodwood with the N1 highway forming its northern boundary and Voortrekker Road the southern boundary. This culturally mixed community was transformed by forced removals between 1958 and 1962. The community is today known as the Kensington/Factreton area[3].

Popular memories are central aspects of identity formation, but silences and the forgetting of past events are also fundamental. Silences around past events are difficult to interpret because they constitute an absence in the stories that people tell. However, in the South African case, the interviewer needs to listen for silences, as they are often created by emotional legacies such as traumatic or painful events experienced by oppressed individuals and groups under the apartheid state. More specifically, the silences within the popular memory of coloured communities need to be carefully analyzed and not simply labeled as 'amnesia', which is a way of pathologizing and stereotyping coloured communities. Rather, for generations of coloured residents, their feelings of loss, evoked by experiences of forced removals during apartheid, are significant. These memories and emotions are carried forward to the present, where fears about others and about the future are influencing the social and political choices these residents are making[4]. I will argue that while people who were classified 'coloured' under apartheid were disempowered they are nevertheless able to negotiate and reinterpret their mixed feelings and fragile identities in empowering ways.

The story of place: memories and feelings of loss

> At the core of the struggle for home lies the struggle for the way the story of place is told. Between what is remembered and what is forgotten, the self takes its bearings home. The question is no longer who is to guard the guardians *of what*, but who's to tell the story, *what story?* Who can bear witness? (Warner 1994, 86)

The stories from Windermere cover a range of topics but central themes are the 'struggle for home' and the 'story of place'. These are common themes for the communities of the Cape Flats. What the 'story of place' highlights is that popular memories cannot survive in isolation. People need to verbally construct their memories into words, sentences and stories, so that others can hear and respond.

But before discussing the intricacies of memory and place it is important to locate myself within this academic text. If interviewees are being scrutinized through the 'academic gaze' then researchers have a methodological obligation to make themselves visible during the research process and within the 'completed' academic text[5].

I write in an unsure way about the memories and emotions of others and about an unsettling past with which we still live in the present. However, to withdraw into silence or self-denial is unacceptable. I am a white male South African. This does not mean that because I am white I am really European and therefore my being African can be conveniently erased by some form of 'ethnic absolutism' (Gilroy 1993). I am white and African, and I was produced by apartheid South Africa. This is the uncomfortably hybrid, at times contradictory, location from which I write. Acknowledging this hybridity makes me feel fragile and unconfident. I have a responsibility to come to terms with the fragility and contradictions of having a hybrid identity and simultaneously occupying a relative position of power as a white South African. While my political activism in the liberation struggle in the 1980s is important it is also crucial that this should never be used to erase how I benefited from gendered, racial and class privileges under apartheid.

I cannot speak for the coloured interviewees quoted in this chapter. Nevertheless, I can present a selection of their stories and attempt to interpret sensitively their words and stories. I exercise power through this process of selection and interpretation. My analysis is an outsider's analysis but it is an outsider's analysis informed and shaped in part by years of political and research work in coloured communities. It is also not that 'the outsider' cannot say anything about 'the other' but rather that all researchers, outsiders and insiders, must try to understand how their identities and research strategies are shaping informants' and interviewees' responses[6]. Even when all the identities of the researcher and researched are identical, unequal power relations will still exist. There is no power-free research nirvana to be reached (Bhavnani 1990).

The retention and telling of memories (in both research and non-research contexts) always occur within a context of shifting power relationships. Access to opportunities to narrate one's memories and stories for audiences is shaped by position, resources and power relations. Memories are vital forms of social and cultural currency that are exchanged between individuals, groups and generations. But social memories are not passive blueprints of the past (Samuel and Thompson 1990). Rather, individual and collective forms of memory are always shaped and filtered in complex ways. As Coleman puts it, 'Memory is much more than recall of past stimuli. It involves emotion, will and creativity in the reconstruction of the past to serve present needs' (1986, 2). Memory is made within a relationship between the past and present, and, in a sense, also in relation to the future, as the presence of wishes and desires for the days ahead make their imprint.

Memories are also not a set of personal experiences trapped in an atomized individual world. In fact, memories are always social constructions. Even personal memories are forged through shared patterns of culture and language. The material of memories is the experiences of the past, but the words, sentences and stories people shape around these experiences, feelings and images have been internalized from the external social world[7]. The culturally accepted practices, rituals and rules that are learnt guide (or fail to guide) people in how to respond to, and make sense of, these memories. Furthermore, for memories to have social significance, they need to be conveyed to others in understandable storied forms, and in the process people are creating and maintaining their sense of self and identity (Lowenthal 1985).

> Groups provide individuals with frameworks within which their memories are localized and memories are localized by a kind of mapping. We situate what we recollect within the mental spaces provided by the group. [...] No collective memory can exist without reference to a socially specific spatial framework. That is to say, our images give us the illusion of not changing and

> of rediscovering the past in the present. We conserve our recollections by referencing them to the material milieu that surrounds us. [...] Our memories are located within the mental and material spaces of the group. (Connerton 1989, 37)

The places and spaces in which people played, worked and lived over time are crucial to their development as individuals and as communities. For example, the areas or spaces which children turn into their 'stomping grounds' are deeply symbolic to growing up and becoming a confident and secure adult. A sense of togetherness at home, in the street, and in the neighborhood is fundamental to creating a community identity. It is the sense of belonging that people develop through these experiences that is central to the construction of identity (Weeks 1991). A sense of belonging to a community is also developed through '[...] place's very same assault on all ways of knowing (sight, sound, smell, touch and taste) that makes it powerful as a source of memory as a weave where one strand ties another together' (Hayden 1995, 18). The stories from Windermere echo simultaneously this assault on the senses and a personal sense of belonging to a particular place. Mrs C.S. lived in the infamous shanty formation called 'the Timberyard'[8]:

> *Ek sê maar elke dag, as ek nou 'n sink huis in Windermere, wat daar nou sinkhuise gewies't, dan het ek soentoe getrek, na my ou dorp toe. Dit was baie lekker gewies. Dit was misvloerhuise gewies, nie soes die huise nie, ons moet maar mis gaan haal't, dan moet ons'e huise gesmeer. Ons plak pampiere in die sinkhuise. Ek maak dit mooi. Jy kan vuur gemaak't as dit koud is (...) soos Sun City is daai plek.* (I say every day, if I can now get a zinc house in Windermere, as there were zinc houses then, then I would move to there, to my old village. It was very nice there. It was dung floor houses, not like houses today. We used to fetch dung and we had to smear our houses. We plastered papers in the zinc houses. I make it beautiful. You could make a fire when it is cold [...] that place was like Sun City).

While she lived in a corrugated iron shanty throughout the 1950s, since the early 1960s she has lived in a sub-economic brick dwelling in Factreton. Nevertheless, she longs for the time when she lived in the shanty. There are elements of nostalgia in her story, but her story is also about a longing for a time when she had some sense of control over the making of her own home. The autonomy she experienced in the past and her sense of losing it after forced removals is a repeated theme in many interviewees' life stories. The degrees of control and autonomy which the individual feels she or he has directly impacts on the sense of agency and potency which she or he has within the immediate social world.

Another issue that affected interviewees' sense of autonomy was constantly rising prices. References to rising prices often have a timeless quality, which crosses the many recessions or changes in prices that interviewees have experienced. The price hikes of the 1980s and 1990s are bunched together in memory, and compared to the 'cheap times' of the 1950s and 1960s.

> Oh very nice, we will never have that time again, never, everything was so cheap, get a lot of things for a, a *sikspens*, nice things you can buy for a *sikspens*. Three pennies, stuff that you won't get today, oh, everything was cheap that time. (Mrs D. S.)

The interviewees who are quoted in this chapter are between 55 and 80 years old. In most cases they are currently living in working class areas and have usually lived in similar or worse economic circumstances for most of their lives. Most of these interviewees told stories about rising prices, housing problems, unrepaired streets, inadequate community facilities, gang violence and many other social issues. Other experiences, such as the forced removal of whites, Africans and coloureds from the Windermere/Kensington area, were woven into their stories. In 1958, under the Group Areas Act, this area was declared a 'coloured group area'. Nevertheless, it took until 1963 before all African residents were removed to Langa and Guguletu or endorsed out to the Ciskei or Transkei (Field 1996). In the process Windermere was bulldozed into the ground. The Windermere/Kensington area was transformed from being a culturally diverse set of community relationships and institutions to being the Kensington/Factreton area for 'coloured residents' only. Due to a lack of housing some coloured residents were removed to other parts of the Cape Flats. Those who remained were in most cases placed in the sub-economic housing project of Factreton. It was particularly the application of 'the Group' which was a watershed in their lives. Mrs D.F. illustrates a common response:

> *Ooo ons was hartseer, dit het gelyk die hele wêreld vergaan, want daai was mense van daar. {...} Daai tyd ryk mense was nie verseer, or rob, pickpocket of dood maak nie. Daai tyd was daar nie ligte nie hier in die pad nie maar ons kon geloop't in die aande. Almal ken vir jou en dit. Maar toe die Groep Areas inkom toe is dit 'n hele verandering, want die mense wat inkom is almal big shot, hulle kyk nie vir jou aan nie, almal het nou grand huise, hulle het grand karre, nie jy moet nou net vir jouself en soe en toe soe. Daai dae hier sal nooit weer nou terugkom nie {...}* (Oooh we had heartache, it seemed the whole world was decaying, because those people were from there. [...] That time rich people were not hurt, or robbed, pick pocketed, or killed, there was none of that. That time there was no lights here in this road and we could walk in the nights. Everyone knew you and that. But when the Group Areas came in then whole world changed, because the

> people that came in were all big shot, they don't look at you, everyone have their grand houses, they have grand cars, no you mustn't keep just for yourself and so and then on. Those days will never come back here again [...])

When people were forcibly removed from areas like District Six, Tramway Road, Harfield (and many other areas) or, in the case of Windermere/Kensington, where the community was transformed by the forced removals of others, this was experienced as a radical blow to the people's conception of their social worlds. As Mr H.B. explains, 'They were unsettled. Lots of people were disturbed by these people being moved away, they were being removed [...] You feel disturbed that this must happen. You know, you see the bulldozer running through these places, running through it.' The impact of forced removals and social engineering is not simply about the loss of physical houses, property and land; it is also significantly about the loss of a sense of home and community. Losing a home and a community is about a loss of security, stability, autonomy and even a sense of family, friendship and self. Most of all it hurts people to feel that such formative spaces, relationships and people have been taken away from them or have been injured in some way. In short, these are powerful feelings of loss, which are experienced as a deep source of hurt or pain. Coping with these uncomfortable emotions day-to-day over decades is a difficult task.

A central part of this difficulty is that 'to acknowledge the radical subjectivity of pain is to acknowledge the simple and absolute incompatibility of pain and the world' (Scarry 1985, 50). This difficulty is also partly rooted in the limits of words and sentences, and that '[...] language can represent pain only in its failure to be language, its willingness to forego sense, its readiness to risk incomprehensibility, implausibility' (Bennet 1997, 98). Emotional, like physical, pain '[...] has no voice, but when it at last finds a voice, it begins to tell a story' (Scarry 1985, 3). There is no easy way to find the appropriate spaces and words to express painful emotions. Furthermore, constructing the connections between 'words' and 'feelings' is itself a difficult endeavour for most people, although there are variations across cultural and gender boundaries (Lutz and Abu-Lughod 1990). Simply put, there is never a precise one-to-one relationship between words and emotions[9]. Therefore, the authenticity of emotions and people's interpretation of these words about emotions are open to doubt and uncertainty. As the survivors of forced removals continue the struggle to verbally 'voice' their experiences and feelings, so the researchers' uncertain, discursive attempts to record and interpret these stories through different mediums continue.

> *[...] daar was nie 'n ding soos apartheid nie. Kyk, die seerheid wat die gowerment kom bring het, die moeilikheid onder mekaar en die haat vandag is waar dit vir my onpliesierig voel het. Ek het nie nog nodig gesien vir daai, daarom is die wêreld vandag soe [...]* ([...] there was never such a thing as apartheid. Look, the

> painfulness that the government brought, the difficulty between each other and the hate of today is where it feels unpleasant for me. I have not seen the need for that, therefore the world is today is so [...]. (Mr H.B.)

All interviewees resorted to mythical reconstructions to deal with uncomfortable feelings of the past and present. Faced with the limits of language, limited material resources and the burden of considerable feelings, interviewees turned to myth making, the myth here being that all was well in Windermere but then the evil of apartheid destroyed that 'tranquility' and brought instability, pain and hatred between people. The need to construct and reconstruct an imaginary inner place where the pain and hatred of the past and present cannot reach or touch is fulfilled by myth (Field 1998). These are the myths that help people to keep on struggling for a better life (Samuel and Thompson 1990).

The memory of loss and losses', for this 55 to 80 year-old generation of coloured residents, is forged in relation to what was once had, experienced and felt, i.e. what existed prior to that loss. Most interviewees repeatedly contrasted 'that time' as opposed to the present time. The sense of community that was remembered from before forced removals was probably a mixture of fact and fiction. However, what is significant is that interviewees live these myths as their truth.

Viewed from a rationalist perspective myths will often seem irrational, unimportant and even naive. Yet it is the internal logic and truths of these popular and personal myths that should be sensitively unraveled and interpreted. This chapter argues that given the harsh socio-economic realities of the Cape Flats, myth making is often driven by people's need to keep hope alive. But these mythical memory constructions are not enough and people's sense of self and identity takes a battering through various losses, betrayals, failures and other disappointing experiences. The process of growing up and maturing is consequently unsettled and dislocated. These social circumstances make it difficult for a positive sense of self and identity to be created and sustained. Nevertheless, it is possible for people to reconstruct or reinterpret their sense of self and community through various activities.

The day-to-day gossip, folklore, urban legends, traditions and other forms of oral storytelling are indelible to the social relationships and emotional fabric of communities. Forced removals obviously shattered many of these relationships and hence many memories and stories have already disappeared. The former residents of District Six, Windermere, Kensington, Harfield, and Simonstown (and many more areas) tend, as expected, to be elderly. Nevertheless, [...] the essential task of old age is the preservation of a coherent, consistent self in the face of loss and of threat of loss. Reminiscence has a valuable role to play in this defence' (Coleman 1986, 14). Whether reminiscence takes place through talking to friends and relatives, giving oral history interviews or speaking to social workers, these are some of the ways in which telling stories of the past can help elderly residents. Furthermore, if the listeners and interviewers are younger members of the community, then there is potential for the strengthening of cross-generational relationships within communities. For example, Mr A.S. expressed his need for greater knowledge about his parents and his family history: 'Only one auntie and one uncle left. I want to trace, to get in touch with them, if I tell them exactly, or I can ask them, they know my father and mother's life before. Then I can get that history.'

The interviewee's plea for more historical knowledge is also a request for assistance with the burdensome feelings he has been carrying for many years. The act of talking about both painful and pleasurable aspects of one's personal past, a past that is always meshed within a collective past, can become a healing process of self review. By giving people the opportunity and space to speak about their experiences it becomes possible to partly understand what their loss (and related feelings) involve. It is also possible to use these stories and understanding to create sensitive development projects for the renewal of urban and rural communities.

Fragile identities: feelings of fear

The cultural hybridity of coloured identities does not necessarily undermine people's ability to make choices and decisions for themselves. However, the explicit cultural hybridity of particular communities, such as people classified coloured, is signified as problematic and disruptive by the dominant discourses of 'whiteness' and 'blackness' (Gilroy 1993; Bhabha 1994). These discourses present the myth of 'pure' identities as the ideal object to be fulfilled. The simultaneous location between and within these essentialist discourses involves contradictory tensions, ambivalences and struggle through a mixture of confusion and clarity in order to reach confident answers appropriate for each person who, or community that, was classified coloured. Therefore, when coloured people 'measure' themselves by these discourses, it usually means that the emotional consequences of living hybrid identities can be confusing, complicated and painful. As one informant said to his friend, *'Jy's soe deurmekaar soes 'n verkleurdemannetjie in 'n smartieboks.'* ('You're as confused as a chameleon in a Smartie box').

Nevertheless, people's responses to their identity location, and interpretations of their feelings, need not be static or fixed. The admitting of mistakes, confusion and weakness allows for the recognition of a fragile identity in the process of perpetual making and becoming. For if a state of mythical 'completion' or 'closure' is ever reached, then the experience of lived identities as being constructed and re-constructed in an open-ended process of becoming is unthinkable (Laclau 1990).

Who we think and feel we are – and who others think we are, and how they relate to us – is shaped by a variety of dialogic power relations[10]. Many of the coloured interviewees I spoke to expressed crude forms of racism towards Africans and a glowing admiration of whites. On the one hand, this was probably an attempt to impress me, as a white interviewer. On the other hand, I think these views were believed by most interviewees. While my relationship to interviewees was in part influencing interviewees' responses, especially with exaggerated type responses, I also think that in most cases the broader power relations that interviewees had been experiencing had a more forceful impact on their consciousness. For example, the following interviewee said:

> *En 'n kaffir al dra hy 'n goue ring, bly hy nog steeds 'n aap. Daai's nou plein gepraat, nè? U gesê ek moet sommer plein praat [...] Kyk hulle sit soe bymekaar, dan praat hulle nog altyd soe hard aaneen. Hulle het niks, hulle sê hulle het 'n culture, hulle het nie 'n culture nie, hulle's rou. Hulle sê onse bruin mense is mixed masala, maar ons bruin mense staanaan die wit mense, as wat hulle aan die wit mense, as wat hulle staan. Want onse culture en die culture en die wit mense se culture is een.* (And a kaffir, even if he wears a gold ring, still remains a monkey. That's now plain talking, hey? You said I must talk plain [...] Look they sit together, and they talk all the time so loud continuously. They have nothing, they say they have a culture, they don't have a culture, they're raw. They say us brown people are mixed masala, but we brown people closer to the white people, as what they are to the white people, as what they stand. Because our culture and the white people's culture is one.) (Mrs D.E.)

This crude racism contains several important themes. Firstly, the 'monkey' metaphor reflects the belief that whatever the social or class position of an African person, their racial identity will remain the overriding, and negative, feature. Secondly, Africans do not have a culture because they are primitive (as in 'raw' and 'talking loudly'). Thirdly, the defence against the attack of coloured people being 'mixed masala' (and the implication of this attack is that coloured people do not have a culture) is to emphasize a closer proximity to white culture, which therefore gives coloured people a greater claim to having a culture. The central theme here is an apparent acceptance of the universal discourse of whiteness as constituting civilized and desirable culture. The above interviewee's racist statements are very similar to the origins of colonial racism which were constructed through a link between skin colour and the heathen/savage image (Foster 1993).

In a similar vein another interviewee said, 'I know I am speaking on the whatsename [i.e. tape-recorder] but I can tell you one thing, I must be honest, it's as the old saying, you can take him (i.e. black Africans) out of the bush, but you will not take the bush out of him' (Mr K.N.). The racial mythology here is rooted in constructions about the 'primitive' Other who comes from the 'bush'. Another interviewee said, 'He was milkie, he had a shanty, but it was beautiful inside. You know, you won't think it looks so nice inside. Some of them (i.e. black Africans) were okay, some of them were raw, you know? But some of them, like the cultured ones, you know, you could communicate with them' (Mrs A.M.). In this instance the African Other was split into those without culture (as in 'raw') and those with culture, a culture that somehow measured up to the interviewee's standard of 'civilized' communication. These myth-laden, racist interpretations of cultural difference were also influenced by language difference; as one interviewee put it, 'Everything they say, they just something uh walla salla salla, something like that, hey? So that's what the Africans talk. Salla salla salla de Klerk uh uh walla walla salla uh ha ha!' (Mrs A.M.). In a racist manner, this interviewee portrays African languages as being crude and primitive.

There were many passages in which other coloured interviewees expressed implicit or explicit racism towards Africans. For example, 'all' Africans were 'unforgiving', 'lazy', 'merciless' and 'dirty'. The differentiating theme of 'primitive' African Other allowed these coloured interviewees simultaneously to distance themselves from the African community and to lay claim to a closer, more 'natural', cultural relationship with the white community. In their relationships with both white and African people, coloured interviewees reflected an ambiguous mixture of fear and desire[11]. As Hall argues, 'Just as masculinity always constructs femininity as double – simultaneously madonna and whore – so racism constructs the black subject: noble savage and violent avenger and in the doubling, fear and desire double for one another across the structures of otherness [...]' (1992, 256).

In other cases, interviewees spoke about their African neighbours in sensitive and considerate terms, but used a racial terminology that many would today regard as racist: 'We had quite a few native people, but very nice. Very nice native people, you know? Very clean, tidy, not like some of them. [...] I got a native doctor and he says he can't speak, aya, Afrikaans. So I thought, oh now, I should have learned their language. I could have spoken their language with them' (Mrs E.C.). This interviewee seems to be conscious of how the inability to speak each other's language inhibits a deeper understanding of the Other.

In contrast, a handful of interviewees initially denied the existence of large numbers of African residents in the area. Only when questioned about who lived next door, across the road and around the corner, did they begin to admit the existence of African residents. As one interviewee said, *'Hulle het eintlik nie hier gewoon nie. Dis net kleurlinges en blankes wat hier gewoon het'* ('They actually did not live here. It was just coloureds and whites who lived here') (Mrs E.G.). I suspect that for these interviewees it was quite threatening to admit to having lived in a community dominated by Africans. The same could be said of the interviewees who exaggerated the presence of black African residents and who extensively drew on racial myths. On the one hand, the African Other is denied, on the other hand, the African Other is presented as an omnipotent, primitive and violent force. In both cases (and the above examples), these responses suggest more about the storyteller than the people referred to. Interviewees who expressed these forms of racial Othering were grappling with a threatened, fearful sense of location and identity within the South African context. It seems that the fear and loss expressed by these interviewees, and the racial mythologies that they constructed around these feelings, are attempts at coming to terms with the ambivalent tensions of cultural hybridity. For example, Mrs E.C.'s mother was a 'German woman' and her father was a 'St Helena man':

> It was very awful when apartheid came, although I don't know who I am, if I am European or coloured. But I used to feel heartsore for people like [...] that the coloured people used to live together with the whitey husbands and the coloured wives and then all of a sudden they had to part and they were thrown out, they musn't live with Europeans anymore. [...] I think it must have been heartbroken for those children, because the other one can go to a European school, but the other one can't because he's coloured. But yes, it's their parents, it's their children. It was very heartsore for me. Very heartsore. (Mrs E.C.)

The pain of living across apartheid's rigid categorization of either being 'white' or 'coloured' meant that interviewees like Mrs E.C. had to confront continual uncertainty and complex decisions about their cultural location and identity. Furthermore, it was common for coloured interviewees to talk about their white ancestry and not to talk about their African ancestry. In many cases the forgetting and silences around black African ancestry goes back so many generations that the current generation no longer has memories of this ancestry. It is difficult to fix when the silencing began but what is explicable is the repeated exaggeration of white ancestry by most of the interviewees. In part these exaggerations are probably related to my white presence but there is also little doubt that this phenomenon exists irrespective of the researcher's identity.

Is the coloured community therefore racist? I think not. For example, as James argues, '[...] to interpret the coloured vote as an act of racism has little basis in fact' (1996, 42); or as a local African National Congress (ANC) leader put it, 'coloureds are not so much racist as they fear non-racialism. The big unknowns for coloureds are non-racialism, freedom and equality' (Rasool 1996, 57). However, the fact that there are instances of racist or conservative political positions within coloured communities, needs to be understood in context. As Mr H.S. argues:

> If they [i.e. African people] can go on with their own people, like they kill them, I mean their own race, what will they do with me and you? I mean will they treat us better, see that's the question on everybody's mind. Cause I mean they have had a raw deal all the time, but the thing is you can't trust them,

> the blacks. The problem is you can't talk their language, you don't know what they are talking about, what they are scheming against you. You must just be on the lookout all the time. But we hope things will come right.

The lack of knowledge created by multiple divisions such as culture, language and resources, combined with differential access to jobs and education under apartheid, created fertile grounds for mistrust and fear of the Other to grow. It is simply wrong to argue that coloured residents were either duped by apartheid ideology or that they were apathetic victims of false consciousness (Field 1990). Moreover, the fashionable 'amnesia' label seems to be a variant of the 'false consciousness' label of the 1980s. On the one hand, in a patronizing manner the false consciousness/amnesia argument represents coloured residents as people who cannot think or remember for themselves. On the other hand, it allows progressive groups the convenience of not dealing with the conservatism that exists within coloured communities. For example, it was common for the coloured population to be labeled as 'fence-sitters' during the 1980s. However, coloured residents of the Cape Flats are not fence-sitters. Coloured residents might be politically divided but then what cultural community is not politically divided? Coloured residents on the Cape Flats have been making political decisions and choices for generations. The problem rather lies with 'us', i.e. the politically correct left. It is 'we' who cannot come to terms with the conservative political choices coloured residents are making and it is 'we' who have failed to explain why coloured residents are making those decisions.

It is crucial to stress that some of the 23 coloured interviewees did not express conservative or racist positions. Several coloured and African interviewees spoke about their cross-cultural relationships as shared experiences of neighbourliness and community.

> *Ek het maar swaar grootgeword hier in Windermere. Ek mien die mense het gesurvive baie mense het hulle eie skape, koeie, varke, hoenders gehet. {...} Die mense is arm, maar hulle het lekker gelewe, lekker ook mekaar verstaan ook. Die Bantoe mense en ons en die Moeslem mense, almal het lekker saam gelewe. Daai tyd jy kan jou huisdeur laat ope gestaan't, jy het nie nodig vir die buurman langsaan te sê, kyk na, want die mense het soe aan een gelewe in daai tyd. En die Bantoe mense en ons het lekker saam gelewe daar was no problem gewees 'ie, daai tyd, nie soe't nou is verdag is nie.* (I had a tough upbringing here in Windermere. I mean the people survived, many people had their sheep, cows, pigs, chickens. [...] The people were poor, but they lived nice, nicely understood each other as well. The Bantu people and us, and the Muslim people, everyone lived nicely together. That time you could leave your house door open, you did not have to tell your next door neighbour, because people lived like that, in that time. And the Bantu people

> and us lived nicely together, there was no problem, that time, not like it is today. (Mr H.B.)

While there are romantic echoes in this story, this interviewee – and several others – are making statements about their community experiences in the 1950s, and more specifically, are describing their affirming personal experiences of interactions with their black African neighbours. In a more painful story, Mr D.S. (a longstanding research guide, informant and friend) gained possession of a baptismal certificate book while working as church scribe in the 1950s. From the late 1950s until 1969 he used this book to help African residents re-classify themselves as coloured. He helped African residents to negotiate the dangers of apartheid bureaucracy, which meant they could avoid forced removal from Windermere to Guguletu or Langa. He was arrested and charged with more than 150 counts of fraud, to which was added:

> *Hulle't my aangeklaar vir invoering van terrorisme, om daardie deel gevind dat ek ek kan 'n kanaal gewies't vir die terrorisme. En die klagtes was toe, aan bedrog en vervalsing {…} hulle't my toe skuldig bevind op tien klagtes en die anner klagte was almal verwerp.* (They charged me for importation of terrorism, because that aspect was found, that I could have been a channel for terrorism. The charges were fraud and falsification ... they found me guilty of ten charges and the rest were scrapped).

For the ten fraud charges and the charges under the Terrorism Act he spent seven years in prison. He says of his prison experiences:

> *Dit was baie dinge, ummm, baie grusaam, nè? Dit was nie maklik soos nou nie, dinge was baie grusaam. Die bewaardes was vir jou treurig, jy moet in jou spore trap of jy word geslaan en jy word aangekla.* (It was many things, aaam, very gruesome, yes? It was not easy like today, things were very gruesome. The warders were terrible, you had to watch your step or you were hit and charged).

Telling these stories was an emotional experience for Mr D.S. – he cried as he told them. While we had been political comrades and research co-workers for several years, it was only when a certain level of trust had been established that he was able to reveal these stories. When responding to intense emotions such as pain and loss, interviewers should heed Erskine's advice, 'Grief is a reaction to loss and sometimes it is not only the presenting loss which the interviewer should be aware of. One may need to skillfully deal with the sharing of past loss that doesn't seem associated with the presenting story. Or perhaps allow the informant a graceful/grateful silence' (1996, 6). Of the 23 interviews, it is significant that mainly male interviewees expressed feelings of sadness through crying. In part, our shared gender identity must have influenced these emotional expressions. In contrast the gender differences between myself and female interviewees probably had an inhibiting effect.

I have selected quotations that highlight the extreme examples of racism on the one hand, and, on the other hand, the major sacrifices that others like Mr D.S. paid for their political beliefs and actions. There were many coloured interviewees who were situated in between these extremes and who expressed a mixture of positive commentary and racist remarks about black and white South Africans. There were also instances where interviewees were able to develop a humane world-view despite experiencing harsh living circumstances. While Mrs C.S. was growing up on a farm in the Swellendam area, the white madam told her that,

> *'Julle is nie dieselfde as wat ons is nie, ons het 'n wit vel en julle 'n bruin vel.' Toe sê ek, die bloed is dan dieselfde bloed, daar's nie 'n swart bloed nie en 'n wit bloed nie of 'n bruin bloed nie. Toe sê sy vir my, 'Jy's te slim. Jy moet wag dat die oubaas die aand kom, dan moet jy vir die baas vra.' Toe sê ek vir die oubaas ek kan't nie glo nie [...] dan kan jy sien van Jan van Riebeeck se tyd hy't gepaar met die bruines, die wittes saam met die bruines. En toe vat hy my na die garage toe, en toe gee hy my 'n pak, want hy wil nie die waarheid leer ken't nie.* ('You are not the same people as us, we have white skins and you have brown skins.' So I said, the blood is the same, there's not a white blood and a black blood and a brown blood. So she said, 'You're too clever, you must wait until the old boss comes tonight, then you ask him.' So I told the old boss and he wouldn't believe it [...] that you can see from Jan van Riebeeck's time, he mated with the browns, and the whites with the browns. And so he took me to the garage and gave me a hiding, because he did not want to learn the truth).

Mrs C.S. is expressing her belief in a common, mythological humanity that is all the same in 'blood'. Her rebellious expression of these beliefs is forcefully and painfully repressed by a gendered, racist *baasskap* which begins with the madam and ends with the male *baas*. At least three other interviewees also used this reference to a common humanity rooted in 'blood'. A common 'blood' which, significantly, is beneath the differing skin colours of people and symbolically understood as beyond apartheid ideology. It is a mythology, which helped Mrs C.S. and others to construct a positive sense of 'humanity' underlying the separations, exclusions and brutalizing apartheid experiences.

It is also important to note that Mrs C. S. cannot read or write. The story of Mrs C.S. is about a young coloured female child facing the old white male baas in the past. Yet, when Mrs C.S. tells her story, she is an old interviewee facing the young white male interviewer. On the one hand, she was expressing legitimate pain and anger at her oppressive experiences in the past, and on the other hand, she displayed a degree of understanding towards me, through telling the story. The story is told because the need is great and the interviewee can sense that the interviewer is empathetically listening. Mrs C.S.'s courage in telling her story filled with pain also suggests a sense of 'hope'. She was neither trapped in fear-driven racial Othering and nor was she captive to her legitimate anger.

However, Mrs C.S., Mr D.S., and a few others, were in the minority. The majority of coloured interviews displayed a mixture of racial Othering, explicit racism or implicit forms of racism. Coloured interviewees' past experiences of loss and their fears of re-experiencing forms of loss and hurt under a black African majority government are important parts of an emerging explanation. Fear of transformation and rapid change and the possible reoccurrence of marginalisation and discrimination are understandable. However, these fears need to be interpreted differently. For example, these fears should not be crudely approached as a defensive protection of social and class privileges. In fact, these fears tend to be more pronounced amongst working class coloured residents, who have less material and social advantages to protect. Fear has multiple meanings ranging from strength, weakness, defensiveness, caution and much more. The same could be said of loss. Significantly, while both loss and fear can be debilitating, finding personal and collective ways to resolve, heal, live with, and move beyond these emotions can make the person or community stronger. Acknowledging and learning to manage constructively the emotions embedded in our memories are a crucial part of signifying fragile identities, not as weak, but as strong. As others have argued in this collection, the struggle over the meanings and ways of living coloured – or any other – identities is never fixed but an ongoing process.

Finally, there is a political need to counter the New National Party's (and other political groups') manipulation of coloured communities' emotions, beliefs and choices. A central question which emerged after the 1994 elections was 'why did the National Party's *swartgevaar* tactics towards coloured communities succeed in the Western Cape and not in the Northern Cape?' Furthermore, research about differing kinds of emotions rooted in shifting patterns of popular memory – and their social and political implications – within coloured and other communities is necessary. Comparative oral history and sociological approaches have much to teach us about how and why coloured residents make particular choices and decisions.

Conclusion

This chapter has argued for the need to include the range of emotions that coloured residents of the Cape Flats have experienced in the past and continue to live with in the present. I have particularly focused on the significance of feelings of loss, hurt and fear and how these emotions have shaped the nature of memory, myth making and identity. This work focused on a generation of coloured residents aged from 55 to 80 years old from the Windermere community. The majority of interviewees resorted to conservative political choices and many in fact expressed racist attitudes towards their image of a 'primitive' African Other. In other cases there were interviewees who expressed progressive political views. However, the role of myth making was central to how all interviewees remembered the past and lived the present. Myths were used to avoid or manage painful aspects of the past or myths were used to deal with fears of the African community and the changes happening in contemporary South Africa. This chapter also suggested that unresolved feelings of loss and fear seemed to be hampering confident decision-making. While the contestation around the meaning of coloured identities will continue, I have an open-ended sense that there are also fragile beliefs in South Africa that need to be defended:

> If racism is an ideology we have one dominant principle in South Africa – non-racialism – to challenge and transform this land. I have argued that racism is a virulent set of changing mythologies; it is not going to be easy to wish it away. It will return in new guises, renewed rhetoric and altered masks. If there is merit in my argument that non-racialism consists of 'fragile threads' then our task for the future should be clear. It will be to struggle, to argue, to analyze and to defend that which is precious, fragile and vulnerable. (Foster 1993, 77)

Finally, I am left with the loose ends of my own fragile thoughts and feelings. These feelings cannot be neatly explained or packaged in an academic text. Nevertheless, the process of critical self-reflection must continue. More crucially, a self-reflection that is motivated by non-racial ideologies and anti-racist practices can make small contributions to personal and collective struggles. We need to make productive use of our privileged positions to speak through different mediums of representation, so that the life stories of the poor and marginalised are being disseminated to as many audiences as possible[12].

Notes

1 See for example, Goldin (1987) and Lewis (1987).

2 This chapter uses many of the labels developed under colonial, segregationist and apartheid governments. For example, the term 'coloured' is not intended to be pejorative and it is argued that people who choose to use this term in reference to themselves, have the capacity to redefine this term in a positive manner. Further-

more, the terms 'race' and 'racial' are used in inverted commas to denote their contested and problematic nature. See Gilroy (1993) who uses 'race' in a similar fashion.

3 For further details about this community see Field (1990, 1996).

4 All the interviews for this chapter were conducted in 1993, and unless otherwise stated, the present refers to when interviews occurred.

5 In the Derridean sense all texts are open to further rewriting and multiple interpretations and are therefore never 'completed' or 'closed'.

6 Researchers have an obligation to 'give back' to interviewees in some form. I originally conducted these interviews for my PhD., and offered all interviewees a copy of the tape recording and a copy of the book that I intend to publish from the PhD.

7 The socially constructed boundaries between the 'individual body' and the 'external world' are blurred and porous. People in most, especially Western, cultures tend to need the mythology of the self-contained 'individual' for emotional survival. It is therefore important that critical analysis be attuned to the social construction of the 'individual body' and 'self' within the context of myriad power relations and discourses.

8 'Timberyard' and 'Strongyard' were legendary structures consisting of a circular formation of inwardly facing corrugated iron and wood dwellings. People would use the open space in the middle to wash clothes, prepare food, and sell liquor.

9 This argument runs the risk of constructing a binary between 'emotions' and 'words'. Post-structuralism and other social constructionist approaches, however, by deconstructing forms of humanism, tend to erase feelings and emotions. Through interpreting the relationships between language and emotions, we can learn much about the construction of the self and its relationships to various internal and external phenomena.

10 It is crucial to understand the possible tensions and contradictions between; on the one hand, how people think, present and talk about themselves, and on the other hand, how people feel about themselves. For example, Lacanian and post-Lacanian analysis tends to miss out these relationships because pre-linguistic feelings are not possible within that approach. In contrast, I think that pre-linguistic feelings do exist.

11 African and white interviewees also expressed forms of racism and racial Othering but these patterns were more pronounced and numerous amongst the coloured interviewees, see Field (1996).

12 I am employed by the Western Cape Oral History Project, which provides opportunities to record and disseminate the stories of economically poor and marginalised people to various public audiences. From early 2001 the project will be known as the 'Centre for Popular Memory'.

Chapter Six

District Six and its uses in the discussion about non-racialism

Crain Soudien

> It was both urban and urbane. It developed a verbal dexterity of its own. It cultivated a macabre and biting sense of humour to laugh to keep from crying [...] It viewed with suspicion and disdain the middle class values of Walmer Estate and Wittebome. Within its boundaries it practiced no form of religious or colour discrimination. There was no observable apartheid since the District was one big apartheid. It practised no class discrimination since almost everyone there was working class. It insulated itself against the outside world that was always threatening it. *Richard Rive*

The events surrounding the dismantling of the formal apparatus of apartheid in 1994 both brought home and emphasized the depth of the identity conundrum in South Africa. On both personal and social levels, long-standing and much used signifiers such as black, white, African, coloured, Indian, Asian, Malay, European and others were, simultaneously, being emptied out, refilled, reconfigured and stabilised. Meanings were taken, given, rolled over, packaged and repackaged, and, in the process, South Africa's past was celebrated and reviled, and affirmed and denied. Sometime blacks came upon a new sense of their old 'colouredness' or their 'Indianness'; there were coloureds who reached into the recesses of their pasts and discovered how much they were really 'Malays' or 'Khois' or indeed even 'Africans'; and there were also whites for whom their 'Europeanness' became important.

What apartheid and the struggle against it had done was to produce what one might now regard as strong 'official' and 'counter-official' identities. In the aftermath of apartheid, both the official and the counter-official have been revealed as constructs which, in the language of deconstruction, are not unproblematic. Class, social and political alignments and the solidarities and schisms which they precipitated came under stress as the political conditions of the post-1994 period opened up new choices and put under threat old ones.

Against this backdrop the struggle to articulate identities which resist the hierarchic and oppressive modalities of times gone by is proving to be profoundly complex. What is more, as Stuart Hall (1990, 222) reminds, if identity needs to be understood as a 'production' which is never complete, 'always in process, and always constituted within, not outside, representation', then the authority and authenticity with which it might be asserted is also being shown up as open to question. In looking for resources in the discussion about identity and its articulation, I try to work within this logic here. The position I take is that the authority necessary for self-representation and the authenticity presumed to underscore its naturalness are invariably inscribed ideologically; the ideological pressures of the contexts in which people find themselves pervade their every experience. It is for that reason, I would argue, that authority and authenticity, as underpinnings of identity, are never unproblematic, written as they are in the idiosyncrasies of the historical formations which have brought them to life.

The thrust of this chapter, bearing in mind this logic, is an attempt to understand the role which the memory of District Six – South Africa's pre-eminent site of forced urban removals – plays in the discursive terrain of 'race'.[1] More particularly, the chapter seeks to understand the concept of District Six as a site for the production of a South African identity, and asks how, and indeed whether, this concept works as a means of articulating the non-racial subject. The chapter is not so much about District Six as a source of empirical data, as, rather, it is about District Six as a site of social construction. It is not, therefore, in the strict sense a history, but rather an attempt to understand *how* District Sixers have written themselves in the range of oral, written and other media that they have used. Beginning from the premise that all reality is human-made, as opposed to natural, the chapter seeks to come to terms with the social meanings with which the idea of District Six is invested. Based on this premise, the point of departure is that 'District Six' as a signifier is understood to embody the qualities of tolerance, mutual respect, and respect for difference which, by contrast, 'South Africa', as a counter-signifier, was, and might still be, presumed to be without. 'District Six' was, therefore, in this way of looking, the opposite of 'South Africa'. It was, as Cape Town-based historian Vivian Bickford-Smith said at a recent meeting, the basis upon which a 'united front against South Africa' was premised. It was, following this logic, not *of* South Africa in its apartheid guise, but a place apart. In these terms, it was an enclave within the wider national context of class oppression and exploitation, racial segregation, religious differentiation and ethnic chauvinism and, indeed, xenophobia.

It is the status and the meaning of the enclave claim with which this chapter seeks to work. I look at the discourse of District Six as it is produced by its major interlocutors. What the features of this discourse are, what the representational strategies which are used in the discourse are, what is silenced and what is privileged, what holds up the coherence of the discourse, and what power and authority are invoked in this coherence, are questions which I pose. While I do not spend much time looking at the conditions of production of this discourse, it is important to recognize how much these conditions lie at the heart of what District Six is presumed to stand for. [2]

Two reasons lie behind the writing of this piece. The first is a concern with the inadequacy of current notions of non-racialism. I would like to suggest that non-racialism, as it has been expounded for the modern South Africa, is a concept which, like many other concepts which serve as the supposed cornerstones of national identity, is almost everything and nothing. In this sense, following Benedict Anderson, it is akin to the founding legends upon which the modern nations of Europe came into being. It is, for example, upon the foundations of non-racialism that the new politics of struggle developed in South Africa in the 1940s, that the government of national unity of 1994 is premised, and upon which the character of contemporary South Africa as a rainbow people is projected.

However, read less innocently, non-racialism also spawned a plethora of political congresses which were, paradoxically, defined racially in the mid-fifties and which came to constitute the Congress Alliance. These understandings, in their turn, gave way to renditions of South Africa as, variously, a single nation composed of distinct racial groups equal in standing, a united country bound together by a common humanity in which 'race' was deemed to be a figment of the hegemonic imagination, or indeed, different cultures united in their diversity.

These tensions have persisted in the new South Africa and have supplied, as and when they have been needed, the arguments for the preservation of racial privilege (the new reconciliationists), the re-ordering of privilege (the affirmative actionists), and the dismantling of privilege (the transformationalists). I want to argue that there is a need to posit a new form of non-racialism in South Africa, one that I would like to call critical non-racialism. This concept is related to what Carrim and I have elsewhere described as critical anti-racism (Carrim and Soudien 1998). I could have used the term anti-racism here, but am profoundly aware that anti-racism as a term only begins to develop a currency in the late eighties and early nineties. Non-racism, on the other hand, was part of the discursive vocabulary of the political and social movements that operated in the Cape from the late forties already.[3]

The notion of a 'critical anti-racism' which is used by David Gillborn (Gillborn 1995), and which draws on the influences of postmodernism on anti-racism in the British context, in particular Donald & Rattansi (1992), bears significant resonances in, and for, the South African situation. A 'critical anti-racism' may be described as a form of anti-racism that consciously seeks to work with, and takes into account, what postmodernists, following Bhabha (1994, 67), have called 'difference'. Difference in this understanding is the articulation of identity as multiplicitous; it is an approach to identity that disavows fixity, originality and singularity. This notion of anti-racism takes issue with understandings of 'race' which homogenize identity and projects the subjects of racial discourse, whatever they might be, as stable unitaries, trapped in fixed dominant-subordinate relations. Instead, it suggests that the epithets of identity are modes of differentiation which are 'realised as multiple, cross-cutting [in their] determination, polymorphous and perverse, always demanding a specific and strategic calculation of their effects' (Bhabha 1994, 67).

Transposing this thinking to the South African discussion of non-racialism, where identity, in the range of non-racial traditions which constitute its political landscape, is presented in the dichotomy of deviance and innocence, identity becomes imbricated as always 'internally divided' (Flax 1993, 96). Subjects, as they are addressed in a critical non-racial discourse are, therefore, seldom entirely oppressive or oppressed; their identities are always in excess of the stereotypes presumed to represent them. In presenting their participation in the world of political choice, they are thus inscribed as contradictory and inconsistent subjects. Critical non-racialism as a way of looking is alert to the possibility, therefore, that the very subjects of domination are capable themselves of being more than just victims and perpetrators of oppression.

A second reason for looking at District Six is that of attempting to understand the relation of its discourse to coloured identity. The extent to which District Six is a 'coloured' place, producing a 'coloured' discourse, is also an issue on which I focus. Constructed by turn as lodestar, spiritual heartland and even as *fons et origo*, the district has been used to legitimize coloured claims for a place within the South African order. Given the racial uses to which the idea of District Six has been put by the apartheid government, and even, in some ways, by the new democratic order, how intrinsically coloured is the symbolism of District Six?

The making of the discourse of District Six

District Six's origins lie in a complex weave of urbanization and modernization processes, similar to those in many other cities in the world. The area abutted what we would understand as the business district of Cape Town and was until about 1840 a largely uninhabited and open expanse of land. Two estates were located in the area, Zonnebloem and Bloemhof. As Cape Town grew economically, stimulated by the export of wool and ostrich feathers, and, later, diamonds and gold (Bickford-Smith 1990, 35), and was structurally opened up to accommodate the need for more homes after the emancipation of slaves in 1838, so the town spilled over into the surrounding areas, and quickly, what would later become known as District Six, emerged as a substantial residential area. The area was officially incorporated into the municipality of Cape Town in 1867 and became known as District Six.

Significantly, prior to this official municipalisation, the area had been known by the name of Kanaladorp – a name rich in portent. The origins of the name *kanala* are said to lie somewhere between the Malay word *kanala* and the Dutch word for canal. Derived from the Malay language brought to South Africa by slaves and used idiomatically in the hybrid Cape patois, *kanala* simultaneously signaled an appeal for help and also an invocation to duty from those in need to those able to help. It is seldom that places acquire arbitrary names. South Africa is rich in names that capture their histories. If the name *Kanaladorp* is indeed derived from the Malay, then it might be argued that District Six's reputation as a haven, a place of refuge or as a place where help would be found, is inscribed in its very origins.

Established as a place of refuge, District Six, long after its establishment, continued to be the first port of call for most of the city's new immigrants and its destitute. To it came rural migrants from every part of the country, speaking a veritable Babel of languages. It was home to the Mfengu, the Gcaleka and the Gaika. It was there at the turn of the twentieth century that wandering African contintentals such as Clements Kadalie, a Nyasa, came to set down their roots. Tennis, it is claimed, was introduced to District Six, not so much by the local gentry, as by visiting African commercial travellers. British workers seeking to find their fortunes in the colonies set up their households there and left behind traces redolent of Victorian Britain. It also provided the first South African homes for Jews fleeing from Tsarist Russia. To it also came thousands from the west coast of India with names such as Surtee, Desai and so on. Added to these were countless St Helenans, Australians, black Americans, people from the Caribbean and from almost wherever one cares to mention. In the fascinating repertoire of ancestral tales told by modern District Sixers, it is not unusual for them to speak of their Palestinian, Scottish, Egyptian, Turkish, Chinese, Bermudan and Bahaman forebears.

It was also, in some senses, the most inscribed and over-determined terrain in the country. While other port cities would have had similar experiences, the scope and volume of traffic through Cape Town put it in a different space to its sister coastal cities. Gateway and home to almost the entire spectrum of modern South Africa's antecedents, social movements of all types first came to light there, not the least of which were the myriad of religious organizations which have come to characterize contemporary South Africa. It was home therefore to the itinerant and the mobile seeking to establish themselves; but it was also home to religious fundamentalism, political vanguardism, cultural idiosyncrasy and artistic innovation.

Together these people, and the forces that swirled around them, produced a community that is today remembered in very specific ways. Reverence and a deep sense of nostalgia surround the ways in which the district is recounted and presented. I have elsewhere (Soudien and Meltzer 1995) spoken of the competing memories of District Six. It is what I called the popular as opposed to the official memory that I wish to discuss here. This memory is one that its producers – in the face of the potent officially proclaimed memory of District Six as a cesspit of evil – have fastidiously cultivated. Of deep significance is the extent to which District Sixers have been able to retain control of their own modes of description and to be able to *speak* themselves.[4] In this process, the interlocutors have been members of the community themselves. Amongst them have been articulate raconteurs, self-taught historians, novelists, painters, and indeed very ordinary men and women, for whom the memory of the district was so precious. This work draws heavily on these interlocutors whom I have called the myth makers of District Six. I use the word myth here in a positive sense and include within the meaning of the term sages, savants and storytellers working in a wide range of expressive media.

What are the features of this discourse?

As discourse District Six is, of course, not a unitary text. It is enunciated in a multiplicity of ways, even within itself. These different ways articulate the very different and contradictory positions in which District Sixers found themselves as Christians, Muslims, Jews, atheists and indeed those who were relatively comfortable as opposed to those who were poor. There have, indeed, been times when community relations inside District Six were subjected to severe strain. These strains were most evident when the district was being dismembered through the Group Areas Act (Soudien 1989), and when proto-middle class and middle-class District Sixers were amongst the first to leave the area, leaving behind a severely dependent and weak working class. However, strikingly persistent and common to the area's evolving discourse were themes of community and solidarity. Despite the different accents in which the district was rendered, iterative in its narrative structure are the themes of *kanala*, telling simultaneously of the area's slave and working class roots. There are three features of this discourse, not all equal in scope, which I try to flesh out here.

The first feature that strikes me is that of sharing. Borne out of its durable slave past, stuck sometimes in Islamic stoicism, and its attendant poverty, a pervasive theme of the district is that of a people managing against all odds. While many descriptions of the district speak of its grinding material poverty, those of insiders speak of an intense will to survive. Rive (1990, 112) makes the point that the district had a mind and a soul of its own. Stories abound of how people shared what little they had. Fortune (1996, 6) talks of how only a few people in District Six owned refrigerators and how when her father bought fish or crayfish he would ask the storekeeper to store it in his: 'The shopkeeper would never refuse and dad always saw to it that the man got a fair share of what he had stored.' She speaks also of how on special occasions a shopkeeper would send a fresh loaf of bread to all the families on a street to show his appreciation for their patronage of his store. It was often thought that this kind of generosity would bring luck to the giver.

Sharing extended also to sharing responsibility for the raising of children of friends and relatives, and the taking in of the destitute and the down and out. Images such as those of Fortune's father trailing up to eight children – his own and their friends – behind him as he made his way to the sea on a crayfish outing were not uncommon. When he was asked whether the children were all his, characteristically he would answer yes. Even the gangsters of District Six, it was believed, were a breed apart. Deborah Hart (1990) cites a reference to a work by Don Pinnock which suggests that gang activity was not only a means of economic survival but also a form of external policing:

> The people, competing for scarce resources at the thin, sharp edge of a fluctuating economy, created for themselves in District Six an elaborate, alternate society; highly co-operative, often violent and tragic; and more often ringing with the laughter of a society with an identity.

Out of these descriptions, District Six emerges as a place undoubtedly mired in poverty, but, in the words of Grogan, an observer of Cape Town in the mid-seventies, 'there was a community spirit that the most advanced urban development will never be able to buy or replace' (Hart 1990, 123). Gangs formed part of a social landscape which understood itself well and which articulated its own identity. Jensen (1997) makes the point that crime – now rampant in the townships of the Cape – was by no means absent from District Six, but was held in check by the social bonds which connected many facets of the place's life. Fortune, for example, tells the story of how her father apprehended a young man attempting to rob a passer-by in their street and how her father physically laid into the man and then, with the support of the neighbours, proceeded to take the youth back to his home.

The second feature of District Six's discourse is that of social harmony. Building on the discussion above, District Six is presented in this discourse as an accessible and open community. All its mediators speak of it as a place which drew in and absorbed new communities. When it was first demarcated it drew in a wide spectrum of the town's citizenry, and was, in the first few decades of its existence, very mixed in class terms. Hart (1990, 119) describes the district as a place which absorbed wave after wave of newcomers. Among the foreigners she describes were 6 500 Jewish immigrants from Tsarist Russia, Germany and Poland.

Amongst its early inhabitants were leaders of the city's business community, some of whom, interestingly, were not white. Rich and poor lived cheek by jowl. Later, when the wealthier moved to other newly developed suburbs, they left behind a distinctly poor community. Even after most of the white bourgeoisie of Cape Town had left the District, those of somewhat middle class standing who stayed behind continued to find occasion to cross the social gulf dividing them from the mass of the poor in their midst. Even the bourgeoisie, located outside the district, found an urbanity in District Six not present anywhere else in the city. Ridd (forthcoming) talks of the intense relations humble District Sixers were able to cultivate with the city's most elevated. District Six made it possible, for example, for Dr Abdurahman, the foremost coloured politician of the day, and a descendant of slaves, to move in the circles of the English elite. She speaks also of an imam from a District Six mosque who used to fish socially with John Dean Cartwright, a parliamentarian whose name is recalled at Cartwright's corner in Adderley Street, and of Harold Cressy, who was a friend and protégé of WP Schreiner, a former prime minister of the Cape.

The 'touch' of the district – the spirit of working across boundaries – did not disappear when its elite moved elsewhere. Significantly, the poor community, as Bickford-Smith (1995) says, was heterogeneous. In an earlier work (Bickford-Smith 1990, 37) he describes the district as consisting of a wide spectrum of different kinds of people. It was not uncommon, he says, to find a white father bouncing a black baby on his knees. Strikingly, Combrinck (1998) speaks of the district as a place where one's background, social or religious, did not work in exclusionary ways. He speaks of Jewish householders with Christian tenants and how combinations such as these abounded. The district was simultaneously home to Jewish, Christian, Muslim, Apostolic, Catholic and Dutch Reformed and it presented itself in the garb, the architecture and the ambience of the disparate communities within its space. Home, as a concept, was an expansive idea central to which was the feeling of familiarity. The place was coded in what one might understand to be a deprivileged symbolic terrain in which symbols overlapped and fused.

This point about the district as being in excess of its parts leads to discussion of the third and possibly most potent claim embodied in its discourse. Central to this claim is the concept of hybridisation. What is meant, of course, by hybridisation is by no means always clear. On occasion it is enunciated as versions of what we have discussed above; District Six is infinitely tolerant, District Six, in its ability to give and take, is the epitome of the cosmopolitan new world. Most often it is the more nuanced explication of the district, as a place of insistent excess, as a place in constant dialogue with itself, as a place able to make and remake itself, which becomes apparent. But how this making and remaking happens is crucial. If this version of hybridity holds discursive sway the material it calls on needs to be understood.

Towards understanding this hybridity, I use Homi Bhabha's (1994) discussion of hybridity. Hybridity, Bhabha (1994, 113) explains with reference to colonialism, is premised on a process of disavowal; power is exercised through small groups presenting themselves as already signifying the whole (of a nation, group or people). What the process of disavowal makes possible is the splitting off, not necessarily the oppressing, of that which falls outside the dominant group. What is disavowed is not repressed but is expressed as something different, a mutation or a hybrid which the signifying power of the dominant groups recognise but are able to disavow as not being the original. The hybrid, in its turn, displays the deformations and displacements of the process of domination and so unsettles the narcissistic demands of power and articulates itself as ambivalence. And thus, as Bhabha says (1994, 112), 'if discriminatory effects enable the authorities to keep an eye on them, their proliferating difference evades that eye, escape their surveillance'. Escape from surveillance is an important element of this explanation. Here, hybridity emerges as a condition rich in political significance. The way people live, their conduct and the forms of social organization they develop are all deeply political in so far as these practices evolve outside of and beyond the controlling gaze of the master.

While I find Bhabha's explanation profoundly insightful for understanding the complexity of the hybrid identity, particularly his understanding of hybridity as an expression of strategic avoidance and subversion, I would like to think that hybridity is premised not only on the deformation of the form of the dominant (which allows disavowal), and that hybridity is, therefore, something which is done to subject peoples, but that what Spivak (1988, 197) calls 'the agency of change' is located within the subordinate groups too. They exist not only as responses to the dominant order in which they find themselves (as they in fact do for much of their lives), but they too force response from those in control. Bhabha (1996, 206) himself talks of the constitution of the subject as an 'intersubjective, performative act that refuses the division of public/private, psyche/social [...] '. Consciousness, he says, is not something which is given, but a process of 'coming-to-consciousness'. Identity-taking is in this process a problem. People, in coming-to-consciousness, negotiate the images of themselves offered to them by the dominant. They are called upon to recognize themselves, and then to decipher and recipher that which they have seen. In reciphering they assume an alterity which is of their own making. Hybridity is, therefore, not only the product of structural forces which surround people, but the expression of popular choice too. It is not a derivative of colonialism in the sense that people waited for it to happen. They were directly responsible for creating their hybrid lives. Mimesis is not the only process of identity-taking in their lives. While their lives are patterned around the rhythms and the order of the dominant, they have their own rhythms and orders which the dominant have to subdue and, failing that, to assimilate. The Cape Town carnival, in its complex taking on of, and playing with, *double-entendre*, is an obvious illustration of this.

Trinh T. Minh-ha (1996, 11), in response to the criticism that the notion of hybridity is now somewhat overused and limp, makes the comment that we should continue to use terms such as these 'as tools of change, and we should keep redefining them until their spaces become so saturated that we would have to couple them with other words [...] in order to go a little further'. Taking this somewhat further, in the context of post-colonial South Africa, is the recognition of how much this hybridity, and the consciousness which emerges in District Six, is, in relation to the dominant colonial mind, an aesthetic and political affront. While this hybridity cannot, on its own terms, displace the dominant order, it persistently disrupts and unsettles it. The presence of the *kanala* mode, for example, forces adjustments on the dominant classes. The example is slight, but the point is an important one to make. People are also the makers of their own histories and destinies.

At the heart of this modification of Bhabha is an attempt to find a way of coming to terms with the presentation of District Six, in the clichéd prose of the everyday, as a particularly cosmopolitan place. What constitutes cosmopolitanness is important in this reckoning. It is a way of life and a commitment to a way of life. In a sense, District Six's credibility hinges on it. It is not the same cosmopolitanness which develops elsewhere in the colonized world, or in the creolized enclaves of the metropole. It is a particular form of cosmopolitanness which takes its shape from the specific ensemble of forces present at the Cape and which produces its own problematics.

Most explanations begin in and with the absorptive and assimilative character of District Six. District Six, goes the refrain, 'was home to [...] ', and so the endless list of nationalities/peoples/'races' is tripped off the tongue. In some versions, the Cape's older past is appropriated as the antecedent for its assimilative properties. The origins of colonial South Africa, for example, are iconicised in two symbolic marriages: the first was that of Krotoa, or Eva in her *evolué* persona, who was the sister-in-law of an important Khoi chieftain and who married an official of the Dutch East India Company; the second was that of Simon van der Stel, the first European-Dutch governor of the Cape, who had married an Indian woman. While both of these marriages are often presented in the tragic 'miscegenation' narrative voice, they are also invoked as the foundations of the new South Africa. Within them, South Africa is at its birth presented as an embrace of difference. Europe, Africa and Asia are figuratively assimilated, incorporated and naturalized on the rich soil of the Cape. There is in this figurative construction, in some senses, the notion of the African cradle of humanity receiving back its diasporic seed. And so, at its very moment of birth, the future South Africa is portended in the coming together at both the apex and the basement of the new society – at the new fort and in its taverns and hunting-grounds – with the physical union of its disparate peoples.

It is this narrative which the discourse of District Six appropriates. District Six is the re-embodiment and the continuation of the foundation moment of South Africa. It takes authority from its ownership of that foundation moment and expresses itself as the spirit of the land. It is, therefore, alongside of its sister locations elsewhere in South Africa, the legitimate South Africa. Not only does the district take in the Irish, the Filipinos and the Indian, but it makes them District Sixers, the true inheritors of the new South Africa. They come as La Gumas, Conchitas, Pastors, Rosenbergs, Kadalies and Smiths, but they emerge embossed with the features of their diverse pasts. Kolbe, pre-eminent rememberer of the District, speaks not only of people living cheek by jowl, but also of living together:

> If you leave any part of the world, whether it's Europe, or whether it's Russia or whether it's Zululand and you come to Cape Town, you're going to become a Capetonian [...] you have to assimilate. And so ultimately, what you leave behind are surnames, like we have surnames like Kadalie, we have surnames like

> Malunga, guys I went to school with. I went to school with Solly Goldman and Max Razenburg who are brown and Catholic [...] I've been called Greek, I've been called an Arab, I was called anything under the sun [...] I'm a product of this creolization and I revel in it [...] When my grandparents married each other, they weren't going to make coloured children. They just loved each other and they were gonna make children.

Central in this explanation might lurk a biological essentialism. Hybridity in this explanation is constructed on the basis of biological difference. Out of it emerges men and women who are marked phenotypically or as mixtures on a palette. They are either brown or a reminder of one or other place from where their ancestors are presumed to come.

The explanation, though, does not stay at the level of biology, but is fundamentally prosecuted as cultural syncretism. From it comes the presentation of District Six as not Europe, Africa, or Asia, but its most generative cultural amalgam. Kolbe, for example, admits to being continentally an African, politically a South African, but culturally what he calls an 'Atlantico'.

> I'm a product of a port city, Cape Town, New Orleans, Rio, Barbados, New York. We have much in common with each other because we are bound by the Atlantic and all that happened on that ocean whether it was slave-trade or commerce or war or whatever and our rhythms and our language and our so-called culture is more outward looking [...] because it's not recognized things [...] I don't speak Zulu, I don't speak Xhosa. I'm not going to learn it to prove my Africanness.

This is echoed several times over in the interpretations of other District Sixers. A well-known historian of the district makes the point that he had lived a life there which demanded of him a form of cultural literacy. District Six called upon him to enter into and engage with its diversity. One, as he said, celebrated life to the full and lived for those times when the end of the Muslim fast came, when Christmas came and participated in Jewish festivities. One participated in all the cultures around one in ways which produced a social and cultural inter-dependence. For Kolbe, this interdependence armed him with the ability to play in his environment,

> District Six was [...] like a womb of the city, a very vibrant, vital east end of the city where the new layers of immigrants came, where the free slaves came, where all this hybridity took place, and [which] symbolizes a tenacity in mankind [*sic*] to resist imposed identities and imposed social structures.

Out of this process emerged people who lived across boundaries and who imbibed and reproduced a culture which was intelligible in what people ate, sang and did. The musical styles of District Six embracing simultaneously the *joie de vivre* of the new Atlantic world and the desperate sadness of its slave past, the polyglot patois taking in and ridiculing the presumptions of racial and class superiority of the colonial order, and the cuisine melding the several worlds of their past. It is this creolization which brings a Kolbe to speak passionately about his love for *Rosa*, the anthem of the Kaapse Klopse, and in his next breath to theorize in the high tones of the academic.

The representational strategies of the discourse of District Six

In identifying three features of the discourse of District Six I am, as some would say, participating in the mythologizing of the district. This I recognise. I am, however, profoundly conscious of the import and power of the imaginative reappropriation of the past. South African history is a panorama of rich imaginaries – creation discourses. In District Six can be found a potent retelling of the South African experience. Recent retellings include a series of exhibitions and publications which have emerged from the District Six Museum. What this work has done, building on the discursive features I describe above, is to construct a District Six which is insistently integrative. The value of this text, as has become apparent in the high-profile attempt by the state to use District Six as the model for its urban land restitution efforts, is at once metaphorical, in the sense that it offers a language rich in extravagant imagery, and also, more critically, political. It offers South Africans a way of imagining, if not retrieving, its past in ways which speak against dispersal and forced removal. It brings a coherence to identities (particularly the racial) fractured in an apartheid world, and restores lost memories. The restoration of District Six is the reconnection of a divided past.[5] The ideal which the district offers is the return of a wholesomeness that was poisoned by apartheid. It is this that provides old and new struggles against apartheid with a text for legitimacy.

The strategic importance of this discourse is, therefore, its availability as a resource for authorizing the authenticity of a counter-apartheid identity. The unity of District Six is the unity of South Africa. District Six, in these terms, is therefore not just an enclave but a point of resistance to the deformation of the real South Africa. The term enclave is therefore an insufficient and inappropriate metaphor for District Six. It is not a place apart. In some senses it is 'the' place.

This discourse might also be read another way, and begins with a recognition that the District is about unity, but that its unity is structured in difference. In this reading District Six is interpreted both in its positive and its negative senses – recognized are that which it privileges and that which it silences. The District is read as a text which is structured in a dialogue of absences and presences. It starts with the acknowledgement (and the disavowal of white supremacist texts which present the district in the voice of 'miscegenation', cultural degeneration and so on) of the unparalleled social and cultural hybridity of the district, but moves to an awareness of the discontinuities and ruptures within the discourse of the district. It moves to recognise the discourse as one which is about being and becoming, as opposed to being about a frozen equilibration. It seeks to position itself as an active agent in the recovery of past memories and the production of future identities. The discourse is thus a discourse which is cognisant and engaging of the power of the racist discourse of white supremacy and emerges, therefore, as a political discourse. The statement 'I am a District Sixer' is thus pre-eminently an enunciation of power. Crucial in this enunciation is the power of self-description. The power which is invoked in this self-description is, as all power, partial, and self-serving and thus capable of defining the boundaries of inclusion and exclusion.

What this second approach does is to understand the discourse of District Six in more complex ways. While the first reading is an attempt to recuperate the district somewhat unproblematically, the second provides ways of seeing the district enmeshed within, not outside, mainstream South Africa. The district might be thought of as a long and continuous moment of engagement with the discourses of hegemony and so manifests itself, simultaneously, as historically continuous and contiguous to South Africa, but also historically disjunct and apart. It is a place which is in constant dialogue with itself and its space. Thus District Six shares the geographic space of South Africa, its people have gone through much the same historical experiences as the rest of the country, but they choose to remember that space and its history and its relation to the broader canvas of South Africa differently. In remembering who they are, they hold tightly to the right to define themselves. The act of doing so, however, is marked with ambiguity.

Central to this remembering is the way in which difference is invoked as strength. In the district, difference was a feature of everyday life. It was, for the most part, able to play with difference. Where the mainstream sought to iconicize difference, in the district one could be a Muslim, but also a worker, one could be a member of the Scouts but also simultaneously a leader of a clandestine left-wing movement, one could be a devotee of opera and at the same time a football player, one could be a ballet dancer and also a social worker. Signification of identity was seldom permanent and finite. It continued to unfold as people re-positioned themselves. In this sense, a district identity challenged the fixed and closed meanings which were given to religious, ethnic and social descriptors. Instead District Six as an idea invited further engagement; it invited additional and supplementary meanings and in the process actively opposed the racial, cultural and class semiotics of the mainstream. Meanings were offered and put up for negotiation and re-negotiation, and manifested themselves as contingent. As soon as they were assumed to have been closed, they revealed themselves as unfinished, enigmatic after-thoughts. District Sixers took the images of their social superiors, played with them, and offered them back in forms which were recognizable but were always different. They participated in the arena in which dominant groups could act out their strategies of disavowal, but were continuously participating in their own processes of disavowal. Their cultural economy was built upon a currency which drew on the resources of the dominant classes but always domesticated those resources. In the everyday language of the district, the ways and manners of the ruling class were taken on board, assimilated but, crucially, turned upon the rulers themselves. District Sixers were always laughing up their sleeves as they addressed those in control.

The notion of domestication/disavowal requires some further discussion, however. Quite clearly, the narratives of Europe, Asia and Africa are complex overlays which constantly obtrude, over-determine and infiltrate the popular consciousness in District Six. In asserting the idea of District Six as a counter-foil to apartheid/segregationist South Africa, it is possible to argue that the district deals with the narratives of Europe, Asia and Africa in particular kinds of ways. In contrast to hegemonic thought which hierarchises Europe, Asia and Africa, in that order, what the district does is to engage in a different kind of dialogue with these narratives. Central to this dialogue is a juxtapositioning in which the figures of Europe, Asia and Africa are taken and remade. The district, following the lead of Kolbe and others, lived across the grain of cultural differentiation and took in and made its own the gamut of cultural forms which were practised within the city. And so, for example, it appropriated Italian opera, it took American jazz and infused it with older musical styles brought to South Africa from the Indian Ocean bowl. The area's cultural socialisation produced men and women who were able to traverse the several cultural idioms within their universe.

Out of this emerged, as I have argued repeatedly, an assimilating District Six. The district was able to take in and appropriate. This process, however, is never without contradiction. Critically, in taking in, assimilating, and domesticating, groups are forced to settle with the complex conceits and presumptions which pervade the languages they use, the accents and underplayings and their prejudices. In this process practices remain, are recontextualised and re-presented. But there is also loss.

Arguably what is lost, and if not lost then certainly subordinated, in the making of the district's discourse is the African presence. The district had difficulty in expressing its locatedness in Africa and its connections to the long and old history of its geographical space. In taking in the narratives of Europe, Asia and Africa, and in crafting the linguistic, gestural and symbolic forms which were its hallmark, it left unspoken, or largely so, its umbilical connection to pre-colonial Africa. The figure of this Africa was absent – an unspeakable presence – sublimated within a hybridized discourse which played mainly in the space of its European colonial history. Silenced were the tales of the ancient hunters and herders who roamed the slopes of the Cape landscape. Evident, and in some ways, celebrated was its slave past. Its music, for example, swelled with the dirges calling attention to the suffering and exploitation of the people and their desire for freedom.

But even there, the African form was domesticated, and rendered bland. By contrast, the linguistic and cultural grammar of Europe, and to a lesser extent that of Asia, was extended and developed. It was into that grammar that Africa was subsumed. The role accorded Africa in this hybridisation was essentially that of a carrier. Africa carried the district's melding of its European and Asian pasts, and when it had played its role, the carrier was ingested and rendered harmless. It is in this sense that the district manifests its connection with, and even its vulnerability to, the dominance of its European past. The presence of Europe conditions the way in which difference is articulated. Play as District Sixers do with their differences, they do so not unaware of the power of Europe. It is the European form which is most evident as they speak, interact and project. They know that they are the disavowed. While they play with their disavowal, it is to the power of disavowal which they are constantly having to respond. When District Sixers express their identities, and proclaim their passions, it is within the aura of Europe that they invariably do so.

Conclusion

In looking at identity-formation, particularly identities of subordinate groups, the claim is often made that subordinate identities are responses to the ideologies of dominant groups. What these kind of claims do is rob people of the specificity of their own experience. They are presented only in dependent relationships to those holding power. While response is a central feature of the character of the District Six discourse, I want to argue here that the lived experience of the district (or indeed, as Kolbe would say, that of the greater Cape Town) is not only a dependent one, or, putting it differently and more triumphally, a subversive or oppositional one, but is crucially also generative in its own right. The District Six experience is defined, in its own terms, as an experience of constant deferment. It is one which refuses to settle within permanent positions (whether they be 'race', religion, class and, as the work of filmmaker Jack Lewis shows in his documentary on Kewpie the *moffie* hairdresser, on gender), but instead chooses to turn its back on essentialist notions of the self. District Sixers live with and through a hybridity which they have constructed for themselves. It is a world which they own.

Attempts have been made to appropriate this hybridity as a specifically coloured experience. While there clearly is a sense of colouredness in District Six, one which emerges out of the specific racial language of the segregationist-Darwinist thinking of the late nineteenth and early twentieth century, what arises, however, in working with the discourse of District Six is the diverse ways in which difference was articulated. Difference was expressed in ways which permitted the epithets of colour to take root, but it was also expressed in a multiplicity of other ways. And so it was that physiognomy provided a frame of seeing, but so did language, cuisine, music, civic and political responsibility, religion and even sporting prowess. One could be a District Sixer in a multiplicity of ways, and the discourse of difference dominated by racial conceit was but one way of presenting difference.

Having made that point, I would argue, however, that these modes of difference struggled to hold Africa in perspective. Hybridity and the ways in which this hybridity was enunciated evolved in District Six in a frame which was largely European. It may be argued that in this sense the European presence in the district constituted the district as a profoundly, and indeed insidiously racial place. It is important, however, to show how wrong this is in so far as the discourse of the district consciously presents itself as more than the sum of its peoples, which include a strong component of people of African descent. The discourse of the district was that of assimilation, a taking in and living with difference. What the displacement of Africa within the discourse does reveal is the complexity of hybridity as an experience and points to the deep entanglement of supposedly non-oppressive discourses with profoundly oppressive elements within them and around them. Discourse comes out of this as always flawed, always problematic.

Interviews

Combrinck, I.
Kolbe, V.
Jensen, S.

Notes

1 I am acutely aware of the politics of District Six in the wider field of forced removals and the special privileging which District Six has received in relation to the wide number of other similar areas in South Africa. While District Six is sometimes emblematic of that wider experience, it by no means either exhausts it or stands for it. I would like to make clear, therefore, that the historical construction which is taking place in the writing of this piece is by no means an attempt to make less of other experiences, or the significance of other experiences which deal with 'race', racism, hybridity and cultural development.

2 These conditions of production are, of course, part of the identity complex which both articulates and is articulated by the different discourses of representation.

3 The specific contribution of intellectuals in the Western Cape to the discussion of 'race' requires a great deal of historical and sociological attention. This contribution is significant coming as it does prior to the significant world-wide shift with regard to anti-biological notions of 'race' which begin to surface after 1950.

4 The significance of this ability to 'speak themselves', or self-enunciation, has to be weighed against insistent attempts for the people to be described and 'spoken'. Clearly, any group of people, in the face of colonial and other oppressive forces which seek to impose names on them which they themselves have not chosen, needs to be understood similarly.

5 Of course, the question, coming from a Derridean point of view, is to ask who District Six's 'others' were. In dealing with this question it is important to note that while absorption and assimilation were very much the order of the day, simultaneously, deep prejudices around colour and gender continued to operate and served to provide, in perhaps less exaggerated ways, the vocabularies by which certain District Sixers continued to be invoked as *Boertjie* and *Kaffertjie*. In raising these with District Sixers, I have been told, and have expressed my reserve in relation to it, that these were minor epithets of prejudice.

Chapter Seven

Writing Hybrid Selves: Richard Rive and Zoë Wicomb

Desiree Lewis

> ... a mixture of degenerate brown peoples, rotten with sickness, an affront against Nature. *Sarah Gertrude Millin*

> Bastard and mixed blood are the true names of race.
> *Gilles Deleuze and Félix Guattari*

The idea of writing as 'black' in South Africa has been largely considered self-evident. It is usually forgotten that the meaning of 'race' is ' 'always already' figural, internally constituted by a system of differences whose relation to the world of phenomena is purely conventional' (Cornwall 1989, 6). In this context it is hardly surprising that both writers and critics often have glossed over the fact that blackness is shaped by dominant modes of address, involves various forms of identity formation, and is predetermined by convention.

Cornwall (1989) helps to explain the enduring salience in South African writing and criticism of 'race' as a signifier which, subsuming others, becomes a persuasively 'natural' marker of collective and individual identity. Assumptions based on the idea that the meaning of blackness (and 'race' generally) is somehow 'natural' do not always indicate overtly reactionary politics; they often simply mean that conventional ideas about 'race' predominate in anchoring explorations of the self and society. 'Race' (generally) and blackness (specifically) have a long legacy of 'obviously' establishing subject positions and conclusively fixing personal and collective being.

The idea that the meaning of blackness is somehow 'natural' and self-evident is clear from the way in which canons have been created in autobiographical, testimonial and confessional South African literature. It is usually argued that the 1950s witnessed the first coherent upsurge in black South African writing, with writers considered central here including Ezekiel Mphahlele, Lewis Nkosi, Nat Nakasa and Todd Matshikiza. These writers, it is commonly claimed, gave literary expression to 'black life' as it confronted the early years of apartheid and institutionalized racism. Following the cultural silence of the 1960s, Black Consciousness politics between the late 1970s and early 1980s shaped a new militancy in black writing. Generally, the period has been associated with what Piniel Shava calls a 'literature of assertion' (1989, 98), a rejection of liberal politics, an espousal of revolutionary didacticism and an associated experimentation – especially in poetry – with language, form and style. Mongane Serote, Sipho Sepamla and Miriam Tlali are often identified as writers whose poems, short stories and novels register a political shift to black militancy and pride.

The publication of Ellen Kuzwayo's autobiography, *Call Me Woman*, in 1985 is customarily seen as introducing a wave of black women's voices in South African writing. Autobiographies and short stories by writers like Emma Mashinini (1989), Sindiwe Mangona (1990), Maggie Resha (1991) and Phyllis Ntantala (1992) soon followed Kuzwayo's and found publishers and readers in a climate that began to acknowledge the inevitable gendering of blackness. Yet it is striking that formulations like 'black life', 'the black family' or 'black experience' – both in this writing and its interpretation – continue an assumption that blackness is largely transparent. [1]

Preconceptions about what blackness must and must not mean partly account for the predictability of much South African writing – in Njabulo Ndebele's words, its fixation with 'anticipated surfaces rather than one of processes' (1984, 45). My main concern, however, is not with writing that demonstrates this predictability, but with two texts that disturb univocality and chart diverse modes for exploring identity. This chapter focuses on works by two writers classified coloured or 'mixed' in the South African racial hierarchy: Richard Rive's autobiography *Writing Black* (1981) and Zoë Wicomb's autobiographical *You Can't Get Lost in Cape Town* (1987). Neither of these books easily fits into the canon described above. For Rive and Wicomb, being black is patently associated with discourses and assumptions that their texts disentangle, rather than assume or blur. In their restless scrutinizing of identity, they represent many past and present meanings of hybridity. However, to approach Rive's and Wicomb's texts it is necessary to examine first the term 'hybridity' and consider key currents in its history.

Hybridity and black identities in South African literature

While the fixing of coloured identity through policy-making is a hallmark of apartheid from the middle of the twentieth century, the semiotic coding of coloured identity in racial ideology has a longer history. The classification of physical features to signify collective identities clearly precedes applications of the concept of 'race'. It was in the nineteenth century that 'race' explicitly became an organizing idea in various forms of specialist and popular thought about groups. Robert Young traces this in detail to show that, with the codifying of racial discourse in the 1800s, physiognomy became the basis for a systematic representation of individuals and groups. Racial discourse produced both distinct scientific concepts, and a particular cluster of connotations, attitudes and icons. These cultural markers – many of which remain implicit – are at the core of uses and disavowals of 'race' in the twentieth century.

The semiotic coding of 'race' surfaces explicitly in definitions of racial hybridity or, in the South African frame of reference, coloured identity. From the perspective of nineteenth-century racial discourse, the term 'coloured' has been linked to a fixation with maintaining racial boundaries. With identity formation being based on an exclusive boundary between black and white, the coloured as debased in-betweener or 'racial mixture', perceived product of the transgression of a sacrosanct boundary, has connoted lack, deficiency, moral and cultural degeneration.[2] In what follows, then, hybridity often refers to a language of 'race' that originates in the nineteenth century and shapes dominant and oppositional formations of identity well into the twentieth century.

In the second half of the twentieth century, racial boundaries in South Africa were policed through various mechanisms. Among these were the Immorality Amendment Act No 21 of 1950 which made 'interracial' sex illegal, the Population Registration Act No 30 of 1950 involving racial testing to establish groups' rights, and the Group Areas Act of 1950 which accorded differential residence rights on the basis of 'race'. This institutionalized racism in South Africa has entrenched a preoccupation with racial and cultural 'purity' or 'contamination' as well as with the fundamental aberrance of the 'racial hybrid' that continues to feature prominently in subjects' self-representations and facets of national mythology.

The codification of 'racial hybridity' in South Africa is starkly delineated in Sarah Gertrude Millin's *God's Stepchildren* (1924). Emphasizing the 'purity' of blackness and whiteness, Millin focuses on the innate corruptness of the 'racial hybrid' – so that her chronicling of coloured characters' degeneracy and doomed lives overtly endorses the biologist term 'miscegenation'. Deborah Kleinhans, the first 'hybrid product' of a union between a missionary and a black member of his congregation, is the founding figure in the lineage constructed by Millin. After describing several generations, the novel concludes with the tragic story of Barry Lindsell, Deborah's great-great grandson. Although Barry is described as looking unmistakably white, he, too, falls victim to the tragedy of the hybrid. He resigns himself to leaving his pregnant white wife and accepting the imperfections of his racial heritage: 'For my sin in begetting him, I am not to see my child. And, for the sorrow I share with them, I am to go among my brown people to help them [...]' (1989, 326).

Concern with the tragedy of 'racial mixing' and its consequences for those considered degenerate and culturally doomed is not, of course, uniquely South African. It features in a widespread racial discourse which peaked during nineteenth century colonialism. J. M. Coetzee (1988) has shown how Millin's text, far from being a bizarre expression of racist cant, echoes legitimately scientific theories of the time. What is distinctive in South Africa is the hegemony of racial theories in dominant policy as well as their currency in popular mythologies that survive political changes. Millin registers this, suggesting that it is within the South African context that eugenics and racial ideology have provided an especially pervasive basis for identity formation and social interaction[3].

The fixation with myths of degeneracy is not, however, confined to overtly reactionary politics. The myths permeate the ideas of progressive writers, Alex la Guma being a case in point. Stressing this writer's self-consciousness about being coloured, Mohamed Adhikari (1995) has correctly criticized the exploration of straightforward black and white dualisms in his work. La Guma's well-known short story, *A Walk in the Night*, is a particularly illuminating example of Adhikari's thesis.

Stephen Clingman explains this preoccupation in relation to Peter Abrahams' *The Path of Thunder* (1948), a novel published in the year that apartheid was officially introduced. Clingman argues that the text deals with 'what it means for those who have to struggle back from the netherworld of an unacknowledged identity' (1988, 7). Emphasizing the psychological and political repercussions of racial classification, he shows how certain South African writers have insistently responded to the symbolic and cultural associations of 'racial hybridity'.

In examining the persistence of nineteenth century views about hybridity in twentieth century texts some of the current theorisation of hybridity and identity is particularly useful. Hall (1996, 130), for example, draws attention to process by offering a way of thinking through identity that involves the dialectic between dominant discourses and marginal positions as well as the performative, provisional and always unfinished motions of identification. Certain post-colonial theorists have wrested the concept of hybridity from essentialising racial and cultural theories and invested it with subversive meanings (Young 1995 and Werbner 1997). In the analysis that follows hybridity and hybridization are used to describe the production of non-unitary, shifting and incomplete subjectivities, a production that interrogates the idea of polarized, complete and essentialized identities.

Rive and Wicomb are pivotal writers for exploring the performative aspects of hybridized identity. Both have been prolific commentators on South African cultural politics. Their writing encompasses criticism and a pronounced self-reflexivity about links between politics, writing and notions of 'race' and identity. Also striking about both writers' texts is the way each demonstrates how identity-formation generates poses that can be provisionally celebrated, interrogated or shed.

Richard Rive's autobiography was published in 1981 when Black Consciousness dominated progressive cultural productions and their reception. An influential public figure both in South Africa and beyond, Rive was under pressure to structure his self-narratives around existing left-wing orthodoxy, a situation probably made all the more urgent by his position as a college lecturer and the intensity of political revolt in black schools.

The strongly performative quality of his autobiography results not only from the way it evidently reveals the constraints on different modes of self-exploration, but also from a habitually flamboyant rejection of political correctness. Interestingly, Rive's autobiography, fiction and non-fictional writings frequently condemn 'Coloured' as an official category and any expression of coloured self-consciousness as evidence of false or imposed identity. It will be argued here that despite this Rive directly and obliquely engages with the entrenched myth-making surrounding an official label in ways that indicate an insistent absorption with areas that his conscious disavowals appear to resolve.

Wicomb published *You Can't Get Lost in Cape Town* in 1987 when she lived in Britain. Influenced by Black Consciousness, yet relatively freed of the South African resident's ties of loyalty to it, Wicomb consistently situates herself as an appraising outsider. While a broadly left-wing affiliation that embraces Black Consciousness is clear in her text, she is generally suspicious about wholesale affiliation with collective identities or projects, and is sharply alert to the political ambiguities of representation and self-representation.

Fictions of community in Rive's 'Writing Black'

As suggested by his reflections on the selective process of his writing, Rive's narrative is carefully structured to take the form of a success story. Charting his development as a public figure, Rive self-consciously takes up the challenge of describing an individual response to 'those whose experiences are as important or unimportant as mine'(1)[4]. Spanning a period between 1931 and 1979, the text chronicles his progress from a young boy raised in District Six, an environment of 'squalid alleys, refuse-filled streets and mean lanes' (2). The selection of incidents recounted later as well as the titles of chapters – often marking the places Rive visited as a student, lecturer and writer – emphatically proclaim that the writer's story of public success is unique and admirable.

In many ways, Rive marks his success as a liberating refusal of and departure from 'colouredism' (3) as it encompasses official labeling, a restrictive sense of community and place, and the general reading of physiognomy associated with marking 'racial mixture'. The start of the text emphatically proclaims a political position when he asserts that the term ' 'Coloured' is offensive in the South African context because it has hierarchic implications – inferior to White and superior to Blacks' (2). Rive describes District Six, a long-established home for Cape Town's coloured people, where he grows up in an 'atmosphere of shabby respectability, in a family chafing against its social confinement to dirty, narrow streets in a beaten-up neighbourhood' (6). Elsewhere, descriptions dwell on the oppressiveness of growing up in the district. In fact, Rive openly disavows the nostalgic representations that burgeoned about the area after it was razed by official decree between 1978 and 1983 and bluntly writes: 'It is notoriously easy to romanticize about slum life and sentimentalize it. In truth the slum was damp, dirty and dank'(4).

The perception of an oppressive community experienced in childhood is linked to explicit criticism of its prejudices when the writer confronts a compulsive practice of interpreting physiognomy as a definitive marker of individual worth[5]. Recounting his participation in an athletics club, he recalls the concern of the 'fair-skinned' members towards his 'dark complexion'(7), as well as the more pronounced hostility towards a 'young man [...] whose hair texture, complexion, high cheekbones, poor education and guttural Afrikaans accent, socially disqualified him'(7). In recollections like the above, Rive self-consciously distances himself from a fixation with marking racial meanings. Yet there is also attention to the hegemony of this practice when he captures his own participation in the language of 'race'. Here the autobiographer's confessional voice admits to childhood memories that are shaped by a past environment and its codes. He recalls, for example, the prostitute, Mary Sausages, as having 'pronounced lips or pronounced buttocks or both' and as being 'the ugliest woman I had ever known' (2). He also writes about another prostitute as being 'fair, I remember' and his sister Georgie as being 'pretty and [having] long hair' (3).

The confessional emphasis on a past self gives way to more complicated recollections. In a revealing account of his lineage, Rive appears to combine retrospective distancing from racialism and a past self with a tacit colluding with racial codes:

> I was born of 'mixed parentage' [...] but I am vague about my ancestry. I remember a mounted print which had pride of place on our dining room wall. He was unmistakably white. I must therefore conclude that my maternal grandmother must have been Black or Brown, as my mother was a beautifully bronze.

Distancing and criticism in this passage are evidenced as quotation marks question racial categories and when Rive mocks his family's pride in a white ancestor. It is in the gratuitous speculation about the colour of his grandmother and the reference to a 'beautifully bronze mother' that the distancing from racial coding seems to teeter. At this point, the author becomes complicit with a representational process that attributes special aesthetic and cultural significance to somatic characteristics. The passage which follows – about a father he never knew – is equally revealing:

> I once competed in some athletics competition, and watching was a very important Black American lady under a sunshade. When I had received my prize from her she remarked, 'They can't beat an American boy, can they?' [...] She was a family friend and knew my mother intimately. So possibly the Black strain came from my father and came from far over the Atlantic (3).

In this extract, Rive seems unable to narrate beginnings without echoing – even if only through conjecture – a fixation with racial lineage. His speculation that the 'dark strain' may have been American is especially noteworthy. The writer tacitly invokes the marker of 'coming from overseas' to confer the 'black strain' with positive meaning. I shall show that this anticipates a recurrent pattern later when the author turns, for example, to class authority as a way of refuting derogatory racial labeling. Generally important here, though, is a consistent preoccupation with the signifying powers of racial markers, and with the centrality of meanings generated by these markers to descriptions of the self. This points to tensions between the retrospective narrator's critical disclaimers of 'colouredism', and a narrator-protagonist who listens to and responds in the language of 'race'. The tension, as it is throughout the text, is between a univocal political persona and facets of self that are intricately entangled in racial discourse.

Crucial to the textualizing of a univocal political persona is Rive's description, emphatically signaled in the title of the autobiography, of a triumphant black self. This self is usually defined through descriptions of entering and being liberated by different black communities. These are not described at length, and overt references to being black occupy little of the text. They are worth exploring in detail, however, since they suggest recurrent conventions in myth making about black identity and uncover the discursive context in which the author negotiates writing the self.

The first of Rive's black communities is the Johannesburg-based group of writers formed around the magazine *Drum,* a group he meets when he starts writing in his early twenties. Rive describes his visit to Sophiatown, the vibrant black area in Johannesburg, before apartheid laws destroyed it between 1954 and 1960. He also implies an intimate knowledge of well-known writers Casey Motsitsi, Todd Matshikiza and Ezekiel Mphahlele: 'Casey was zany, Todd was reserved, Lewis starry-eyed and opinionated and Zeke the Grand Old Man' (13). Emerging from a milieu that he has 'explained' mainly by mentioning names and places, Rive feels 'inspired and worldly wise' (17). The superficiality of his account of the Johannesburg community is obviously evidence of brief visits and casual acquaintances; there is little substantive attention to how this world affects his politics, personality or writing. The gap between the cursory descriptions of a milieu and the liberating significance the author accords it is therefore interesting. It suggests that the black milieu is important not as it explains how Rive develops, but in naming a self vis-à-vis an influential site of black literary and cultural expression. In other words, it is a community that offers the author a persona of being black.

The inclusion in the text of largely formulaic representations is not a strategy exclusively used by Rive. It is evident also in other South African writers' constructions of blackness. The *Drum* writers' ethos was celebrated at a time of growing interest in and curiosity about black South African township life – both to those who were familiar with it and to those for whom it was inaccessible. On one hand, the history of the magazine, started by white editor Anthony Sampson and owned by Jim Bailey, reveals the marketability of textualizing black life and the positioning of writers as windows on a world for readers who desired self-affirmation. On the other hand, the publication of many *Drum* writers' short stories and autobiographies, together with the marketing of many cultural and musical events, indicates considerable general interest in an inaccessible subculture. For many writers of the time, the broad interest both in and beyond South Africa meant interpreting a world in ways that conveyed its uniquely oppositional and different identity.

The profound sense of the optimistic mood of the 1950s was linked to political protest and the Defiance Campaign, to innovations in music, dress and dance, and, generally, to an ethos captured in pithy descriptions like the 'Drum Decade' or Lewis Nkosi's often-quoted phrase, the 'fabulous fifties'[6]. Writers' representation of this black community – whether or not it involved detailed description – implicitly marshalled the popularized glamour with which it was associated. In this way, writers could easily exploit circulating meanings about the 'fabulous fifties' to give substance to 'black identity'. When Rive mentions this world and writers he meets in exile at later stages in his autobiography, it is therefore a wealth of accumulated extra-textual meanings that anchor 'being black'. It could be argued that the 'outsider' status which allows Rive to offer only a limited account of a milieu leads him also to draw attention to the way the meaning of 'being black' in South Africa during the fifties is always already written and signified. In his cursory treatment of the 'fabulous fifties' the writer is unwittingly telling about the construction and reproduction of blackness as this may simply involve gesturing towards a world of meaning and myth-making beyond the text.

For Rive, the provisionality of the 'fabulous fifties' as a signifier of black identity becomes clear when the autobiography proceeds to other non-South African definitions of blackness. After invoking the 'Drum decade', he affirms blackness through a tour to Africa and Europe in 1963. The journeying through Africa becomes the basis for a largely implicit claiming of pan-African identity, a testimony of belonging to a dispersed group of African writers and activists. Thus, the description of his departure from Africa is resonant with nostalgia about an African homeland:

> As I left the African mainland I was acutely aware of the fact that this was the first time I was leaving the only continent I knew from experience [...] Flying over the Mediterranean I experienced a feeling of being cut adrift, of the umbilical cord having been severed. (58)

It may seem meaningless for a young man who has spent most of his life in the western Cape to claim – after briefly visiting three African countries – knowledge of the 'continent from experience'. But the sense of Rive's claim rests on its recourse to African nationalist thought, prominent during the 1960s and the period that Rive deals with here. In African nationalism during the 1960s, the postulated homogeneity of Africa and

African identity signified a common legacy of colonial political and cultural domination. The signifying potential of Rive's description is especially evident in his metaphors of birth. Here he directly enlists nationalist myth making as it emotively symbolizes communal rights, belonging and identity in terms of gestation, birth and the preservation or loss of 'natural' laws. Rive therefore uses dense shorthand to invoke meanings beyond his text, in this case, a sense of belonging with the victims of colonial domination and of alienation from the West. The explicit codifying of a pan-African self is echoed in a comment made when Rive visits Rome. In claims reminiscent of many African writers' cultural nationalism in the 1960s, he writes:

> Africans' excitement is the development and nurturing of our potential. Europe's torpor is her inability to give up her glorious past. The sophistication of that past is her embarrassment today. Africans are a contemporary people because our yesterday is so recent. We live in terms of today and the excitement of tomorrow. Yesterday is meaningless. In fact we cannot remember clearly what it was like before the white man came, because he has deliberately obliterated the past. But we do remember conquest by fire, subjugation by force, slavery and discrimination. (58)

While this account seems pretentious and offers some baffling claims, its meaning derives primarily from the mythologies it cryptically echoes. Rive invokes the Negritude ideas of Aime Cesaire and Leopold Senghor in his optimistic celebration of a vibrant Africa versus a sterile West, while at the end he turns to the standard declamatory rhetoric and imagery of African nationalist indictment.

As is the case with Rive's claims of alignment with *Drum* writers, the pan-African community defined in his autobiography revolves around writers. Again, the text provides frequent, although dispersed testimony of Rive's encounters with other African writers – as though the author were determined to offer conclusive evidence of the world he inhabited. He writes: 'At the transcription centre I met the best-known Nigerian writers, John Pepper Clark, Christopher Okigbo, Chinua Achebe, and [...] Wole Soyinka'(79). There are times when he does not actually encounter the writers he mentions, yet is at pains to imply intimate knowledge of the world they are associated with. Thus he writes: 'In 1962 I again missed the opportunity to meet other African writers and critics. Chinua Achebe, Wole Soyinka and Christopher Okigbo [...] were present' (37). Thereafter, he appears to offer a first-hand account: 'The conference proved controversial from the moment Soyinka posed the question 'What is African literature?' Okigbo added fuel to the fire [...] What really mattered was the opportunity for writers to meet, to exchange ideas and to stimulate controversy' (37). It is tempting to consider accounts like these as straightforward examples of name-dropping. But Rive's name-dropping, a limited resource for defining a conventionally understood sense of being black, reveals his constraints in constructing a more 'substantive' sense of belonging. Once more, then, Rive's strategy broadly exposes the extent to which the claiming of black identity may rely on textualizing well-known fictions.

Another black persona is adopted later in the text when the autobiographer describes American experiences in black areas or with black Americans. His meetings with the American writer Langston Hughes are central here, especially when he describes their first encounter in Paris. Rive implies that he establishes a moment of instant rapport, with Hughes inviting him to the performance of one of his musicals. The occasion is described in detail:

> Langston grinned at the ticket clerk and said conspiratorially, 'I would like two tickets for Dick and myself. I'm Langston Hughes. I wrote the book.' He was really enjoying himself. She looked as if she was going to pass out [...] Langston chose two seats in the middle row where no one could miss us.

It is not only Hughes' delight in public recognition that this description records, but also that of Rive as he textualizes his public visibility through proximity to Hughes. Again, the self-definition vested in knowing famous people is not the main point. More important is how proximity to a potent symbol of black success becomes a way for Rive to claim a racially inflected authority and public recognition.

Like previous definitions of black community, Rive associates black identity strongly with place, recounting visits to Harlem where he teaches, attends Langston Hughes' party and meets an insurance agent whose book collection amounts to 'over ten thousand volumes and every one of them concerning Blacks' (120). Reminiscent of his descriptions of Johannesburg, accounts of Harlem are cursory, a result of Rive's having spent very little time there. Again, then, the text suggests that being black is not necessarily about intimately knowing or describing places, but about the way particular places automatically connote meanings. Like 'Sophiatown' in South Africa, 'Harlem' gestures to a complex of myth making, so that Rive's meanings are anchored by conventions that do not require explanation in the text.

When Rive published his autobiography in 1981, the black personae described above did not explicitly connote the blackness associated with South African identity politics during Black Consciousness. In the context of South Africa in the early 1980s, then, the images are politically obsolete, rooted in liberal protest against apartheid in the 1950s, African nationalist opposition to colonialism in the 1960s or a broad African-American indictment of white racism. A 'relevant' definition of blackness surfaces at the end of the autobiography, when the writer recounts events surrounding the Soweto revolts in 1976. In this section he uses a rhetorical style, images and tone strongly reminiscent of literary representations – especially in poetry – of the 1970s and 1980s.[7] While he often perceives political events as a witness, he emphatically stresses a personal connection and emotional entanglement. In a chapter titled 'Soweto', he provocatively repeats the phrase '16 June 1976 – Soweto exploded', and goes on to write: 'We identified strongly with the Transvaal blacks [...] There is much I could record of this period; about friends detained and people hurt, of others shot and still others killed' (151). The author does not in fact go on to describe this period in any detail, so that he relies again on an established code for linking signifiers like 'Soweto' and 'June 1976' to the spiralling implications of 'friends detained', 'people hurt', 'others killed'. Yet the tone of this section is clearly unique, and conveys a compelling sense of the urgency, the relevance, the immediacy of being black in South Africa during the 1980s.

That this 'relevant', contextual and strongly emotive definition of blackness concludes the autobiography is not only evidence that Rive lived through the evolution of black political postures. It is also a reminder of the context that shapes the writer's presentation of a political persona, and his insistent although often superficial claiming of black communities. During the 1980s, being black in emphatically collectivist, exclusionary and militant ways loomed for many writers as an authorizing frame for writing selfhood. The collectivism and sense of communal responsibility associated with black identity during the 1980s are evident in the way well-known writer Mongane Serote changed his proto-modernist novel about individual angst, *To Every Birth Its Blood* (1981), to a social realist novel about communal black militancy and struggle. Rive was similarly positioned, and his autobiography subjected to a related, although less contrived and self-conscious, framing.

Defining himself as an emphatically political figure of the 1980s, a black writer with a sense of collective commitment, Rive consequently turns to past experiences and frames them with the range of definitions of blackness at his disposal. While these definitions are politically outdated and often superficially sketched, they help to sustain the impression of a univocal black narrative. Although the complexities of his life experiences may strain against monolithic definitions, provisional definitions of blackness convey the impression of a consistent black self and give 'substance' to a culturally valued persona. The act of writing signaled by the title is therefore revealing about how blackness is constructed in a process of making fictions through and about other fictions, a process through which the subject discovers a textual home.

I have argued earlier that one important indication of the discursiveness of blackness in Rive's text is its provisionality and performativeness. A more direct indication is its frequent registering of unease with black communities. At these moments, Rive often confesses to their 'insubstantiality' and admits that being black is only ever contingent on fiction making. Disagreeing with a group of Africanists in Ethiopia, for example, he expresses his impatience with all nationalisms and concludes: 'Our approaches were poles apart [...] Which makes speaking of the African experience as a common and unified one such a futile exercise' (43). At one stage, citing Wole Soyinka, he comments cynically on Negritude, and mocks the 'professional African' who 'flourishes in Europe and America when he can smoothly slip into character' (163). The pronouncements here emphatically reinterpret the African nationalist and pan-African belonging delineated elsewhere. The text similarly repositions black American identity. When Rive teaches African-American students in Harlem, he is taken aback by their 'crude nascent Black Consciousness', 'some kind of identification with "The Continent"' and finds their questions 'naive' (123).

Such pronouncements register impatience at the stages when Rive does reflect analytically on the composition of his constructions of black identity. At moments like these, the author disturbs formulaic constructions with a diagnostic appraisal of the reductive and, most importantly, individually stifling positions they offer. This impatience is emphatically marked in a chapter dealing with a visit to Mozambique. Considering the way that blacks are stereotyped in dominant discourses and often repeat those stereotypes in counter-colonial identities, Rive remarks:

> I cannot be what the propounders of Negritude or the African Personality would have me be. I am Johannesburg, Durban and Cape Town. I am Langa, Chatsworth and Bonteheuwel. I am discussion, argument and debate. I cannot recognize palm fronds and nights filled with the throb of the primitive. I am buses, trains and taxis. I am prejudice, bigotry and discrimination. I am urban South Africa. (23)

This outburst is a fascinating departure from the restrained voice that dominates elsewhere, and functions as a defiant rejoinder to political correctness. It also registers the autobiographer's pleasure in disavowing a unified self. The flamboyant celebration of hybridization in this passage is an index of unevenness throughout the text, unevenness which – it often becomes clear – Rive seeks neither to conceal nor to resolve.

While constructions of blackness are central to the self-conscious political alignment in the autobiography, much of the text focuses on idiosyncratic, personal and – clearly for the autobiographer – more meaningful modes of exploring selfhood. When dealing with desires, yearnings, moments of pleasure and fulfillment, Rive turns to non-racial markers of identity. One of the most insistent emphases in *Writing Black* is the autobiographer's emphasis on his proximity to western European culture. When he visits Mozambique, he responds with outrage to those who see him as the cultural convert who can still show the 'savage beneath, the telltale marks of the primitive' (23) and reflects:

> I am personally able to sympathise with no world other than Western European sophistication and unsophistication. I have never had the opportunity to identify, like Langston Hughes in *The Weary Blues* with The low beating of the tom-toms

> The slow beating of the tom-toms [...]
> I cannot be what the propounders of negritude or the African Personality cult would have me be. (23)

On one level the passage is obviously another refusal of prescribed black subject positions. Rive explicitly distances himself from black myth making ranging from African-American reclamations of an African homeland to negritude. But equally important are assertions of a more comfortable self-immersed in European sophistication. This self is textualized when Rive, describing a visit to Tanzania, explicitly associates creativity with high culture, and not the 'night clubs and coffee bars and cinemas, figures made out of wood' (32).

The impression of Rive, a cosmopolitan traveller who needs the stimulation of high culture, is sustained in descriptions of his experiences in Western Europe. Describing a visit to Germany, for example, he writes, with evident confidence in his appraisal of high culture, 'I found the level of creativity, especially in the performing arts, exceptionally high. I attended a performance of *Die Drei Groschen Oper* by the Berliner Ensemble and was afterward introduced to Helene Weigel, the wife of Bertolt Brecht. I was taken to plays, opera and ballet, all magnificently mounted and produced [...] We went to see an outstanding performance of *Swan Lake* by the *Deutsche Staatsoper*'(90).

It could be concluded that the emphasis on high culture and education here implies a non-racial mode for asserting identity, that Rive finally eludes the language and codes of 'race'. This is complicated when we consider the links – comprehensively explained by Robert Young[8] – between racial theories and notions of culture and civility. In racial formulations of hybridity, ideas about 'degeneracy', 'taint' and 'impurity' are also connected to stereotypes about the cultural and moral imperfections of the hybrid. Popular mythologies have often articulated this as innate hybrid culturelessness. It is therefore not surprising that assertions of 'being cultured', of being civil and respectable, surface continually in a range of popular, literary and theoretical expressions of self among those defined as racial hybrids in South Africa. Rive reveals some of this in references to his childhood in a family 'whose hankering after respectability became almost obsessive'(6).

Thus, Rive's compulsive testifying to Western European sophistication is often an emphatic rejoinder to stereotyped hybrid culturelessness. In many ways, the success story of slum-boy turned successful writer anchors a positive sense of self in conventional assumptions about respectability, culture and civility. This concern in the autobiography is interestingly reflected in its style and tone. Drawing attention to his urbanity, Rive often uses extremely formal expression, while his political commentary frequently exploits urbane irony, rather than emotive and explosive protest and exhortation (interestingly, a voice which dominates much Black Consciousness writing). The following passage, describing Rive's encounter with a British settler on a train and a moment that illustrates Homi Bhabha's views about 'ambivalence at the source of traditional discourses on authority'(1985, 154), reveals some interesting features:

> An elderly British settler [...] waded into an attack on local savages, niggers and the Mau Mau, constantly reminding me that we from the South were different. He kept nudging me and expressing his admiration for the way the Whites and Coloureds in South Africa were handling the Native and keeping him in his place. Too tired to argue, I sought out the steward and changed my compartment. (39)

Long complex sentences and a formal register evident in phrases like 'sought out' as opposed to 'looked for' are recurrent patterns in the text, especially when the author is addressed by or represents exchanges with socially dominant subjects. In this passage, the effect is to contrast an 'uncivilized racist' (who, ironically, tries to establish a bond with Rive) with the politically defiant yet consistently urbane author, who maintains a dignified silence and eventually simply withdraws. In this way the autobiographer identifies his radical distance from a white racist world at the same time that he displays the standards of decency, civility, urbanity and dignity conventionally associated with that world.

Homi Bhabha uses the phrase 'White but not quite' (1984, 132) to explain the subversive effects of subaltern speech through mimicry. His comments on the ways in which subversion repeats the dominant discourse suggest a description for the embedded politics of Rive's 'assimilation'. Bhabha notes: 'For it is between the edict of Englishness and the assault of the dark unruly spaces of the earth, through an act of repetition, that the colonial text emerges uncertainly' (1985, 126-7). With Rive, it is also important to consider how the display of metropolitan Englishness, both in language and in behaviour, asserts a form of superiority in the context of colonial South Africa and Afrikaner Nationalism. There is a pronounced pattern of what could be termed anglophilia in the text, with the author painstakingly testifying to his enjoyment and performance of attitudes, manners and conventions that are customarily considered English. In a striking criticism of another black man's constructed Englishness, Rive appears to denounce the aping of English ways by a 'dedicated anglophile'(14):

> He was very black, round-faced, podgy and bow-legged. He tended to waddle in an undignified manner. He dressed in the way he imagined an English gentleman would, in a dark suit, waistcoat, white shirt and sober tie. The effect was spoilt at both sartorial extremities. His shoes were two-tone and sizes too small for his sprawling feet, and his hat was round and sizes too small for his large head. A feather was stuck jauntily into the narrow band. (14)

What strongly filters through here, though, is not so much a principled opposition to mimicking Englishness, as it is a condemnation of the inadequate way it is done. Elsewhere, Rive in his manner and tone, demonstrates what it is to be 'properly' English. English image-construction and the dignity it is seen to confer are persistent themes in *Writing Black* and perform a signifying function of self-vindication in the context of 'barbarous' South African 'race' laws. The pervasive image of Englishness is clearly linked to being 'urbane', 'cultured' and 'respectable' and appears to be one authoritative way of resolving anxieties about hybridization. Racial domination is challenged not by speaking the language of 'race', but by sidestepping this language and speaking the language of culture and civility. Simply claiming, therefore, that Rive's anglophilia reflects an assimilation of dominant English or metropolitan standards misses the performative ways in which assumed identities play self-individuating roles in certain contexts. Rive's adoption of Englishness cannot simply be reduced to his 'wanting to be like an Englishman'; it is evidence of deploying a persona to define a distinct subject-position, an authority vis-à-vis white South African racism and stereotypes about the 'degenerate' and 'uncultured' coloured.

The authority conferred by Englishness, civility and 'being cultured' is inextricably entangled with class. This is made clear in Rive's lengthy descriptions of being a PhD student at Oxford and later being an Oxbridge graduate. Insisting that he is not an unnatural cultural convert, he writes that 'I took quite easily to most Oxford customs' (131) and establishes the idea of his being innately – in refutation of stereotypes about the hybrid – 'cultured' and at ease in positions of class superiority. Central to the autobiographer's poses of social authority are the ways they affect how others see him. The emphasis on class status is therefore emphatically discursive as it positions both addressee and addresser through messages about class authority and formal education. This is obviously one way in which the autobiography positions the reader: by constantly demonstrating Englishness, class superiority and civility, Rive seeks to elicit our respect. But this is also revealed in the way he recounts encounters with others in the text, for example, when a waitress in an Oxford restaurant shows disrespect in serving him. He immediately assumes that she is being racist. It is with obvious delight that he realizes the class basis of her resentment when she says:

> 'You know, I'm sick and tired of you Oxford snobs. You think because you're gentry and we are waitresses you can treat us how you like. Just because you're a toff doesn't mean you can treat us how you like. Just because you're a toff doesn't mean you can speak posh to me and think you can get away with it.'

The class markers of authority, even when they are sometimes ironic, become valuable avenues for testifying to authority and dignity. Their value rests on the way they both signal an emphatic authority and elude the language of 'race'. Generally, class authority can become a powerful way of countering the debasement of self as 'racially impure' or imperfect. Because claims to authority within the logic of racial discourse rely on notions of 'uncontaminated essence' (precisely the notions that 'racial hybridity' defiles), the transformation of racial discourse into a discourse of resistance presents unique difficulties from the perspective of 'racial mixture'[9]. In other words, subjects who are labeled coloured cannot enlist the same signs or signifying logic used in ideologies like Negritude or Black Consciousness, ideologies which invert negative evaluations yet retain a binaristic and essentializing logic. For many coloured subjects, therefore, authority can be claimed by side-stepping the language of 'race' and looking to other signifiers to inscribe dignity, respectability and social superiority.

Rive's autobiography forms a complex and revealing tangle of discourses and signifiers which often draw attention – directly and implicitly – to codes through which signals of identity generate social meanings. 'Race' features prominently in this writer's construction of identity, but as a patently constructed category and in ways that differ from many other South African assertions of black identity. Of key importance is the way in which a range of fictions and discourses are mobilized to substantiate, complicate and also unravel the logic of racial discourses. In this process, Rive writes a hybridized identity that not only responds to 'racial hybridity', but also charts multiple subject positions and unstable subjectivities. Fictions of community are clearly central: it is by connecting the notions which community draws together – collectivity and place – that identity is named. And in the same way that communities and the sense of belonging they confer are constantly discarded, so too are unified identities and their fixity.

That belonging within black communities for Rive often features as a restrictive location is clear in the way his text celebrates 'new' and constantly changing communities. He often describes his ease, contentment, and spontaneous periods of joy when recounting incidental or fleeting encounters with individuals and groups with whom he has little in common politically or ideologically. It is often here that the author celebrates a personally liberating sense of belonging. Maybe the text's most telling celebration of hybridity is the implied message that it is mainly within communities that have not already been defined by convention or existing fictions that the subject finds freedom.

Identity's labyrinths in Wicomb's 'You Can't Get Lost in Cape Town'

Zoë Wicomb has criticized the tendency to interpret black women's writing as unmediated personal testimony. Yet the central character and narrator of her connected stories represents psychosocial experiences which encode those of the author. Like Frieda Shenton, Wicomb grew up in Little Namaqualand, attended the University of the Western Cape in the 1960s, and returned to South Africa after living in the United

Kingdom. As I shall show, the stories' self-referential orientation draws attention to the author's retrospective assessment of subject positions that punctuated her life story. Commenting on the structure of the stories, Sue Marais claims that they are 'a composed cycle with a unifying directional impulse', so that 'they approximate the novel rather than the short story collection'(1995, 33).

With their heavy emphasis on return through memory and the body, the stories seem to register a determination to capture a lost, elusive, or previously undiscovered self. Yet Wicomb ends up dealing primarily with the impossibility of this discovery. What Frieda inevitably confronts are interruptions, shifting locations and a diversity of subject positions for writing the self. Frieda's journey consequently illustrates Hall's comment that identity, inevitably 'incomplete', is always negotiated around master and counter-narratives yet never finds a stable home (1996, 130). The language of 'race' in the stories is seen as a particularly precarious yet oppressive site for representing the subject. To a greater extent than Rive, Wicomb maps the way racial discourses crowd the subject, shaping responses and being in relation to others in ways which cannot be transcended. While Wicomb's sequence of the stories traces the narrator's development from childhood to adulthood, this analysis of the sequence traces key themes in Wicomb's exploration of racial myths and hybridized identity.

In a paper subtitled 'The case of the coloured in South Africa'[10], Wicomb deals theoretically with the legacy of racial thought that constitutes the category 'coloured' and also, she shows, profoundly shaped coloured subjectivities and political responses. The argument is couched in a discussion of the biologist idea of 'miscegenation' and its association with shame. Shame, for Wicomb, is what a culture declares when its sacrosanct order is disturbed. In South Africa this disturbance is registered in the visible reminder of 'race mixing'. Wicomb is obviously concerned with the way that 'racial degeneracy' and shame are discursively marked. Shame is not, as it is for Millin, an ontological condition of the blood, but a construct of ideology and deeply entrenched racial theories. Shame is acknowledged not only in the dominant group's obsessive naming and separation of a coloured 'race'. It is also internalized by the 'hybrid' bearers of shame, so that talking about reinventing or refuting coloured identity always reinscribes the original story and language of 'race'.

Wicomb's deconstructive forays into identity, naming and language are suggestively allegorized in the title story, 'You Can't Get Lost in Cape Town'. Central to this story are ways in which shame is named, projected and obsessively probed – always through or by the explosively figurative language of 'race'. Frieda has an abortion after becoming pregnant by her white boyfriend. In the filthy rooms of the abortionist, a woman who cynically checks that Frieda is white and reassures her that she has never had any coloured clients, Frieda's body is violently probed. The story cryptically raises questions about the sources of perceived guilt and complicity in relation to the unborn child, who is a marker of shame. It therefore shows how exploration of the origins of coloured identity always occurs within the master narrative of eugenics. Wicomb problematizes the possibilities for a subversive reading of and resistance to discursive positioning. Whose action, the story seems to ask, is not shameful: Frieda, who chooses a humiliating abortion rather than carry a child fathered by a white man, or the white woman who performs the abortion, a 'grotesque bridegroom with yellow teeth'? (80)[11]? Or the abortionist's coloured assistant whose 'brown hand falls on my mouth and stifles my cry'(79)? Or her boyfriend, who impregnates his coloured girlfriend and then leaves her to find her own way to an abortionist in the city because 'you can't get lost in Cape Town'? The cycle of complicity widens and makes it impossible to decide who is ultimately responsible – both for the shameful act and for naming shame.

Allegorically, this suggests how all responses to original shame lead to an endless displacement of interpretation and – ultimately – a reproduction of the original story of disgrace that must be erased. The story's image of erasure is the abortion. But the erasure of shame finds echoes in identity politics, and can be identified in both dominant and ostensibly oppositional politics. Thus the Nationalist Party's obsessive policing of racial boundaries during apartheid, the left-wing coloured Unity Movement's denial of racial categories and calls for the more authentic language of class, or the upsurge in essentialism among many coloured politicians and subjects in the 1990s, can all be seen as ways of erasing the subject's entanglement with the shame connoted by 'coloured'.

The title story therefore deconstructs coloured identity in ways that reach beyond conventional indictments. Unlike these, Wicomb dredges up the symbolism of racial ideology and locates a deterministic mood of gloom that is strongly reminiscent of Millin's writing. Embodied as the discarded foetus, coloured identity is excavated as the old story of 'miscegenation' and unwanted 'hybrid' offspring. At the end, this old story of shame and 'degeneracy' is captured in the sordid image of an abandoned foetus, a 'newspaper parcel dropped into a dustbin [...] [absorbing] the vinegary smell of discarded fish and chips [...] ' (81). Although an old story originating in nineteenth-century myth making, the story of shame morbidly invades the cultural imagining of the present. It is clearly not only coloured identification that is explored here, but more generally the obsessive return to stories of 'race'.

'You Can't Get Lost in Cape Town' is in many ways Wicomb's exploration of the difficulties of discursively locating Frieda's independent choices in the face of a legacy of racialized thinking in South Africa. The story insists on identifying Frieda's body as the locus for others' inscriptions, namely, the sexuality of her white boyfriend, the operating of the abortionist (starkly reminiscent of Victorian probing of black female bodies), her relatives' perceptions of the 'disgrace' of black women who 'go with white men' (66), and the compound meanings which will make her body the 'source' of a 'mixed race' child. Apart from tracing the constant reinscription of shame, then, the story shows how guilt is written onto the bodies of black women. Denied subject positions in masculine and white-centred discourses, they become the bearers of, and projections for, others' guilt.

Yet the story is not only about the impossibility of making new meaning, and does not entirely invalidate scope for individual or political agency. Importantly, Frieda's reasons for aborting her child are not explored. This therefore allows the reader's writerly interpretations in ways not possible in Wicomb's theoretical article. These interpretations would revolve around how Frieda *negotiates* different subject positions. Thus, as Driver observes, the text opens up a space for considering Frieda's agency in relation to subject positions such as 'black', 'coloured', 'woman' and 'writer'. Driver further notes that the authority afforded by speaking, at times with and at times against these subject positions, is suggested when Frieda defies her boyfriend's vision of their romantic experiences at a beach resort by writing a poem entitled, 'Love at Loggiesbaai (Whites Only)'. His vision is unsettled by her Black Conscious vision of 'warriors charging out of the sea, assegaais gleaming in the sun' (75-76). Overall, however, the story is insistent about situating Frieda's agency within and through the oppressive fictions surrounding her.

While 'You Can't Get Lost in Cape Town' unravels the semiotics of racial ideology, Wicomb elsewhere focuses sociologically on coloured locations. Three stories that deal especially clearly with coloured identities in relation to changing political circumstances are 'A Clearing in the Bush', 'Behind the Bougainvillea' and 'Ash on My Sleeve'. The first of these describes Frieda's education at a 'Coloured university' during the obsessive Verwoerdian[12] era of separate development. 'A Clearing in the Bush' concentrates on the officially ordained complicity of coloureds with apartheid. Frieda is situated firmly within the state's ideological apparatus when she attends the University of the Western Cape (UWC), established by the Extension of University Education Act of 1959 that rigidly defined educational institutions on racial bases.[13] While UWC became the locus of anti-apartheid struggle in the late 1970s and 1980s, it was – at the time the story is set – part of an apartheid grand plan. Its teachers were often Afrikaner nationalists, its methods dominated by rote learning, and its ethos shaped by Calvinism and Christian nationalist austerity.

This is clearly conveyed when Frieda is seen to struggle with an essay on *Tess of the Durbevilles* – to be marked by a lecturer who relies on rote learning, and who 'does not know me, doesn't even know any of us, and will not recognize Frieda the next day' (40). Frieda's battle with the trappings of a dominant educational system is echoed in the struggle of a rural coloured working-class woman, who works in the university cafeteria and whose story runs parallel to Frieda's. Like Frieda, Tamieta is pressurized into measuring herself in relation to an authoritative white world. A campus ceremony is organized to commemorate the shooting of Prime Minister Verwoerd, engineer of the state's separatist educational policies in the interests of white supremacy. The ceremony is boycotted by most of the students, although Tamieta, alienated both from student politics and from the urban political knowledge of her co-workers, dutifully attends. During the ceremony she experiences a crisis of self-worth: 'Oh what could she do, and the shame of it flames in her chest. Wait until she is asked to leave [...] She longs for a catastrophe, an act of justice, something divine and unimaginable [...] '(57).

The source of Tamieta's insecurities in her racial ascription is made obvious when, unable to see herself as an addressee in the white rector's address, she broods obsessively about her appearance: 'How could she, Tamieta Snewe, with her slow heavy thighs scale such heights?'(59). What aligns the two women's crises is the extent to which both are trapped in an ascribed position of intermediacy and complicity, a position which compels dependence on the status quo for the meagre dignity withheld from Africans. This entrapment is clearly implicated with gender and place of origin, since both Frieda and Tamieta are coloured rural women. It is therefore suggested that both their responses foreground feminized behaviours like duty, deference and obedience. Tamieta muses about herself in the following way: 'Why should she not be called a lady? She who has always conducted herself according to God's word? Whose lips have never parted for a drop of liquor or the whorish cigarette? And who has worked dutifully all her life?' (59).

While Tamieta's extreme self-flagellation seems to make her even more of a victim than Frieda, both are profoundly constrained by their marginality within existing discourses of authority. Although these are myriad, coloured hybridity, as it generates anxiety about self-worth and an associated quest for dignity, is central. In this sense the story conveys the mood of mainstream political protest in the 1960s especially as this affected a group uneasily situated as a buffer, privileged class. This was partly made possible by the Coloured Labour Preference Policy of the mid-1950s and the range of limited rights for coloureds in the 1960s in relation to 'pure Africans'. While the 1960s ushered in a vigorous Nationalist streamlining of apartheid, it was also associated with a national clamp-down on oppositional politics. Coloureds were situated in the Nationalist Party's elaborate plans for white supremacy in ways that led to an entrenched sense of political powerlessness or conservativism. The 'clearing in the bush', directly referring to UWC's location at the periphery of Cape Town, also symbolizes the induction of an interstitial group into the racial hierarchy, as the rector puts it, 'its liberation' from 'the barbarism, the immense task that lies ahead of the educator' (59).

In the face of this, Frieda, like Tamieta, aspires to respectability and decency along the avenues that the state-controlled university offers her. Thus her reading of *Tess* is constrained not only by the mechanical expectations of her lifeless educator, but also by an imbibed moral creed, echoing Calvinist austerity: 'Murder is a sin which should outrage all decent and civilised people' (42). While Frieda is deeply disaffected by and uneasy with existing paths for self-definition, she seems to be trapped in a white supremacist educational system and the racial hierarchy more generally. Unlike some of the other stories in the collection, then, 'A Clearing in the Bush' does not trace cryptic moments of rebellion. Tamieta and Frieda are shown to be trapped, rather than to be able to forge independent routes to decency, dignity and respectability. Both end up leaving the campus to walk into the bush, their paths leading neither to the dominant society's vision of salvation nor to any alternative ideal of liberation and self-realization.

'Behind the Bouganvillia' and 'Ash on My Sleeve' deal with Frieda's return from Britain to a rural community when she visits South Africa. While the stories are set in the 1980s when Frieda has developed politically and when the political mood among many coloured South Africans was militant, they do not insist that earlier patterns in identity politics entirely disappear. 'Behind the Bougainvillea' describes Frieda's encounter with a man she knew when both were children, and when his dark skin alienated him from obviously 'mixed' coloured people. Frieda recalls her abortive love affair:

> All through the summer we composed delicious letters of love. Secret, for Father said I was too young to think of boys; besides, Henry Hendrickse, I had heard him say many times, was almost pure kaffir. We, the Shentons, had an ancestor, an Englishman, whose memory must be kept sacred, must not be defiled by associating with those beneath us. We were respectable Coloureds. (116)

The story tantalizingly suggests that Frieda has the option, in adulthood and on her return to South Africa, to disavow coloured exclusivism by renewing her relationship. When she meets Henry Hendrickse at the doctor's then, she agrees to visit his home. Yet their meeting and subsequent love-making are marked by unromantic awkwardness. The idea of Frieda successfully redressing the past and recapturing a romantic moment is consequently undercut. Later, she also learns that Hendrickse could be a spy for the government. Thus the liberatory meanings he seems to encode (the antithesis of hybrid respectability, the romantic lover of her childhood, a black man who speaks Xhosa) are belied by his social role. Frieda is forced to confront the way she has clung to fictions that promise an ultimate self-discovery and fulfillment.

This theme is developed in a story focusing on coloured involvement in political struggles in the 1980s. Set in an ethos shaped by the politics of the United Democratic Front (UDF)[14], the story describes a period and mood totally different from those of 'A Clearing in the Bush'. In 'Ash on My Sleeve', Frieda visits a former girlfriend, who, unlike herself, has remained in Cape Town, acquired a family and 'settled down'. Although the path of her development appears conservative, both she and her husband are active in the turbulent politics of the 1980s. Yet Frieda is struck by the limitations of this protest as it affects subjects like her friend. She is appalled by the boorishness of Moira's husband and acutely conscious of her overwhelming social roles in combining child-care, domestic work, a full-time job and political activism. Even Moira's apparent sense of security is fractured when she momentarily admits: 'Jesus, I don't know. Sometimes I'm optimistic and then it's worth fighting, but other times, here in this house, everything seems pointless' (160).

Thus the story raises the theme – to which Wicomb returns – that political struggles in South Africa have been masculinized processes which ignore gender and domestic politics; women's involvement in politics opposing racial hierarchies often leaves intact their oppression within gender hierarchies. The story also turns specifically to the gap between the postures and practice of protest by highlighting the family's paradoxical location in UDF politics. Although Moira's family appears to be deeply involved in black progressive politics, the story offers hints of their privileged location. At one stage, Moira's child rushes in to announce: 'There are two African men in the playhouse, and they've got our sleeping bags. Two grown-ups can't sleep there' (161). This detail might be a description exposing the ambiguities of white liberal political involvement. It shows that while the socially advantaged progressive might be aligned consciously with opposition to the state, a structural location inevitably complicates conscious or principled alignment with collective black struggle. Thus, the story exposes tensions both in coloured alignment with black politics, and women's relationships to a national liberation movement. Broadly, it highlights how individuals occupy a range of subject positions – which makes conventional strategies, ideologies and organizations for collective resistance very tenuous. As Driver has observed, Wicomb 'steadfastly insisting on creating more complex subject positions than those of the past' shows how 'new subjectivities [are] continually emerging at the critical point between stereotype and representation, and between one discursive subject position and the other' (1996, 52).

Many of Wicomb's stories deal with the ways in which fictions of identity and belonging constrain subjects' agency. Others trace moments of rebellion and resistance, as characters enlist strategies at hand to assert moments of freedom and assertive processes of identification. The sustained ironies in Wicomb's stories make it tempting to stress their broadly deconstructive thrust while underplaying the extent to which this thrust is itself a socially-positioned appraisal of identity, shaped by the author's encounters with South African politics[15]. The self-referentiality of the stories is important not only in the way it maps the central character's return to past memories and places, but also as it charts the author's return. This return involves not only going back to subjects, places and people – an autobiographical emphasis described by Carol Sicherman (1993) – but mainly reconfiguring a mood and political outlook which profoundly affects Wicomb's enduring sense of the individual's entrapment in a distinctively South African fixation with racialized positions, markers and meanings. The stories powerfully encode the period shortly before the writer went into exile, a period in the 1960s when oppositional politics was heavily constrained by apartheid and clamp-downs on opposition, and when the state seemed impervious to conventional collective political acts of resistance.

The encoding of this mood of forbidding authoritarianism has led one critic to describe the stories as both 'terrible and wonderful' (Mukherjee 1987), and it can be traced even in stories that signal forms of political triumph. Each of the stories either symbolizes or narrates an overwhelming atmosphere of social and cultural sterility. All the stories therefore seem to gesture towards the political stasis and gloom of a period described in 'A Clearing in the Bush' or the haunting stories of racial obsession described in 'You Can't Get Lost in Cape Town'. In stories dealing with agency and political revolt, Wicomb turns emphatically away from conventional trajectories of struggle and stresses a profoundly individualist self-liberation. It is primarily by endorsing idiosyncratic and individualist processes of subversion that Wicomb celebrates a liberating agency and self-discovery. For a number of reasons, then, Wicomb, like Rive, explores political agency in ways that consistently disavow conventional collectivism and the hallmark of much black South African writing.

The first story of the collection invites comparison with Rive's preoccupation with respectability, with a language and social posture that defy debasement within the racial hierarchy. Frieda is a child in 'Bowl Like Hole', a story which traces her induction into political behaviour when she closely observes her parents. Frieda, we learn, habitually skulks beneath the kitchen table, suppressed within a domestic domain that is already marginal. Unlike the title story, 'Bowl Like Hole' does not centre around a traumatic or important event, yet defines the important social and psychic influences on a young coloured girl in a rural community during the early years of apartheid. Key influences are her father, a figure of authority in the public world of the local community; her mother, repository of discipline and a figure who connects authority in the family home to worlds beyond it; and Mr Weedon, a white figure of authority in the area. The domestic world and local community are defined in relation to Mr Weedon, symbol of economic and political power both in and beyond the rural community, who 'came like any white man in a motor car, enquiring about sheep or goats'(1). The title of the story refers to the white man's pronunciation of the word 'bowl' as hole. The story concludes with Frieda reflecting that her mother, despite initial scepticism, will adopt the pronunciation of Mr Weedon: 'I knew that unlike the rest of us it would take her no time at all to say bowl like hole, smoothly, without stuttering' (9).

Like Rive, Wicomb refers to an ethic of respectability, configured through language usage, through which subjects construct positive identity. Frieda's mother is defensive about the way her pronunciation reflects social status, yet quickly gauges the advantages of echoing a white English-speaking man. The narrator disparagingly comments on her mother's mimicry. Yet the story also establishes the legitimacy of the mother's quest for dignity through the restricted avenues open to her. Circumscribed by the home, denied access to a public world in which her husband is active, Frieda's mother can only enlist the behaviours that are conventionally considered petty. Frieda is sharply aware of her father's contrasting authority, and registers that he is part of a world in which neither she nor her mother plays an influential role. When her father interacts with the white Weedon, he is assertive, and self-confident, refusing to capitulate to the white man's authority. The narrator proudly refers to her father's refusal of the routine packet of cigarettes doled out by the white *baas*: 'Father seemed very tall as his rigid arm held out the box' (8). Frieda exults in her father's manly self-assertion, disparaging what she sees as her mother's collusion. While Frieda does not read against gender politics, the text, drawing attention to the father's masculine physicality, does, and invites us to consider the gendered locations of Frieda, her mother and her father as each inhabits a different location for confronting the power of Mr Weedon. Thus, the story starts to consider how public and influential defiance of white racism can be shaped by masculinity, with women being interpellated into positions of protest already marked by male authority.

Another story focusing on Frieda's relationship with her father represents the daughter's separation from her father. The story describes her departure for a white school in Cape Town, an event that becomes emphatically public when she and her father encounter boys and girls of her age on the station platform. Apparently reversing the pattern of the previous story, Frieda ventures into an authoritative public world while her father remains at home. While this journey seems to reverse a traditional gender pattern, filial obligation (and not choice) underpins Frieda's departure for a white and masculine world; as a daughter, she is simply her father's emissary. An index of this role is the paternal message communicated by her father: 'You show them, Frieda, what we can do'(27). This command refers to the *boers*, cited in the previous few lines when members of the community say, 'a clever chap old Shenton, keeps up with the Boers all right' (27). The father's struggle for success, dignity and authority is therefore evident in the way he urges Frieda's empowerment in class terms.

Like Rive, then, Wicomb foregrounds class mobility in the face of 'race' laws and myths that construct hybrid inferiority. Generally, Frieda and her family, who use English, rather than Afrikaans, occupy a superior position of respectability and civility in the Afrikaans-dominated community. At the station, Shenton, speaking loudly in English, positions Frieda as an extension in his narrative of respectability. Frieda's discomfort results not only from recognizing the resentment of others on the platform; she is also painfully aware of her position as a young girl, both lacking and desiring the femininity of the other girls on the platform. While Frieda chafes against the confines of an empowerment offered by her father, she cannot envisage liberation through the dominant languages of black South African struggle. When one of the boys on the platform taunts her with the story that trains, usually carrying white people, are destroyed by black activists, Frieda experiences only intense outrage: 'I would like to hurl myself at him, stab at his eyes with my blunt nails, kick at his ankles, until they snap' (34). Frieda's experiences on the platform therefore mark her alienation both from her father's paternal (and politically conservative) story of success as well as from the dominant progressive (and masculine discourse) of black political struggle.

Yet the story does not simply chart her helplessness, and illustrates Driver's claim that 'the self-knowledge with which Wicomb imbues many of her major characters involves their active engagement with their world rather than their being passive victims of hegemonic control' (1996, 48). Using an urban dialect which combines English and Afrikaans she utters a taunt used by Cape subcultures to call attention to the boys' predatory scrutiny: 'At what you look and *kyk gelyk* / Am I *miskien* of gold *gemake*'? (35). Here Frieda demonstrates what Mikhail Bhaktin (1981) has referred to as intentional hybridity, the destabilizing in language of authority through the simultaneous speaking of different languages. This derives both from code-switching (when Frieda mixes English and Afrikaans grammar rules and vocabulary to corrupt the fluent Afrikaans spoken by members of the rural community) and from the way she disobeys her father's strictures about 'good English'. The story shows how emphatically language and speech mark communal boundaries, and how linguistic mixtures can jar established boundaries and become ways for individuals to articulate rebellion against fixed communities.

The story therefore celebrates the way moments of subversion may give self-defining identity to subjects whose positions often appear hopelessly complicit or marginal. This affirmation is evident also in 'Jan Klinkies', dealing with Frieda's uncle who refuses to drink rooibos tea because the package bears a potent Afrikaner nationalist icon: a depiction of the Great Trek. It surfaces also in 'Another Story', in which the rural and apolitical Deborah Kleinhans suddenly pours out the cups of coffee she has prepared for two policemen[16]. The most startling posture of protest in the story, then, is not the routine political activity of her niece, a teacher of history at the university, but the violence of the older (and apparently very conservative) woman's unpredicted defiance and rage. By using these kinds of interruptive languages, Wicomb tells the other stories of political resistance: self-assertion among individuals and groups conventionally considered beyond the mainstream of progressive political organizations and struggle. It is particularly significant that most of these individualist acts of revolt are demonstrated through processes of signification, especially within speech. Here Wicomb foregrounds the centrality of representation in her exploration of power and the politics of identity.

I have shown how Wicomb disavows conventional representations of fixed identity and collective action. Like Rive, her stories affirm individualistic processes of identity formation, unchartered spaces, and interruptive languages. Part of this celebration is a vigorous condemnation of 'home'. Thus, homelessness, not as loss but as the absence of a coherent locus of return, is the explicit theme of 'Home Sweet Home', the first story to deal with Frieda's return from exile. The story explicitly registers her alienation from the world she is a product of as she returns to her childhood and earlier memories. But the story also interrogates alienation, which suggests the comforting notion of home as the subject's 'natural' origin and desirable place of return. Neither 'natural' nor desired, home is only ever the fiction constructed through the sentimentalizing of Aunt Cissy's 'There's no place like home' (99) or her father's 'home is where the heart is' (99).

This implies that 'home' (like Rive's community) has none of the resonance of completeness or fulfillment often celebrated in writings that claim collective identity. The 'return home' may allow new perspectives, even broader understanding, but no final discovery or recovery of definitive identity. Wicomb consequently inverts a conventionalized theme in much black South African writing with its preoccupation with lost and recovered homes, with collective and denied spaces, with the inextricable connection between collective agency and individuals' liberation. The writer's celebration of hybridization is thus a powerful reminder of her individualistic, idiosyncratic and performative affirmations of self. While this individualism never amounts to the speaking of wholly new languages, or the discovery of subject-position outside of existing discourses, its anchorage in mixing, blurring and refusals of fixed positions proclaims triumphant and emancipatory meanings.

Conclusion

Emphasizing the centrality of myth making about 'racial hybridity' to an understanding of 'race', Deleuze and Guattari have argued that 'bastard and mixed-blood are the true names of race' (1988, 379). The claim seems to be confirmed in the writings of Rive and Wicomb: both trace the myths and politics of 'racial hybridity' to shed light on a pattern of repetitious compulsion in constructions of racial identity, and on the range of conventions that underlie racial identifications in South Africa. Although South African writers have constantly evoked the category and politics of 'race', they have rarely drawn attention to the discursive processes through which 'race' constitutes and excludes individuals and collectivities, to the signifying processes that this involves and the codes that this assumes. We could therefore speculate that attention to hybrid spaces, as opposed to analysis of univocal and essentialized identities, is more likely to uncover entrenched assumptions. Such attention might more easily explode the tendency to fixate on what Ndebele calls 'anticipated surfaces' and encourage exploration of the actual production of 'race' in South Africa. These hybridized versions might more readily allow insight into a complex and unstable terrain, rather than merely confirm conventions whose meanings are established through ritualistic interpretive and representational practices.

While Rive and Wicomb focus emphatically on racialized processes, they also chart what Young (1995, 173) refers to as a paradigm of 'palimpsestual inscription and reinscription' for exploring the complexities of cultural expression, identity formation and political agency. These hybridized cultural practices that speak in-between and through established ones do not involve discovering substantively 'new' identities, or speaking entirely different languages. Yet it is perhaps in these palimpsestual models, previously dismissed as politically suspect or contradictory, that new processes of resistance (and ways of exploring them) can be mapped. There has been much preoccupation in present-day South Africa with actively constructing new identities, with discovering original fictions, and, especially, with rewriting, rediscovering or renaming coloured identity. All this disturbingly recuperates an old obsession with 'essences', 'purity' and normativeness. The autobiographical projects of Rive and Wicomb offer evidence of the ways in which 'new' fictions of freedom and selfhood inevitably gesture to old and oppressive ones. Yet in the same way that hybridity has been redefined to give different meanings to a traditional concept, so too can the repositioning and reappraisal of 'old' identities.

Notes

1 Trajectories in the canon described above have been constructed in book-length criticisms like Ursula Barnett's (1983), Jane Watts'(1989) or Piniel Shava's (1989), in seminal articles, or in university courses and indicate ways in which a corpus of writing has been categorized, organized and represented through largely unexplained assumptions about blackness. The extent to which the reception of writing codifies, exhorts and levels 'black identity' is evident in Jane Watts' emphatic yet curiously tautological statement: 'By focusing on the negation of freedom and identity black writers attempt to reflect back to their readers an authentic sense of being' (1989, 30).

2 Nikos Papastergiadis discusses hybridity as follows: 'For as long as the concepts of purity and exclusivity have been central to a racialized theory of identity, hybridity has, in one way or another, served as a threat to the fullness of selfhood. The hybrid has often been positioned within or beside modern theories of human origin and social development, mostly appearing as the moral marker of contamination, failure or regression' (1997, 257).

3 Narrative point of view in certain omniscient comments about the conditions when 'race' myths are invoked is particularly revealing. At times it is possible to read Millin's novel as an expose, rather than simply as an endorsement of the racial hierarchy.

4 Page references are to Richard Rive, *Writing Black*. Cape Town: David Philip, 1981.

5 Adhikari has described the fixation with the minutae of features like hair texture or skin colour among coloured people. The surveillance of physiognomy is obviously not the fixation of only one group in South Africa, but the obsession with degrees of 'blackness' or 'whiteness' within a particular group can be traced to criteria for including and exclusion within it.

6 See the 'The Fabulous Decade' in Nkosi's *Home and Exile* (1965).

7 This school of poetry has been codified in numerous anthologies, including *Voices From Within* (1982), *The Return of the Amasi Bird* (1982), *To Whom It May Concern* (1972) and *A Century of South African Poetry* (1982).

8 See especially 'Culture and the History of Difference' and 'The Complicity of Culture' in *Colonial Desire*.

9 This is clearly evidenced in current fraught and contradictory expressions of coloured identity - which range between claiming Khoi-San 'essence' (so that somehow the 'mixing' and 'contamination' of other racial strains is simply wished away) to exulting in 'mixture' at the same time that essentializing labels are invoked.

10 See 'Postcoloniality and Postmodernity: the Case of the Coloured in South Africa', keynote address at Auetsa Conference, University of the Western Cape, July 1996.

11 Page references are to Zoë Wicomb, 1987. *You Can't Get Lost in Cape Town*. London: Virago.

12 Hendrik Verwoerd is often known as the 'architect of apartheid'. Leading the Nationalist Party he played a central role in developing the apartheid state's ideological apparatus.

13 Thus, white students attended universities like the University of Cape Town, black students attended universities like Fort Hare, Indian students the University of Durban-Westville.

14 The UDF, formed in 1983, mobilized supporters through a politics of non-racial opposition to apartheid. Divisions between coloured and black were strongly condemned as apartheid reflexes.

15 See for example Sue Marais who writes that Wicomb 'project[s] the contemporary situation in South Africa as a state not only of political and existential but also of aesthetic breakdown, similar though not identical to the postmodern crisis' (1995, 32).

16 As I show earlier, the stance of protest is not explicitly celebrated or interpreted by the narrator. But the idea of Deborah's performing an action which is not only difficult to explain, but also profoundly interruptive, is stressed.

Chapter Eight

Crossing the colour(ed) line: Mediating the ambiguities of belonging and identity[1]

Heid Grunebaum & Steven Robins

> The over-integrated sense of cultural and ethnic particularity is very popular today, and blacks do not monopolize it [Nazi Germany, the Balkans, apartheid South Africa ...]. It masks the arbitrariness of its own political choices in the morally charged language of ethnic absolutism and this poses additional dangers because it overlooks the development and change of black political ideologies and ignores the restless, recombinant qualities of the black Atlantic's affirmative political cultures. *Paul Gilroy*

How are narratives of personal and subjective experience displaced or silenced in the production of collective identities? How is the tension between the personal and political, the individual and the collective, represented and understood in the testimonies to the Truth and Reconciliation Commission (TRC)? How do the cultural politics of location get played out within the memorializing framework of an institution such as the TRC? This chapter attempts to examine these questions, particularly in relation to coloured identity. We analyze a particular Human Rights Violation testimony that draws attention to coloured identity but refuses to celebrate it as a transgressive hybridity, or to embrace it as an immutable and biologically essentialist racial identity. We focus on the Human Rights Violations testimony of Zahrah Narkadien, an ANC activist and Umkhonto we Sizwe (MK) combatant who was imprisoned and held in solitary confinement during the 1980s. Narkadien later appeared before the TRC hearings on human rights violations perpetrated in South African prisons. In this chapter, we investigate how this testimony draws attention to the complexities of the identity politics of colouredness and challenges the homogenizing discourses of ethnic essentialism, non-racialism, and 'rainbow' nationalism.

Narkadien's testimony alerts us to the difficulties of speaking about coloured identity both during and after apartheid. These difficulties involve finding a vocabulary to speak about complex and heterogeneous identities and histories that were collapsed into the single overarching apartheid category of coloured. It has become increasingly clear that coloured identity is highly contested and unstable and involves claims to Nama (Khoe Khoe), San, European, African, and Asian ancestries, histories and identities. We acknowledge that these difficulties cannot be reduced to nor crystallized in one fleeting moment of Narkadien's life immured in testimony.

This chapter is not only based on Narkadien's testimony to the TRC. We also include subsequent interviews with her because her commentary on her testimony and identity speaks about the impossibility of closure of both the coloured identity question and her own experience of torture and solitary confinement. She asserts the necessity of an ongoing working through of pain, of identity issues and of the layers of meanings that she makes and that are imposed on her. In this way, both Narkadien's TRC testimony and her ongoing commentary point to two important issues around identity in general and coloured identity in particular. On the one hand, they question current post-modern celebrations of hybridity as an anti-essentialist and transgressive cultural politics of resistance and empowerment. On the other hand, Narkadien's testimony is instructive in how it reveals the making of collective memory and national identity as a highly contradictory and ambiguous process which highlights, in turn, the complex relationships between personal and collective memory, between individual and imagined experience, symbolic and real solidarities.

The dilemmas, ambiguities, and anxieties of belonging experienced by coloured activists such as Narkadien have not received much media or scholarly attention. Interestingly enough, however, the radio commentary which framed Narkadien's testimony at the prison hearings sought to resolve some of the tensions between personal and collective memory through silences and erasures, and by splicing Narkadien's account of solitary confinement on to a heroic national narrative of collective suffering, resistance and sacrifice.

TRC testimony and identity: psychic landscapes of imprisonment

> I think prior to my experience of my black comrades, I was denying this history that was forced on [me] by the South African government, that you are a coloured. And I was trying to shake it off and be this African woman that my parents tried to encourage me to be. But I think when I came out [of prison] I realized that was being too much of a dreamer, too idealistic, that even though I'm achieving this African woman status this coloured woman status may not be in the inside of me but it is on the outside of me. I had to [see] that reality painful as it was. It was like taking a good few steps back or eating your own vomit, that's how bad I felt it was. But it was reality and I decided to rather embrace and deal with it. I make it my business whenever I talk to

> black colleagues or black friends, and if they make remarks about coloured people as coloured people, I correct them immediately [...]. (Transcript of Case JB04418, testimony of Narkadien, TRC Special Hearings - Prisons, Johannesburg, 21 July 1997)

The Human Rights Violations (HRV) hearings of the Truth and Reconciliation Commission (TRC) have assumed a central role as the repository of a collective memory and public histories of apartheid. An understanding of the framing and mediations of individual testimonies has alerted us to the silences that inevitably occur. As the testimonial utterance is appropriated and contained by the discourse of the 'new' nation, alternative ways of speaking about identity are displaced. And it is precisely these silences and displacements in the name of the nation with which we are concerned in this chapter.

The Human Rights Violations testimonies presented to the TRC are constructed as matrix of a 'shared memory' of personal sacrifice, heroism and national redemption. The testimonial moment, however, is a multi-faceted one. It challenges, in its very structure, the linear and teleological emplotments towards which national narratives tend. Testimony intersects the boundaries of the personal/political, and the public/private. It disturbs 'a number of discourses, [which] do not function discretely, but usually overlap: legal or judicial, religious, and, of course, poetic as well as psychotherapeutic and ethnographic' (Brodski 1997, 5). Nonetheless these many layers of testimony coalesce in ways that allow for the production of stable collective narratives of national unity.

Human Rights Violations testimonies have presented us with a powerful instance of the trauma of recalling and telling of trauma (very often for the first time). In the instance of political detainees, part of that trauma is often constituted through an inner conflict: between the demands of the disciplined political persona, and the pain, trauma and denial of the deeply personal, which is sometimes seen as self-indulgent. Often these tensions are revealed through expressions of complex inner turmoil (or, conversely, firm resolve) in moments of self-definition, explanations of subjectivity and ethnic identity. This chapter examines how Narkadien's account of her traumatic experience, and her own struggles with identity, are interpolated during the presentation of testimony.

Trauma theorists and psychotherapists Bessel van der Kolk and Onno van der Hart gloss Pierre Janet's distinction between traumatic memory – the voluntary or, very often, involuntary recollection of traumatic experience – and narrative or ordinary memory (1995, 163) in a way that highlights the sociality of narrative memory as being an address to community. They point out that narrative memory is an integrative and 'social act' (163) which, we would contend, is the underpinning logic of the highly public nature of HRV testimony. According to van der Kolk and van der Hart, traumatic memory, on the other hand, often 'has no social component; it is not addressed to anybody, the [witness] does not respond to anybody; it is a solitary activity'. However, we would qualify this by acknowledging the important role of audience and listener in the passage of traumatic memory towards narrativization. The HRV hearings present us with an instance when the environment can either facilitate or block such passage.

The Special TRC Hearing on Prisons, held during July 1997, focused on the theme of human rights violations within the South African prison system. This was the framework within which Narkadien's testimony was presented.

As Greta Appelgren (Narkadien's name before her marriage and conversion to Islam), Narkadien's personal history presents her progressive questioning of apartheid constructions of 'race' within a trajectory of increasing politicization beginning in 1976 when she entered University of the Western Cape as a social work student (interview with Kevin Ritchie, *Argus,* 3 May 1997). Linking her political awakening to a questioning of apartheid identity construction, she maintains that 'I began to question why I was called a coloured'; she explains, 'God creates all of us equal, with different hues and hair textures, yet the white government was making us different' (interview with Ritchie).

Her TRC testimony initially presents us with an almost superhuman story of survival: political activism, arrest, interrogation, torture and gross abuse during her period of incarceration. But her storyline is paused/collapses when she breaks down during her recollection of an incident, articulated specifically around her colouredness. As we will see, this recollected moment becomes a turning point in the testimony, enacting a break in the testimonial and national narratives of resistance, and asserting instead the alienation and trauma of being literally imprisoned in a disavowed identity. While acknowledging the limits of representivity in this focus on a single TRC testimony, we nonetheless believe that the way that Narkadien's story is mediated through the radio allows us to reflect upon the more general process of creating collective accounts of apartheid violations.

Narkadien's presentation at the special hearing is remarkable precisely because of the controlled manner in which she speaks of her inhumane, humiliating and brutal treatment during long sessions of interrogation and torture. As the subject and narrator of the testimony her recollections are linear, chronological in progression, her voice is steady, unwavering even, and the presentation controlled, almost detached.

Narkadien's testimony begins by explaining her commitment to a cause: as an MK combatant she is dedicated to the liberation struggle and it is clearly this identity which endows her with a resolve that remains unbroken by torture and the brutal, relentless interrogation to which she is subjected by the security police. Indeed she explicitly establishes this causal link between her commitment as an activist and her ability to withstand interrogation and torture after her arrest. Narkadien continues to describe solitary confinement and its devastating and sustained effects. This, however, is counterpoised by her recollections of being transferred to Klerksdorp prison with three other activists. Coming out of isolation and joining like-minded activists was initially a source of tremendous emotional and psychological support. This initial experience of solidarity and camaraderie becomes all the more ironic when it is followed by her account of exclusion from this group, solitary confinement and psychological breakdown.

Having previously subscribed to the notion that the designation of apartheid categories of 'race' and ethnicity could be transcended as a form of political 'false consciousness', the testimony highlights her expulsion from political community (in prison) as one of the radical dilemmas of her identification.

> [....] I came out of isolation [...] It was a wonderful day to get to Klerksdorp prison, I was there with three other comrades of mine. It was a big celebration for us because I was ending my solitary confinement now. But it didn't last. I was with them for only about six months when a fight broke out between two of the comrades from KwaZakela [Port Elizabeth], and they strategized amongst themselves that, 'Let's blame it on the coloured woman'. And unfortunately they knew that the prison wardresses, especially the head of the section, was a very racist woman and she believed that coloureds were violent, they were gangsters. So because of that hmnn, racist, you know, stereotype I was taken one morning, it was about five o'clock, when all the other prisoners were sleeping, out of my cubicle, everything, my mattress it was taken, and I had to go down to the basement in isolation for seven months. And that was very, very, very painful. I don't even want to describe psychologically what I had to do to survive down there. I will write it one day, but I could never tell you. But, hmnn, it did teach me something that, no human being can live alone [cough] for more than, I think even a month, or even three months. Because you, there is nothing you can do to survive all by yourself, every single day.

It is significant to note that in other mediations of Narkadien's story (TRC Special Report interview aired on SABC3, 5 November 1997), she offers a gloss on her primary testimony which, in its description of the incident that precipitated her expulsion from her support community and her second bout of solitary confinement, highlights precisely what cannot be spoken about within the TRC's 'official' testimonial space. In this secondary narration Narkadien recounts how it had been her rejection of the sexual advances of one of her comrades that had led to the incident that brought about her punishment in solitary confinement. Gail Reagon, the SABC Television Special Report interviewer and producer, couches Narkadien's prison experiences in the language of trauma and betrayal:

> But Zarah [sic] was damaged in more complex ways: she spent seven months in that basement because of some of her comrades. There was racial tension; she was belittled for being coloured. One woman [...] made sexual advances. Zarah [sic] rejected her. In retaliation she was blamed for a fight [that] broke out between two prisoners. And once again, Zarah [sic] was confined to the sound of nobody but herself.

It is within the space and duration of this interview that categories of the universal soldier/activist are further collapsed and the questions of gender and sexuality complicate the notion further. Narkadien describes her fellow combatants as:

> [all] strong women, at least that's what it seemed. Till after about the third or fourth week [when] the honeymoon was over. And I saw how damaged my comrades were. They had been in prison longer than I was. But okay, I know sex is a good, hmmm, what can I say, [it] releases a tension in the body and it is also reassuring for each other, whether it's between two men or two women. But I hadn't been in prison long enough to need that, so I wasn't ready for a sexual relationship with anybody, and least of all this tough, masculine woman who was determined to bully everyone left, right and centre. Okay, I know that she was the most damaged. We all understood that we were all older than her and we were all willing to mother her but I wasn't willing to be her sex partner so to speak. So I paid dearly for that.

It is significant to observe that it is within the context of this interview that the psychic aftermath of trauma – the language of damage, deferral, and the assertion of non-closure – is presented as an empowering response to the prison experience. The language of trauma in this interview therefore marks a notable contrast to the original testimonial performance where the political imperative of the TRC's framing of testimony attempts (unsuccessfully in our opinion) to subsume the identity of the narrator in its quest to represent a seamless collective narrative of community. In its invocation of testimony as metonymically representative, the TRC's testimonial forum seems to 'evoke an absent polyphony of other voices, other possible lives and other experiences' (Beverly 1996, 28). In Narkadien's testimony, however, it is the disruption of community that is highlighted. So where the hearing of human rights abuses in prisons calls on testimony to represent the experiences of all political detainees, irrespective of gender, ethnicity and 'race', it simultaneously highlights the subjective voice of Narkadien's testimony as that of an isolated and alienated prisoner.

The painful experience of enforced marginalization and alienation is expressed around Narkadien's colouredness. In this way this account of the trauma of torture simultaneously narrates the inescapable trauma of apartheid as enforced isolation[2].

In the moment of testimony when the breach of solidarity of political community is retold Narkadien frames her experience as the severed possibility of any or all community. Her description of enforced isolation is presented as the disturbing experience of living one's own death:

> And the basement was an entire wing of the prison, it was like so much at the bottom with high walls [...] I felt as the months went by that I was going deeper and deeper into the ground. I mean I physically wasn't but psychologically I was. And had to live in this basement with long passages with all the other cells which used to be locked, and I was in this one tiny cell which was the size of my parent's bathroom at home. It's a two-bedroomed house and if you know the size of a bathroom in a two-bedroomed [...] If I get up from my bed I would have to take two steps, let's say four steps to get to my toilet. I only had a bed and desk in there. And I became so psychologically damaged that I used to feel that all these cells are all uhmn, uhmn [...] kind of, they were like coffins and there were all dead people in them. Because no one was there. It was like I was alive and all these people were dead. I was so disturbed but I would never, never let the wardresses know [breaks down and cries].

Clearly the conflation of Narkadien living her own death with the devastating rejection by her fellow combatants enacts a remembering of pain which is both a cause and a consequence of her colouredness. Although it is her rejection of the sexual advances of her comrades that precipitates her expulsion from political community, it is the aspersions cast on her coloured identity that seem to be most devastating to Narkadien's sense of self. Her testimony collapses precisely at the point that narrative memory recalls the limits of a political community that had been defined in terms of a disavowal of racialized identity. It is the striking and painful description of the carceral space – the psychological experience of solitary confinement figured as the shrinking, sinking space of the prison – that endows this testimony with its performative impact. At the same time as the testimony narrates the devastating psychic effects of solitary confinement, it offers a powerful comment on the effects of the incarceration in disavowed racialized identities. Indeed, in the televised TRC Special Report interview with Gail Reagon, Narkadien describes how during her imprisonment she would burn her hands in boiling hot water, in acts of self-mutilation. Initially, we understood this act of burning as a gendered and racialised gesture of self-directed anger, as an attempt to burn through the visceral embodiment of a metaphoric imprisonment within the fixed and legislated boundaries of racialized identities. Narkadien, however, contests this idea. Responding to a draft of this chapter in an interview with Steven Robins (Kimberley, 10 April 1999), Narkadien states:

> Okay, I agree with it. I agree with all the stuff. It's just the part about the burning of the hands that was possibly burning off my skin colour or my racial identity, whatever. Whereas I don't think so. I think it's purely that I was just trying to distract myself from the psychological pain of being lonely. I would agree that maybe you can speculate that perhaps deep down I really was burning or destroying my coloured identity, which got me down there [in solitary confinement] in the first place. So somewhere in my sub, sub-consciousness [laughter] it could have been but I don't think so [laughter].

Narkadien goes further than this. Later in the interview she distinguishes between colour and colouredness when she links her brownness to colouredness in a gesture of affirmation claiming that

> as much as my brownness is linked to colouredness, and that's [what] I was being tortured for. But the colour of my skin, I mean, I like this colour. We always talk amongst ourselves, my sisters and my cousins, because we're all this colour [laughter]. We say, 'Anytime we want to we can just declare that we're from Tahiti or from certain parts of Italy where you know the people are really olive skinned or this tanned [laughter].' So for us it's beautiful, I would never want to destroy the skin colour, or make it browner, or darker or whiter.

By making such a distinction between skin colour and colouredness, Narkadien lays claim to an aesthetic of colour, to a sensual dimension, that escapes state-defined ethnicities and racialised essences.

Significantly it is Narkadien's powerful performance of incarceration, seclusion/setting apart, which challenges the community of memory on which nation-building and new national identities are constructed. This is precisely what is effaced in the radio transmission of this testimony. Narkadien's narration is paused as she sobs and the commissioner intervenes briefly in order to comfort her, by telling her to take her time. The voice-over of the radio commentator literally drowns out the incessant sobs that punctuate her unsuccessful attempts to continue the narration within the linear confines of the original plot of the testimony. He claims that Narkadien is

> [...] telling the Commission of her experiences behind South African prisons. She is one of the two women who testified before the Commission about how they were shabbily treated, telling very horrible experiences behind South African prisons. Let's cross back to the Commission to get more information about what really happened behind the South African prisons [...].

Possibly the radio commentary could have presented Narkadien's breakdown as a powerful metaphor of the pain of a literal incarceration in an identity which results in her being set apart. Instead the radio commentator draws the narrative back into the containing and privileged discourse of the focus of the hearing – human rights abuses in South African prisons – and in the process subsumes Narkadien's recollection of her colouredness into that discourse.

At the institutional level, TRC vice-chairperson Alex Boraine seems to endorse the trajectory of the radio announcer's commentary. Referring to precisely the medium by which Narkadien's testimony is made public, Boraine's last word response to her testimony enlists Narkadien's voice in the collective narrative of courage and healing:

> We trust that the courage that you displayed will be taken into this new country of ours, and the very tough thing you had to say about discrimination, which is much, much wider than we ever imagine, much more hurtful. [It was] not easy for you to say that, and to say it publicly. I'm not sure if you know, but your voice is being carried all over South Africa, on radio, and I'm very glad of that because I think the whole country [needs] to be healed. Thank you very much. (Transcript of Case JB04418, testimony of Narkadien, TRC Special Hearings Prisons, Johannesburg, 21 July 1997)

The testimony, however, provides a discursive framework in which the affectivity of these raw, immediate and painful memories are performed. So while both the commentator and Alex Boraine reconfigure Narkadien's testimony according to the theme of the prison hearing, the testimony itself places colouredness at the centre of the breach of community as well as the desire for community:

> So I [suffered] just for being a coloured person. It was the first time I had to face up to the fact that I was part of a minority. I mean I thought I was just an African woman. So even my comrades used the fact that I was not really in their eyes an African. It was painful for them to also deny me that right to be an African woman. Because my parents have always taught me that my ancestors were African [breaks down crying]. So it hurt to be tortured by your own comrades. Okay I understand that they had been in prison longer than me, and that they were more disturbed than what I was. But I suffered unnecessarily because of this coloured issue. Okay, I think I should end on this isolation bit [...].

By ending with 'this isolation bit' Narkadien's testimony indicates how the personal is reinserted within the testimonial space in a way that attests to the radical trauma of the experience described. Moreover the testimony signals a residual unassimilability of that trauma into the epic narratives of courage and resistance (without invalidating the tremendous courage which such resistance entails)[3]. Narkadien's painful encounter with colouredness as a breakdown in political community ends up being elided in the name of the TRC narrative of heroic suffering and resistance, non-racialism and nation-building.

The politics and reclamations of coloured identity in South Africa after apartheid highlight the persistent embeddedness of apartheid identity, categories and constructs in individual and collective modes of perception, cognition and meaning making. Narkadien's testimony reveals the insidiousness of 'race' discourse precisely in its persistence, in the way its discourse naturalizes ways of speaking and experiencing identity. It is precisely this ungraspable and unavoidable dimension of apartheid that cannot easily be seized within the testimonial space of the TRC. As Mamdani (1996) and others (Robins 1997) have reminded us, the TRC's mandate highlights the criminality of apartheid in the forms it took in terms of suppression of the resistance and opposition of the liberation struggle. This focus displaces the way that apartheid state discourse propped up and was supported by legal, social, cultural and political discursive constructs. It also elides the ways in which racialized identities are played out within the TRC, but not taken up by it.

Crossing borders: reflections on hybridities and national identity

Hybridity has become a fashionable keyword in post-structuralist academic discourse. It has also, however, produced criticisms because of its inescapable biological connotations rooted in its etymology and epistemology in scientific racism (Ifekwunigwe 1999). As such, it is a term that implies the transformation of 'pure' essences into 'mixed' hybrid and 'degenerate' forms. In this regard one could argue that all identities are culturally hybrid, although in certain usage hybridity, as a conceptual category, allows the construction of convincing fictions of 'ethnic' purity (Robins, 1999).[4] In other cases, the celebration of *métissage* can also be an expression of resistance to ethnic absolutisms (Gilroy, 1993). And yet, when speaking about colouredness in South Africa, given its regional and historical specificities, the complexities that are associated with living the legacy of this category make it difficult to generalise about what it means to be coloured.

There is no single coloured experience, nor any single voice that speaks in its name. Similarly there is no single trans-historical hybrid condition. Identity is located, as always, in its multiple and specific sites and contexts. As such, we are impelled to question any reductionist argument about what colouredness might imply. For example, it becomes important to question how academic prescriptions about colouredness could figure into essentialist political projects that deny the multiple ways of being coloured. Similarly, when hybridity is contextualised within specific gender, 'race', class, geographical and historical configurations it becomes clear that being a 'hybrid' Third World migrant intellectual at Columbia, Yale, Harvard or Chicago universities differs radically to working class experiences of colouredness in, say, Manenberg, Cape Town.

Our particular personal and intellectual engagement with hybridity is one that questions uncritical celebrations of hybridity as a radical and empowering cultural politics of location. In recent years hybridity, indeterminacy and in-betweeness have come to be celebrated as spaces of radical openness that refuse to embrace essentialist myths of origins and totalizing narratives of ethno-nationalism[5]. Hybridity and 'third space' (Bhabha 1994; Soja 1996; Gilroy 1993), invented traditions (Hobsbawm and Ranger 1983), and staged ethnicities (Boonzaier and Sharp 1993) are common currency in these social constructivist and anti-essentialist cultural politics of identity. They are part of a conceptual vocabulary that signals the fluidity, contingency, and diversity of cultural identities. We do not wish to dismiss entirely this anti-essentialist challenge to the potentially dangerous rhetoric of blood purity;[6] however, we are cautious of the tendency to romanticize these in-between 'third spaces'. While the anti-essentialist politics of location are especially attractive for 'progressive' intellectuals, ethnic absolutism (with its conceptions of timeless, bounded cultures and immutable ethnic differences) is likely to continue to appeal to cultural nationalists. After all, these conceptions of creolization, *métissage*, *mestizaje*, and hybridity are, from the perspective of ethnic absolutism, sure signs of racial pollution and impurity.[7]

Representatives of a postmodern black diaspora intelligentsia, based mainly in the United States and Britain, have drawn on notions of hybridity to challenge the ethno-nationalisms ranging from Molefe Asante's Afrocentrism to Louis Farrakhan's black nationalist rhetoric. By celebrating diasporic and hybrid identities, borders and margins as radical and emancipatory subject positions, these writers seek to implode black/white binaries. Such strategies also challenge homogenizing and monolithic notions of black communities that obliterate class, gender, region, language and sexual orientation differences between black people. Stuart Hall, for instance, calls for the end of the innocent notion of the essential black subject, recognizing that 'blackness', like 'whiteness', is a politically and culturally constructed category (West 1990). Similarly, Cornel West argues that since 'whiteness' is a politically constructed category parasitic on 'blackness', it requires that we conceive of the profoundly hybrid character of what we mean by 'race', 'ethnicity' and 'nationality'. For instance, European immigrants arrived in North America thinking of themselves as 'Irish', 'Sicilian,' 'Lithuanian', 'Jewish' and so on (West 1993). They learnt what it meant to be 'white' by adopting an American discourse that attributed positive value to whiteness and negative value to blackness (West 1993). Whiteness, in other words, has been historically constituted through homogenizing essentialist discourses that have erased the complex hybridity of white identities, whether in North America, Europe or South Africa.

Whiteness in South Africa, as in the United States, continues to appear as an unmarked and undifferentiated category, a monolithic, homogenous and hegemonic substance of power. This gives whiteness its taken-for-granted status, thereby rendering it unseen and unremarked upon.

In South Africa, while the originally contested whiteness of certain ethnic groups has been solved through becoming unambiguously white,[8] colouredness remains a contested and unstable identity. Zimitri Erasmus (2000) describes the dilemmas and difficulties of being both coloured and black as a painful process of living the 'moments of entanglement' – of living with the fragments of her slave, Khoi-San and Dutch ancestry. For Erasmus, like Zahrah Narkadien, this 'kind of blackness' is not a romanticized, radical and celebratory space of in-betweeness, but is instead a way of living without certainty that can evoke pain, nostalgia and a sense of loss of 'pure' origins and coherent memory.

The search for a dignifying, self-defined and appropriate vocabulary of identity is not new to the South African political and academic lexicon. Throughout the 1980s the anxiety caused by the category of coloured to anti-apartheid activists was evident in the disavowal and negation of colouredness. This was the outcome of the consensus amongst 'progressive' South African academics and activists that ethnicity was being appropriated and produced by the apartheid state for divisive agendas. This view of coloured identity as an apartheid construct, and an obstruction towards black working class solidarity, was endorsed in the political culture of the mass democratic movement of the 1980s. Within academic and political discourse, the ambiguity of coloured identity was signposted by the uncertainty about whether to use the 'so-called' appellation, as well as doubts about whether to use a capital C, the lower-case c and/or to encapsulate the term within inverted commas. This anxiety revealed the uncertainty and instability of this category even within anti-apartheid political and academic discourses.

The rhetoric of the new rainbow nation of the 1990s and the flourishing of multicultural discourses that valorize African culture and roots, have created the space within which to challenge the homogenizing definitions of colouredness imposed upon people dispossessed of histories, communities and ancestries under apartheid. This reclamation of Africaness is evident in a recent resurgence of KhoiSan ethnic-nationalism by people who were previously identified as coloured, largely because of the derogatory and derisive associations colonialists attached to indigenous peoples labeled 'Hottentots' and 'bushmen' (Boonzaier and Sharp 1996). The 1990s witnessed San, Nama (Khoi), Baster, and Griqua groups becoming increasingly involved in asserting indigenous (KhoiSan) identities and vigorously reclaiming cultural and political rights[9]. These various claims were symbolically embodied in the person of Benny Alexander, a Pan Africanist Congress (PAC) former Member of Parliament who in 1995 decided to publicly disavow his 'slave name' for that of 'KhoiSan X'.

What Zahrah Narkadien's testimony suggests is that such choices do not automatically lead to unproblematic and seamless inclusion. Her story testifies to the fact that living in the grey zones between the essentialized and racialized blocs of whiteness, colouredness and blackness is not necessarily an easy space to occupy. Her story draws attention to some of the cracks, fissures, ambiguities and continuing difficulties in negotiating this politics of location, identity and history in contemporary South Africa.

Notes

1 During the past year this chapter has been presented in various stages of development and with varying emphasis on argumentation to various audiences. We would like to thank the many respondents whose critical discussions contributed to many of the issues explored here. In particular, we would like to thank Joanne Prins for her thoughtful comments and Claudia Braude for an ongoing dialogue around many of the ideas explored in this chapter. We are grateful to Zahrah Narkadien for sharing her public testimony to the TRC, her time and her critical comments. This chapter is a tribute to Zahrah Narkadien's strength, courage and honesty.

2 Yet something still remains outside of the narrative expressed in this tension between writing and saying. The testimony indexes the unsaid by performing the trace of this pain as something which remains but which cannot be contained as narrative by the articulation of the inability to 'speak' about 'something which remains that was very, very, very painful. I don't even want to describe psychologically what I had to do to survive down there. I will write it one day, but I could never tell you.' Clearly, this statement also anticipates the refusal of the listener who is less materially present in a written address to hear what cannot be said.

3 Dislocation, the incommunicable alienation of the individual after torture and the persistence of this rupture in the narratives of the post-imprisonment self in the present, is performed within this testimony. As such, the split between the pre- and post-imprisonment selves, located at the centre of the testimony, is indexed as a break with language (Narkadien breaks down) and in the representation of the self as altered, as other ('I am damaged' she claims).

4 In South Africa cultural hybridity has been incorporated into a repertoire of resistance to essentialising apartheid ideas about racial and ethnic separateness. Many urban Africans refused the apartheid constructs of rural tribal purity that underpinned the 'homeland' system. For instance, in the 1950s, a group of black African journalists working for *Drum* magazine self-consciously opposed this tribalist discourse by embracing urban African-American cultural styles emanating from movements such as the Harlem Renaissance (Robins 1999; Nixon 1994).

5 (See Appiah 1992; Bhabha 1994; Gilroy 1993.)

6 Writing about blacks in the West, and in particular the contemporary black English, Paul Gilroy (1993, 2) notes that the Manichean dynamics of the antagonistic relationship between black and white has supported 'a special rhetoric that has grown to be associated with a language of nationality and national belonging as well as the languages of 'race' and ethnic identity'. Gilroy traces these modern ideas about nationality, ethnicity, authenticity, and cultural integrity to the revolutionary transformations of the West at the end of the eighteenth and the beginning of the nineteenth centuries. He concludes that shifts to 'the postmodern condition' will not easily dislodge these modern subjectivities whose tenacity and longevity have defied the belief that the universalistic languages of class and socialism would surpass them.

7 Paul Gilroy's *The Black Atlantic: Modernity and Double Consciousness* (1993) questions the 'continuing lure of ethnic absolutisms in cultural criticism produced both by blacks and by whites' (3). What emerges from Gilroy's work is a keen sense of how rhetorical strategies of national belonging depend on the construction of the nation as an ethnically homogeneous object. Whereas many contemporary cultural critics seek to embrace 'hybridity' as a radical critique of these ethnic-nationalisms, Gilroy reminds us that 'appeals to the notion of purity as the basis of racial solidarity' are considerably more popular than politics that retreat from the stability and coherence of the racial solidarity. It is for these reasons that the fragmentation of self (doubling and splitting) that fascinated modern black intellectuals such as W.E.B. Dubois, Richard Wright and Delany, and more recently Paul Gilroy, Hommi Bhabha and Kwame Anthony Appiah, is of such little interest to cultural nationalists drawn to the hyper-coherence of black nationalism and Afrocentricity (Gilroy 1993,188).

8 It is generally forgotten that Jewish whiteness was at one point in question. Working class East European Jews arriving in South Africa during the early part of this century experienced rabid anti-Semitism as they disembarked from the ships docking at Cape Town harbour. Anti-Jewish sentiments in the press and amongst the public contributed towards the calls for Anti-Alien Immigration legislation. This legislation was specifically directed at what was perceived to be the inassimilable 'nature' of the East European Jew (Shain 1994). Many South African Jews would probably no longer recall that their whiteness was ever in fact in question.[9]

10 Compensation from the British Crown is currently being demanded by people espousing a 'Griqua' identity, based on claims of misappropriation of 'Griqua' land by Britain in the 19th century (Robert Ross 1993).

Chapter Nine

Black thing: Hip-hop nationalism, 'race' and gender in Prophets of da City and Brasse vannie Kaap

Adam Haupt

> Hip-hop nationalists are organic *cultural* intellectuals to the degree that their activities are directly linked to the everyday struggles of black folk and that their music critically engages the popular knowledge of which they are a part
>
> *Jeffrey Louis Decker*

Jeffrey Louis Decker's Gramscian discussion of hip-hop nationalism in *The State of Rap: Time and Place in Hip-Hop Nationalism* speaks directly to hip-hop in the United States and may appear to have little application to the everyday struggles of black individuals on the Cape Flats. But the notion of the organic cultural intellectual is one which is compelling in discussions of the South African bands Prophets of da City (POC) and Brasse vannie Kaap (BVK), a more recent brainchild of POC's Ready D. Both rap groups are with the Ghetto Ruff label, which has POC's Shaheen and Ready D as its key creative forces, and draw upon black nationalist ideals in a manner which recalls Decker's discussion of Ice Cube and Afrika Bambaata. The significant difference, however, is that these performers create black nationalist narratives upon their own terms and do not mimic aspects of American mainstream or underground hip-hop. They employ codes and speak to experiences that are specific to everyday black South African experiences. The bands do this through their use of *gamtaal* (a Cape Flats dialect of Afrikaans), as well as non-standard dialects of English, Xhosa and Zulu.

This chapter looks into the ways in which POC and BVK employ *gamtaal*, which has stereotypically been associated with notions of the 'authentic' working-class coloured, in order to problematise hegemonic representations of black subjects. In this regard I would like to suggest that a double process of inscription and subversion takes place through both rap groups' use of the sign *gamtaal*. While POC and BVK are set apart from American hip-hop artists through their use of *gamtaal*, what does seem to link their music with the work of 'old school' artists such as KRS-ONE, for example, is their continual commitment to the Black Consciousness ideals of spiritual and intellectual upliftment. These ideals are often expressed in hip-hop by the phrase 'knowledge of self'. Ultimately, I will relate my discussion of POC and BVK's work to the intersection between 'race', class and gender by analysing problematic representations of black female subjects in their music.

Setting the scene: state repression of black theatre and music

While it may be possible to guess why hip-hop appealed to black South Africans, I would like to suggest that it was particularly during the early eighties that hip-hop began to fill a gap which was left by the hegemonic cultural and political practices of the white minority. In order to understand this it is necessary to discuss the conditions under which cultural production, specifically theatre and music, took place during apartheid.

Black theatre and music in South Africa have been characterised by direct and indirect state intervention, restriction and censorship. It was with the introduction and implementation of Bantu education in 1953 that the Afrikaner nationalist state started intervening more closely in cultural matters. In line with the introduction of Bantu education, Afrikaner nationalists saw to it that 'suitable plays in Bantu languages' were published 'under the government's auspices and published by companies owned by the growing Afrikaner capitalist section' (Kavanagh 1985, 48). By the sixties, the extent to which the state intervened in cultural production became more far-reaching. Legislation such as the Separate Amenities Act 49 of 1953 and Group Areas Act 36 of 1966, along with pressure from white musicians, saw to it that black musicians were forced out of city venues (Coplan 1985, 191). The Publication and Entertainment Act 26 of 1963 prevented black and white people from associating or collaborating 'outside working hours and working relationships' (Kavanagh 1985, 51). This act also prohibited mixed audiences and prevented black performers from performing in white venues. These laws had adverse effects on black music because the only venues left were 'big concerts and outdoor jazz festivals in Soweto', which were often sponsored by South African Breweries and organised by United Artists (Coplan 1985, 191). According to Coplan, these concerts were not very successful due to 'social, organisational and programme conflicts' (1985, 192). The deterioration of the black urban music scene forced musicians such as Abdullah Ibrahim (Dollar Brand) into exile and others into early retirement or 'an early grave' (Coplan 1985, 192).

Ultimately, state intervention created a gap in the development of musical talent in the country as many leading musicians were no longer present to act as mentors and role models to young musicians (Alperson 1993, 26). The gap in the market created by the unavailability of South African music was filled through the promotion of American artists which, according to POC's Shaheen, is more profitable because record companies merely have to distribute units which have already been marketed and processed (Haupt 1994).

On the contrary, black theatre was not necessarily negatively affected by apartheid legislation (Kavanagh 1985, 52). Instead, it shifted the positions of power in collaborative theatre involving white English-speaking directors and playwrights. White producers were now at a disadvantage because if they

> wished to involve themselves in black theatre or entertainment on a commercial or other bases [they would have to produce a product which pleased black, and not white, audiences]. (Kavanagh 1985, 52)

Black playwrights and directors such as Gibson Kente and Sam Mhangwani, pioneers of township theatre, became more successful. By the late sixties, the independence which black theatre began to enjoy from English-speaking white management contributed to the rise of a form of political theatre which advocated Black Consciousness ideology (Kavanagh 1985, 53). The students who were involved in this form of theatre moved away from avant-garde models provided by the works of Pinter, Beckett and Sartre to adapted African-American, West African or Caribbean material and the 'creation of material "relevant to the black experience" in South Africa' (Kavanagh 1985, 48-53). However, censorship of work by serious political theatre groups or township theatre directors such as Kente became more restrictive by 1973 (Kavanagh 1985, 55).

For the purposes of this chapter, it is important to observe that serious political theatre in the late sixties and early seventies was interested in material which narrativised the black experience of oppression – however erroneously homogenising such narratives may be – and thus directors and playwrights turned to African-American and Caribbean material. Coplan observes that within African intellectual circles, at least, 'there was a clear association of Afro-American performance culture with urban cultural autonomy' (1985, 149). The tendency by black artists to use American material has a history which stretches as far back as the forties:

> Only a few jazz musicians of the 1940s brought anything identifiably South African to their playing of American swing. The reason was simply the identification of traditional music with the rural present and tribal past. Begun by the missionaries, this negative association grew until the 1950s, when the Afrikaner government's policy to 'develop along their own lines' entrenched the attitude for the next twenty years. (Coplan 1985, 148)

Internalised colonial ideas thus initially accounted for urban musicians and performers' preferences, but the shift towards material which was specifically relevant to the black experience was brought about by apartheid policy. Within South Africa's jazz history at the very least, the contribution of American jazz was positive because it relied upon much interaction between South African and American musicians. According to Coplan:

> American [musicians] who looked to Africa for inspiration like John Coltrane were leading South African jazzmen to re-examine their own indigenous resources. (Coplan 1985, 189)

Interaction between South African and American musicians brought musicians such as Philip Thabane closer to their cultural roots and affirmed their identity as African. Thabane and his band, Malombo Jazz Men, combined a pastiche of musical styles that included

> neo-traditional music, African church melodies, *marabi*, *mbaqanga*, and the jazz guitar work of Wes Montgomery and John McLaughlin [which gave] it a feeling at once indigenous and rural contemporary and urban [...] Intensely theatrical poetic recitation was vital to the Malombo's music, and the group soon became associated with African cultural nationalism and the emerging aims of the Black Consciousness Movement (Coplan 1985, 196)

Jazz itself and the interaction between South African and American jazz musicians, therefore provided a cultural alternative to the repression of apartheid. It could thus be said that the censorship difficulties which POC faced with the 1993 release of *Age of Truth* is consistent with the experiences of black artists involved in cultural production in the past[1]. It also appears that the group's use of an African-American art form, rap music, conforms with black artists' reliance on African-American or Caribbean material in their attempt to construct black nationalist narratives that rely on the notion of a global black experience of oppression and resistance.

Hip-hop in/on South African terms: ghetto code/*gamtaal*

However, a crucial distinction to be made is that POC's work consciously positions itself within South Africa through its use of a number of dialects of Afrikaans, English, Xhosa and Zulu. BVK raps exclusively in the Cape Flats dialect of Afrikaans and, like POC, attempts to address social, political and economic issues in ways which would engage its target audience. In this regard, Fat (an MC for BVK) says that the group is keen to prove that '*gamtaal* is legal' (Haupt 1998, 113). In '*Laat Dit Rik*', Ready D makes BVK's position on this issue clear:

Yo man, what's up, kid. Let's do this for the honeys.
That's not the way we *praat in die Kaap*.
Jy moet wys raak of waai want jou valse accent don't make you *kwaai*.
You not Chester Williams so don't even try to try
before I *skop* your *gat* like Popeye (BVK, 1998)[2]

These sentiments are echoed in POC's 'Wack MC's (It's All Your Fault)' (POC 1995), which commences with a parody of the gangsta rap genre, and criticises the tendency of some hip-hop fans and performers to mimic mainly American gangsta rappers such as Dr Dre, Tupac Shakur and Notorious BIG. This criticism is a real one in the face of the Cape Flats gangs' appropriation of aspects of the West Coast/East Coast split in American gangsta rap into the ways in which they represent themselves. Murals of Tupac Shakur in gang strongholds such as Manenberg, for example, are not an uncommon sight. This appropriation is hardly surprising, since local gangsters have long been fascinated with American gang subcultures as South Africa has always been bombarded with Hollywood's sentimentalised representation of gangs. The conflation of hip-hop in general with a particular type of rap (gangsta rap) which sentimentalises gangsterism could thus undermine the attempts of rap groups such as POC and BVK to engage critically with issues such as gangsterism and the negative representations of coloureds in the media. The group attempts to initiate critical thought about this issue in *'Kaap van Storms'*:

Jy moet hoop dat jy nooit geboorte skenk aan 'n jongetjie baby nie.
Daai's wat hulle sê op Agenda.
Hulle wys altyd lelike prente van onse mense.
Hoekom moet ek altyd 'n gangster of 'n klops
soos al wat ons sien in 'n koerant of TV's.
Hulle trek hulle neus sê, 'Sies, jy's a low-class coloured' (BVK, 1998)[3]

Here BVK exemplifies Decker's claim that the 'hip-hop nation understands that, today, control over the media means the ability to control representations of the real as well' (Decker 1993, 61). The group's concern over the monolithic way in which coloureds are represented in the mainstream media speaks directly to the bias of South Africa's largely conservative white-owned press. It is arguable that there is substance to their concerns when considering the frenzied obsession of certain Cape Town newspapers with gang violence.[4]

BVK's attempts to engage with the representation of gangsters in the media goes beyond POC's engagement with gangsterism in their 'Dallah Flet' songs, which extol the folly of aspiring to gangster ideals. However, POC's consciousness-raising and overtly political songs such as 'Blast From Da Past', 'Dallah Flet' and 'Understand Where

I'm Coming From' (see Haupt 1996, 51-61) and BVK's *'Kaap van Storms'*, *'Op die Jaard'* and *'Tronk Storie'* do confirm Decker's claim that 'nation-conscious rap' employs 'postmodern information technologies' to 'inform and mobilise the black community' (Decker 1993, 61).

Self-representation: Black Consciousness and the 'coloured' thing

Fat's assertion that *gamtaal* is legal provides an important point of entry into both groups' largely overlapping positions with regard to the ways in which they represent themselves. Initially, POC faced the danger of being perceived exclusively as a coloured group addressing coloured issues for a coloured audience. By the time they achieved a significant measure of success and independence in 1993, they re-constituted themselves. Jazzmo left and was replaced by two black artists: Junior 'Danisa' Dread, who left after the release of *Age of Truth* to form the kwaito group Boom Shaka, and Ishmael, who is currently in Ghetto Ruff's kwaito group Skeem and has released his debut solo album.

The introduction of these performers not only changed the perception of POC as an exclusively Cape Town group, but also made it impossible for audiences to view it as a coloured group. The range of languages and different rap styles within which POC was now able to perform also meant that a larger national audience could be reached. Consider the linguistic range of songs such as 'Zulu Muffin' and 'Remember Where You Came From' (POC, 1993). Its explicitly hybrid African representation of itself also appealed to European and British audiences and the group continues to do tours in other countries.[5]

POC and the decidedly less cosmopolitan BVK's use of Cape Flats dialects of Afrikaans might suggest that their work would appeal to a specifically Cape Flats audience. Their work might also be read as a confirmation of stereotypical associations with colouredness. But POC's Shaheen's explanation of why he employs *gamtaal* suggests that POC's very specific youth township appeal is goal-directed and counter-discursive:

> We want to be street, you know? When we do interviews and shit like that and we speak *gamtaal*, or whatever, that shit's on purpose so the kid at home can say, 'Fuck, they're speaking my language,' you know? They're representing, you know, what comes out of the township and shit. So if some middle class motherfucker comes, *'Oe God, skollietaal.'* The shit's *not* for them, you know what I mean? I don't care if some white-ass dude at home thinks, 'Oh shit, look at this . . . uncultured,' you know? I want some kid from the ghetto to think, 'Naa, we can relate to that,'. (Haupt 1994)

Shaheen therefore expresses a desire to remain organically connected to the community in which he lives and to produce a discourse that engages this community. POC's *'Net 'n Bietjie Liefde'* provides an interesting example of the group's engagement with the everyday details and struggles of Cape Flats dwellers. The song covers Ramone's, Ready D's and Shaheen's narratives of love relationships. All of the narratives contain details of their personae's difficulties of getting *bymekaar* with their lovers. Shaheen's narrative hints at a fairly serious difficulty:

> Here girl, *jy het my by my koppie.*
> *Jy's poenankies, ek wil jou sommer opiet.*
> *Jy is my dingetjie* diamond.
> But time and time again your *tannie* wanna chime in.
> *Sy's net aspris en oorlams.*
> *Sy sê jy is kris en ek is slams* (POC, 1996)[6]

The universal narrative of lovers' difficulties is presented in ways which would only appeal to specific South African audiences. We find that *'Net 'n Bietjie Liefde'* hints at the divisions within coloured communities, which have conventionally been represented as homogenous, through the suggestion that the two lovers have to contend with the cultural and religious intolerance which still pervades the South African consciousness.

Despite POC and BVK's use of the Afrikaans vernacular, Ready D and Shaheen are very wary of having either group being labelled as coloured groups (Haupt 1999, 68 ; Haupt 1996, 58). They use *gamtaal* as a counter-discursive voice, which signals their refusal to be co-opted into conservative and essentialist readings of colouredness. This has been an important issue for POC because they were actively involved in the voter education programme *Rapping for Democracy* before South Africa's first democratic elections. On songs such as 'Dallah Flet 2' off *Age of Truth* they went through great pains to persuade Cape Town's largely coloured electorate not to vote for the National Party (Haupt 1996, 57-58). 'Dallah Flet 2' ensures that its message is unmistakably clear to its imagined audience:

> Don't let FW puzzle you.
> *Hy praat jou kop vrot.*
> *In sy oe is jy nog altyd 'n kaffer en 'n hotnot.*
> *Hulle* sponsor township violence *en gee vir smokkelhuise* licence.
> *Want hy wiet die wyn fok op die brein*
> *want dan vang jy kak aan dan word jy ge*blame.
> *Die* move *is beplan wat jy gat nou mang jy gat nou hang*
> *want die vark is 'n slang* (POC, 1993)[7]

It is therefore *gamtaal* that is used to convey the message that it was National Party policy that was responsible for the continued racist appellations of individuals as *kaffers* and *hotnots*. As in BVK's *Afkoel* (BVK, 1998), a connection is made between alcohol abuse and violence in the townships. What sets 'Dallah Flet 2' apart is that POC suggests that it is the NP which is responsible for the township's social problems and that coloured voters are being manipulated. In 'Black Thing', off *Phunk Phlow*, POC make their Black Consciousness position clear and allude to the politics behind colouredness:

> The term 'coloured' is a desperate case of how the devil's divided us
> by calling us a separate race.
> They call me 'coloured' said my blood isn't pure, but G,
> I'm not *jakking* my insecurity.
> So I respond to this and ventilate my mental state with Black Consciousness
>
> And I believe in each one teach one reach one from the heart 'cause that's where the beats are from . . .
> But racism is a trap and the nation seems to lack knowledge of self.
> But what it means, what it seems
> We're attracting anything but a black thing (POC, 1995)

Here the agents/devils who are responsible for separating black people are the white minority or, specifically, the National Party if one reads this song in relation to the previous quote from 'Dallah Flet 2'. The use of the verb 'ventilate' suggests the act of refreshing one's mindset with an ideology which is able to do away with the stagnation and lack of growth associated with the internalising of racist conceptions of blackness. A typically Afrocentric black nationalist allusion is made to the notion that black subjects were united prior to colonialism and, more recently, to apartheid through the claim that 'we' were 'divided' and 'called a separate race'. While this conception of Africa as homogenous may be problematic, its motivational value in re-conceptualising black subjectivity should not be underestimated. In '*Kaap van Storms*', for example, the reference to the dominant media representation of coloureds is met with this response:

> *Hulle wys altyd lelike prente van onse mense.*
> *Hoekom moet ek altyd 'n gangster of 'n klops*
> *soos al wat ons sien in 'n koerant of TVs.*
> *Hulle trek hulle neus sê, 'Sies, jy's 'n* low-class coloured.
> *Jou voorvaders was* whites *en slawe*. So it must be a bastard.'
> But, wait a minute, if you trust my story and not his story *sal jy sien*.

> My *voorvaders* was a king a queen and never knew drugs, guns of *'n kantien.*
> *Hulle was altyd daar om God te bedien* (BVK, 1998)[8]

Here Ready D expresses an awareness that history is 'his story' and that the dominant narrative of history is but one version of the past. The version of history which he offers to those who are willing to listen presents coloured subjects with the opportunity to re-conceptualise themselves outside of the master narrative of apartheid and its own myths about 'miscegenation', the shame of slavery, the legacy of the *dopstelsel* [9], alcoholism and violence. The 'ventilation of mental states' of which Shaheen raps in 'Black Thing' is therefore offered by the act of de-legitimising the master narrative of coloured history and presenting the choice of an alternative narrative. This choice therefore coincides with the work of American rappers such as Queen Latifa, X-Clan and Lakim Shabazz , who 'contest the Western notion that pre-colonial Africa was barbaric' (Decker 1993, 76).

Ironically, the chorus in 'Black Thing' conveys a sense of the tension which coloured subjects feel with regard to conceptualisations of blackness. The recurring chorus is 'Sometimes it feels like I'm not black enough' (POC 1995). This line is repeated a few times and Ishmael croons a response to the anxiety which this admission provokes: 'But I am' (POC 1995). The chorus suggests that despite the certainty which Black Consciousness narratives offer, racial identity is unstable and is always fraught with contradictions and anxieties about belonging. It also speaks to the claim that the 'nation lacks knowledge of self' and that 'we are attracting anything but a black thing' (POC 1995). The tension between their interpretation of Black Consciousness and many other South Africans' conception of 'race' is therefore alluded to.

Whilst there are aspects of Black Consciousness that might be problematic due to its tendency to oversimplify certain issues and overlook crucial gender issues, the necessity for ideologies which retrieve positive black subjectivities in post-apartheid South Africa should not be overlooked. A recent discussion in a *Y* magazine column between Breyton Paulse, a coloured Western Province rugby player, and Emile, the leader of a Cape Town rap group called Black Noise, supports this contention and complements my discussion of POC's employment of Black Consciousness in 'Black Thing' (Haupt 1999, 28-29). It becomes very clear that Emile comes from a left-wing position, whilst Breyton Paulse is somewhat more conservative:

> E: My opinion is you're the only one who deserves to be on the team. *Naai*, serious, because where you're from, the resources you have growing up. These *ouens*, their whole life they've been comfortable, nice facilities. For them it's a breeze. You're the one that worked extra hard to be on the team.
> BP: That's what I said to myself when I started to take the game up seriously. And our okes, really I hate to say it, they're really not working hard to get

> to the top, man. They just want to get the things for free. That's the problem with these okes.
> AH: Do you agree with that?
> E: I don't think so.
> [We move on. There is a word count to observe, you dig? Breyton does, however, mention Sarfu's development programme]. (Haupt 1999, 28)

Here Paulse subverts what Emile is trying to say and confirms white conservative assumptions about black people who place black empowerment on the agenda. It's interesting to observe how Paulse and Emile's political differences are signified through their language usage. Paulse's consistent use of the term 'okes' aligns him with the largely white male Afrikaans rugby team to which he belongs and Emile's usage of the terms '*ouens*' and '*naai*' aligns him with Capetonian people who speak the non-standard dialects of English and Afrikaans. Their political differences become more apparent at the end of the column:

> BP: We gotta get a culture like in my team. We got an unbelievable spirit where sometimes they tease me a bit. They call me *hottie*.
> [Emile and Adam take a deep breath. Their pupils dilate.]
> BP: No, no. In a positive way! We play. We tease each other. We understand each other. We gotta try and create that kind of culture where the okes are together, we understand each other.
> E: *Ouens* using such words that used to or still have a lot of feeling attached to it, like *kaffir*, *hotnot*, *boer*, whitey, albino – it can't be in pure innocence if you're not healed. Almost nobody in this country is healed. It's almost like detoxing.
> BP: It takes a while.
> E: *Ja.* (Haupt 1999, 29)

In hip-hop terms, what Breyton Paulse lacks is 'knowledge of self' as he has not become critical of the ways in which racist discourse has labelled him. Instead, he seems to have become complicit by internalising this discourse. This is interesting because he is a role model who has emerged in post-apartheid South Africa and he, much like Chester Williams, has become one of the mainstream media's signifiers of political change in the world of sport. The irony is, of course, that his political perspectives and anecdotes do not signify that real political transformation has taken place. Instead, Paulse inadvertently suggests that there still is a dire need for the sort of self-discovery that hip-hop nationalism offers black subjects.

'Race', gender and class intersections

BVK's work is performed in a context which differs remarkably from the one in which *Age of Truth* was produced and is not as explicitly anti-National Party as POC was on this album. In theory, freedom of speech is less of a contested issue, but many issues with regard to constructions of racial identity are not resolved any more significantly than they were in 1993. BVK's *'Jy Smaak My'* explores some of the problems in this regard. Hama takes the lead in this song and addresses a woman who will not reciprocate his advances because she 'only speak for English' and he 'don't speak it so *lekker*' (BVK, 1998). It is clear that a class dynamic is at work here as he knows that the odds are against him because he is from the township of Mitchell's Plain and she is from Garlandale, a middle-class suburb. His perspective is presented in the form of a sound bite and it becomes clear that the discourses of 'race' and class intersect:

> His hair is, well, *kroes* [kinky]. There's no other way for me to say it. And I don't think that I want to have anything to do with him. I mean, can you imagine the embarrassment? There'll be no way I can stand for that. Not with my status. (BVK, 1998)

This speaker's motivations are similar to that of the mother in *'Net 'n Bietjie Liefde'*, who objects to her daughter being involved with a Muslim person. But in *'Jy Smaak My'* the link between language and class aspirations is clear enough. It also becomes difficult to speak about these aspirations without discussing racism, which Hama refers to as 'your coloured mentality' shortly after the sample (BVK, 1998). This song also recalls some of Kay McCormick's findings about District Six interviewees' attitudes towards the Afrikaans vernacular and English. McCormick's claim that her 'interviewees were always quick to assert that the Afrikaans they use is different from *suiwer* [pure/standard] Afrikaans' (McCormick 1990, 91) resonates with a sample from POC's *Gamtaal* (POC, 1995), which seems to celebrate the vernacular through a pastiche of sample from everyday conversations of mostly women: *'Ons praatie suiwer Afrikaans nie. Ons praat kombuis Afrikaans'* [We don't speak 'pure' Afrikaans. We speak 'kitchen' Afrikaans][9]. The interviews reveal varying attitudes towards the Afrikaans vernacular:

> They sometimes referred to the local dialects as 'colloquial Afrikaans' or as 'a patois' but most ways of describing it are less neutral, more pejorative: *'onbeskof'* [impolite/unrefined], 'stupid', 'bastardised', 'cheap', 'careless', 'messing up the language'. They know from experience that outsiders stereotype speakers of this dialect as lazy, feckless, poor, and street-wise rather than well-educated. (McCormick 1990, 91)

It is the awareness of outsiders' perceptions which Hama reacts to in *'Jy Smaak My'*. These perceptions are not held by racial outsiders, but belong to the addressee in the song. As suggested earlier, her position alludes to the view that class and racial tensions do exist within the seemingly homogenous coloured community, which are themselves a product of racist socialisation under apartheid. It is also interesting to note that *'Jy Smaak My'* is as much of a masculinist narrative as POC's *'Net 'n Bietjie Liefde'* because the problematic 'coloured mentality' – of which Hama speaks – is located in the minds of female subjects. A consolation which is offered to the lover's seemingly hopeless situation in *'Jy Smaak My'* is that she is 'gonna *stoot my laaitie in die pram*' (BVK, 1998). In this regard, Decker's discussion of American hip-hop nationalism's inability to confront sexism might be illuminating. He contends that the 'historical conditions for new thinking on gender relations have yet to be realised by the largely male-dominated organic intelligentsia' (Decker 1993, 68). Hip-hop in South Africa is still largely male-dominated and Ghetto Ruff has a small number of artists, many of whom are kwaito artists.Rare representations of the female subject in POC's more explicit Black Consciousness performances raise this issue more clearly. An analysis of 'Dallah Flet 2' would be incomplete without considering the second stanza, which leads up to the song's anti-National Party climax. In this stanza Shaheen denies a paternity claim:

> *Ek issie vaakie nege maande gelede was ekkie eens in die Kaapie dis 'n haatie,*
> *Jy't nie 'n saak nie hou jou mond, moenie eers praat nie want jy kan niks maak nie*
> *Genoeg van daai ek praat van 'n meid wat dink sy is kwaai*
> *By sy is hard deur die (naat ek gattie sê nie)* (Prophets of da City, 1993)[10]

Here we find that POC internalise a racist appellation by referring to the woman as a '*meid*'. This word is defined by the *Beknopte Verklarende Woordeboek* as a:

> *Kleurlingvrou, vroulike Bantoe; jy is 'n ~, papbroek, lafaard*
> (Kritzinger 1980, 312)[11]

This dictionary was first published in 1960 and was widely in use in black schools during the seventies until pupils objected to its racist content. POC's inability to position themselves critically against such abusive language suggests that they have not yet realised that factors of 'race', class and gender are inseparable.[12] Decker's discussion of the 'male-dominated organic intelligentsia' being unable to 'confront sexism' is echoed here (1993, 68). In a discussion of racist and sexist oppression in America, Murray Forman recalls bell hooks' claim that

> racism is fundamentally a feminist issue because it is so interconnected with sexist oppression. In the West, the philosophical foundations of racist and sexist ideology are similar. (Forman 1994, 36-37; hooks 1984, 52)

The denial of paternity in the second verse and its rhetoric thus doom POC's political aims to failure because POC do not steer clear of sexist ideology. Instead, they undermine the attempts by students of the late seventies and early eighties to do away with the institutionalised discourse of apartheid by confirming stereotypical assumptions about coloured men.

The rhetoric with which the woman (who remains anonymous and may very well not be a fictional character) is addressed is thus sexist as well as racist and what is also significant here is that she is not afforded the opportunity to speak. In fact, the speaker violently silences her by claiming that she does not have enough power to do anything about the situation. Shaheen absolves himself from parental responsibility by stating that he was not in Cape Town nine months ago and therefore relies upon his status as a musician who is always on the road. His claims therefore rely upon what Hazel Carby calls the myth of the lone wandering male, which conventionally refers to the notion of the blues performer who travels from town to town without fixity or responsibilities (Carby 1992, 755). While the anonymous woman is spoken to and about in the song, she does not speak and any possibility of hearing the female voice is therefore foreclosed. It is thus only the male voice which is to be associated with the political position which POC takes in the final section of the rap song. The sphere of political action is therefore gendered male by the rhetorical and discursive violence of the second stanza, which effaces the role that women play in the political sphere.

The video of *Age of Truth*'s single, 'Understand Where I'm Coming From', carries out this effacement on a visual level in a more subtle manner. In line with the album's overall attempts to advocate critical awareness in the minds of the electorate, this music video aims to shock viewers by presenting video material about township violence and police brutality during unrest situations.

The SABC would not ordinarily have broadcast this sort of material during the apartheid years. For example, shots of corpses and mass funerals are shown with shots of right-wing political figures and we see scenes where the police fire at crowds, followed by scenes of an *Afrikaner Weerstandsbeweging* meeting. The visual clips thus support the anti-National Party message which this rap song, along with others on the album, contains. Various left-wing political figures are shown as well during the video, but all of them are male. In fact, the entire focus of the video is on men, regardless of their political positions. At the beginning of the song we see Dion on stage as he addresses his audience:

> This is a song I'd like to dedicate to Nelson Mandela. I'd like to dedicate this one to Oliver Tambo, Chris Hani, Steve Biko. (POC, 1993)

The group therefore strongly ally themselves with the ANC as well as Black Consciousness ideology. They also identify with Black Consciousness explicitly on 'Black Thing' off *Phunk Phlow* in response to being labelled as coloured by the NP government. In this video we see merely one shot of protesting women and no female political figures and the active role which women have played in political transformation is once again effaced. It is therefore men who are presented as the active figures in South Africa's public sphere. Bhekizizwe Peterson makes a similar observation about black theatre in the apartheid state. He states that

> black theatre has been unable to organise its internal structures differently from those characterising the social formation. African males predominate as performers, whites as 'skilled technicians' who mostly direct, and African women are reduced to the periphery in both numbers and status.
>
> (Peterson 1994, 52)

POC and BVK's tendency to place black women on the periphery thus does not differ significantly from the way in which black theatre was organised during the apartheid years. This is especially true when one considers that the voice of the black female subject is absent from all of the rap songs, except when it features in the chorus of a song such as *Phunk Phlow* (POC, 1994). Whilst POC and BVK's texts do not reflect much of a shift within hip-hop in the country, initiatives are under way to make hip-hop more participatory. The inclusion of 4 Feet Deep is one example of Ghetto Ruff's attempts to deal with this issue. The recent inclusion of a female rapper into POC is also a positive indication in this regard.[13] Shaheen has also been in planning sessions with Bush Radio about a hip-hop initiative, which involves a number of female participants.

Conclusion: making sense of sexism in hip-hop nationalism

In our analysis of POC and BVK's texts we have encountered the demarcation of the public sphere, the sphere of action, as one which is reserved exclusively for the male subject. The demarcation of the public sphere as male and the private sphere as female can be traced to the birth of modern civil society. In her discussion of the social contract, Carole Pateman contends that civil freedom is not universal, but is a 'masculine attribute' (Pateman 1988, 2). Pateman explains that civil society

> is not structured by kinship and the power of fathers; in the modern world, women are subordinated to men as men, or to men as fraternity. The original contract takes place after the political defeat of the father and creates modern *fraternal patriarchy.* (1988, 3)

It is for this reason that civil society is divided into two spheres and only the public (male) sphere is regarded as relevant (Pateman 1988, 3). This gendered division of the public and private sphere, which commenced roughly during the eighteenth century, coincides with the rise of the 'domestic woman' of the middle-class in an emergent capitalist world order (Armstrong 1987, 59). Pateman argues that as capitalism and its sexual and class division of labour developed, 'wives were pushed into a few, low status areas of employment or kept out of economic life altogether' (Pateman 1989, 123). The rise of the new domestic woman of the eighteenth and nineteenth centuries therefore plays a crucial part in the development of capitalism and imperialism.

A similar dynamic seems to operate in black nationalist texts because such texts often require the domesticity, silence or passivity of the female subjects. Jeffrey Louis Decker contends that hip-hop nationalism follows in the steps of sixties black militancy by positioning black women who do not conform to the ideals of the patriarchal family structure as ungrateful wives or gold-digging lovers (1993, 68).

Much like black nationalism in general, hip-hop nationalism attempts to position women within the confines of patriarchy and the struggle against racism is seen as a confrontation between black men and white men. This view is consistent with the patriarchal belief that the public sphere, the sphere in which the aims of imperialism and colonialism are furthered by men, is an exclusively male sphere. Pateman's claim that civil freedom is not universal, but is a 'masculine attribute' (1988, 2) is thus supported because black nationalist texts such as 'Dallah Flet 2', 'Understand Where I'm Coming From' and *'Jy Smaak My'* put to the fore black masculine activity and interests in their articulation of political resistance.

Despite the fact that hip-hop nationalism has placed women largely on the periphery, Decker singles out New Jersey rapper Queen Latifa as a hip-hop artist who has managed to balance the interests of the black female subject with that of black nationalism. He analyses her 1989 debut music video 'Ladies First' (off *All Hail The Queen*) in order to argue that the video is 'simultaneously woman-centred and pro-black, feminist and Afrocentric' (1993, 77). He states that Queen Latifa restates the anthropologist Claudia Mitchell-Kernan's revelation that black cultural practices such as 'Signifyin(g)' and 'playing the dozens' 'were fundamentally not male' (1993, 79). By asserting her position as a female rapper within the largely masculinist hip-hop subculture,

> Latifa not only reveals the severe limitations of nationalism as a language of equality for women in general; she also clears a space within hip-hop nationalism for the empowerment of black women. (Decker 1993, 79-80)

On a later album titled *Black Reign* (1993), Latifa largely addresses the misogyny in gangsta rap and female rapper Da Bratt's internalisation of gangsta rap's rhetoric. On the album's single, 'U.N.I.T.Y.', she speaks out against the physical and emotional as well as rhetorical abuse of women and on 'Listen To Me' she situates her feminist concerns within Black Consciousness ideology:

> Momma taught me black was beautiful when I was young
> And told me all about where babies really came from
> So you can hit the door with the theory that all black women are ho's
> (Queen Latifa, 1993)

Here Latifa appropriates the positive elements of Black Consciousness, conventionally perceived as a discourse of 'race' which is separate from gender politics, in order to support her attempts to challenge dominant representations of black women in work by gangsta rappers such as Snoop Doggy Dog, Da Bratt, Dr Dre or Ice-T and nationalist rappers such as Public Enemy. Decker's claims about 'Ladies First' thus seem to hold true for 'Listen To Me' as well. Latifa's work therefore seems to indicate the extent to which hip-hop artists could take rap as an expression of political resistance as well as a vehicle for change within the cultural sphere. In my earlier discussion of BVK's *'Kaap van Storms'*, I invoke Decker's claim that the 'hip-hop nation understands that today, control over the media means the ability to control representations of the real as well' (Decker 1993, 61). These artists therefore realise that it is crucial that they control the means of production. Due to the shortcomings in both rap groups' gender politics, however, it is doubly important for specifically female hip-hop artists to gain control over the means of production.

Notes

1 See Adam Haupt's 'Rap and the Articulation of Resistance: An Exploration of Subversive Cultural production during the early 90's, with particular reference to Prophets of da City' (1995: 5-8). In this thesis I summarize POC's attempts to establish themselves as artists as well as political commentators in the face of repressive laws. In 1993 and 1994, the band used music from their third album, *Age of Truth*, to undermine both the National Party and African National Congress' calls for South Africa to 'forgive and forget'. POC urged the electorate to be crit-

ical of all politicians preaching the philosophy of reconciliation. To them, the idea of reconciling the nation and the euphoria associated with the metaphor of the 'Rainbow Nation' amounted to 'reconning the nation'. *Age of Truth* was also explicitly anti-National Party in its sentiments and it was banned soon after its release. In the late nineties POC's live performances in South Africa decreased significantly subsequent to the release of *Ghetto Code*. Ironically, Ready D has become incredibly popular as a DJ and Brasse Vannie Kaap has also catapulted into the mainstream. In fact, Ready D and BVK have performed at most of the major South African music festivals in 2000 and have secured a solid following in the traditionally white rock music world. They have also managed to follow in POC's footsteps by performing in Europe. See Adam Haupt's 'Roer Daai Potjie, Brasse!' in *Mail & Guardian Friday* 16.31 (4 –10 August 2000): 3; James Reynard and Adam Haupt's 'BVK Goes Yskoud' in *Friedjam.com* (19 June 2000): http://www.friedjam.com/news_artist_archive_details.asp?id=16);
Adam Haupt's "Brave New World" in Friedjam.com (30 March 2000)
http://www.friedjam.com/news_artist_archive_details.asp?id=11)
Adam Haupt's 'POC's Still Bouncing' in Friedjam.com (26 June 2000):
http://www.friedjam.com/news_archive_details.asp?id=49) for more details about both bands' development.

2 Translation:
'Yo, man, what's up, kid. Let's do this for the honeys.
That's not the way we speak in the Cape.
You must get with it or scram because your fake accent doesn't make you cool.
You're not Chester Williams (a black rugby player) so don't even try to try
Before I kick your butt like Popeye.'

3 Translation:
'You'd better pray that you don't have a baby boy.
That's all they say on *Agenda* (an SABC actuality programme).
They always show ugly pictures of our people.
Why must I always see a gangster or a coon in the newspapers
or on TV?
They sneer at us and say, "Sis, you're a low-class coloured."'

4 A recent *Cape Argus* article about Americans gangster Mogamat Kadika Madat, for example, features a colour photograph of him posing in designer clothes showing off two pistols. The article is based largely on an interview with him, in which he claims to be 'the biggest Mandrax merchant in Tafelsig, Mitchell's Plain' (Smith, 29 April 1998: 3). The page three article, a prominent space in many newspapers, spends much time providing Madat's perspectives and provides a glamorous representation of the subject, which recalls representations in Micky Spillane novels, Martin Scorcese movies and American TV series such *as Miami*

Vice: 'Mr Madat showed the 'price' he paid to become the leader of the Americans gang in Manenberg at the age of 14. Beneath the veneer of the designer clothing is a body raked with the scars of street warfare' (Smith, 29 April 1998: 3). Whilst such masculinist representations implicitly valorise violence, they also confirm the negative perceptions of black men and life in the townships.

5 They have also participated in programmes such as Northern Ireland's recent Youth Festival, which was meant to promote understanding and reconciliation amongst that country's youth.

6 Translation:
'My God, girl, I'm all yours.
You're so cute that I want to eat you up.
You're precious to me.
But time and time again, your mother wants to intervene.
She's full of crap.
She says that you're Christian and I'm Muslim.'

7 Translation: 'Don't let FW (De Klerk) puzzle you.
He's a smooth talker.
He still thinks of you as a kaffir (nigger) and hotnot (Hottentot).
They sponsor township violence and give licences to shebeens.
Because they know that wine fucks up your brain
and then you get involved in shit and you get blamed.
The whole thing is planned because you're going to jail and
you're going to get hanged
because the pig is a snake.'

8 Translation:
'You'd better pray that you don't have a baby boy.
That's all they say on *Agenda* (an SABC actuality programme).
They always show ugly pictures of our people.
Why must I always see a gangster or a coon in the newspapers
or on TV?
They sneer at us and say, 'Sis, you're a low-class coloured.
Your ancestors were whites and slaves. So you must be a bastard'.
But, wait a minute, if you trust my story and not his story, then you'll see.
My ancestors were kings and queens and never knew drugs, guns
or pubs.
They were always there to serve God.'

9 Farmers often used the dop-stelsel (tot-system) to pay their black employees. In this system, farm workers were remunerated with alcohol, as opposed to cash. This system has left many communities with the social, economic and physical problems related to alcohol abuse. Over recent years, the media has reported that certain farms still observe this practice.

10 This statement recalls the history of Afrikaans being used as a language between slaves and their Dutch slave masters in domestic situations.

11 Translation:

'I'm not stupid. Nine months ago I wasn't even in Cape Town.
It's too bad you don't have a case, be quiet, don't even speak
because you can't do a thing.
Enough about that, I'm talking about a '*meid*' (bitch) who thinks she's cool
Meanwhile, she's (no I won't say).'

The intervention, '*naai ek gattie sê nie*' ('no I won't say') is deliberate. Many black Capetonian Afrikaans speakers would realise that Shaheen is about to say, '*Sy is hard deur die naai.*' This statement could mean that she is a 'jerk' or 'asshole', but may also imply that she is a slut. This interpretation is possible because the word '*naai*' could refer to the act of sewing as well as 'fucking'. '*Naai*' also means 'no' or 'nay'.

12 Translation:

'Coloured woman, female Bantu; *you are a ~,* coward, fool.'

13 In all fairness to POC, it should be pointed out that they do speak out against misogyny in, particularly, gangsta rap. In his criticism of the music industry, Ready D points out that the 'industry encourages that kind of rap because it sells, but we [POC] have deliberately steered away from the gangsta route. That's not what we are about' (Dlamini, 1995, 25). The problem we encounter in POC's texts with regard to gender discourse therefore points to the presence of an aporia in black nationalism.

14 4 Feet Deep has not been signed to the label, but has performed under the guidance of Ready D. Subsequent to writing this paper, Shaheen has left POC. One of the performers who have replaced Shaheen is a female rapper named Eloise, who impressed new and old POC fans at the Woodstock Pop Culture Festival (Heidelberg) in 2000. See Adam Haupt's 'Brave New World' in *Friedjam.com* (30 March 2000) at
http://www.friedjam.com/news_artist_archive_details.asp?id=11 for an interview with Shaheen about his departure from POC.

Bibliography

Abrahams, Yvette. (1997) 'The Great Long National Insult: "Science", Sexuality and the Khoisan in the 18th and early 19th Century' in *Agenda*, 32

Adam, Heribert. (1971) *Modernizing Racial Domination*, Berkeley, University of California Press

Adam, Heribert and Giliomee, Hermann. (1979) *Ethnic Power Mobilized*, New Haven, Yale University Press

Adhikari, M. (1992a) 'God, Jan van Riebeeck and 'the Coloured People': The Anatomy of a South African Joke' in *South African Discourse*, Vol 4

– (1992b) 'The Sons of Ham: Slavery and the Making of Coloured Identity' in *South African Historical Journal*, Vol 27

– (1993) 'Protest and Accommodation: Ambiguities in the Racial Politics of the APO, 1909-1923' in *KRONOS*, Vol 20

– (1995) 'Race and Identity in Alex La Guma's 'A Walk in the Night' and Other Stories', colloquium on Alex La Guma: Journalism, Writing and Representations of Race and Place, University of the Western Cape

– (1997) 'Voice of the Coloured Elite: APO, 1909-1923' in (ed.) Switzer, Les, *South Africa's Alternative Press: Voices of Protest and Resistance, 1880s-1960s*, Cambridge, Cambridge University Press

Agarwala, Shelly. (1999) 'A Literary Politics of Reinscription: Embodying and Transforming the Subject in Toni Morrison's Paradise', unpublished paper

Alperson, Myra. (1993) 'I've got those walking, talking, blowing, slowing, downright growing Jo'burg blues' in *Leadership*, 12, 5

Althusser, Louis. (1971) 'Ideology and State Apparatuses (Notes Toward an Investigation)' in *Lenin and Philosophy and Other Essays*, London, Monthly Review Press

Anzaldua, Gloria. (1990) 'Haciendo Caras, Una Entrada: An Introduction' in (ed.) Anzaldua, Gloria, *Making Face, Making Soul, Haciendo Caras: Creative and Critical Writings by Feminists of Color*, San Francisco, Aunt Lute

– (1990) 'En Rapport, In Opposition: Cobrando Cuentas a las Nuestras' in (ed.) Anzaldua, Gloria, *Making Face, Making Soul,* Haciendo Caras: *Creative and Critical Writings by Feminists of Color*, San Francisco, Aunt Lute

Appadurai, Arjun. (1991) 'Disjuncture and Difference in the Global Cultural Economy' in *Global Culture. Nationalism, Globalisation and Modernity. A Theory, Culture and Society Special Issue*, London, New York, Sage Publications

Appiah, K. (1992) *In My Father's House: Africa in the Philosophy of Culture*, Oxford, Oxford University Press

– (Winter 1991) 'Is the Post- in Postmodernism the Post- in Postcolonial?' in *Critical Inquiry*, 17

Armstrong, Nancy. (1987) *Desire and Domestic Fiction. A Political History of the Novel*, New York and London, Oxford University Press

Ashforth, Adam. (1990) *The Politics of Official Discourse in Twentieth-Century South Africa*, Oxford, Clarendon Press

Attridge, Derek, Bennington, Geoff and Young, Robert (eds) (1987) *Post-Structuralism and the Question of History*, Cambridge, Cambridge University Press

Bahktin, Mikhail. (1981) (trans.) *The Dialogic Imagination: Four Essays*, Austin, University of Texas Press

Ballahachet, K. (1980) *Race, Sex and Class Under the Raj: Imperial Attitudes and Policies and their Critics, 1793-1905*, New York, St Martin's Press

Banton, Michael. (1967) *Race Relations*, London, Tavistock

– (1977) *The Idea of Race*, London, Tavistock

Barnett, Ursula. (1983) *A Vision of Order: A Study of Black South African Literature in English (1914-1980)*, London, Sinclair Browne

Barrow, Christine. (ed.) (1998) *Caribbean Portraits: Essays on Gender Ideologies and Identities*, Kingston, Ian Randle

Bekker, S. (1997) 'Rainbow nation – dream or nightmare?' in *Cape Times*, 1 February

Bennett, J. (1997) 'Credibility, Plausibility and Autobiographical Oral Narrative: Some Suggestions from the Analysis of a Rape Survivor's Testimony' in (eds) Levett, A., Kottler, A., Burman, E. and Parker, I. *Culture, Power and Difference, Discourse Analysis in South Africa,* London, Zed Books

Bhabha, Homi. (1984) 'Of Mimicry and Man: the Ambivalence of Colonial Discourse' in *October*, 28

– (1985) 'Signs Taken for Wonders: Questions of Ambivalence and Authority under a Tree Outside New Delhi, May 1817' in *Critical Inquiry*, 12,1

– (1990) 'Dissemination: Time, Narrative and the Margins of the Modern Nation' in *The Location of Culture*, London and New York, Routledge

– (1993) 'Remembering Fanon: Self, Psyche and the Colonial Condition' in (eds) Williams, Patrick and Chrisman, Laura, *Colonial Discourse and Post-Colonial Theory: A Reader*, New York and Singapore, Harvester Wheatsheaf

– (1996) 'Unpacking my library ... again' in (eds) Chambers, I. and Curti, L. *The Post-colonial Question: Common Skies, Divided Horizons*, London and New York, Routledge

Bhana, S. & Brain, J. (1990) *Setting down roots: Indian migrants in South Africa, 1860-1911,* Johannesburg, University of Witwatersrand Press

Bhavnani, K. (1990) 'What's Power got to do with it? Empowerment and Social Research' in (eds) Parker I. and Shotter, J. *Deconstructing Social Psychology*, London and New York, Routledge

Bickford-Smith, V. (1990) 'The Origins and Early History of District Six to 1910' in (eds) Jeppie, S. and Soudien, C. *The Struggle for District Six: Past and Present*, Cape Town, Buchu Books

– (1995) *Ethnic Pride and Racial Prejudice in Victorian Cape Town*, Johannesburg, Witwatersrand University Press

Blair, M. Elizabeth. (Winter 1993) 'Commercialisation of the Rap Music Youth Subculture' in *Journal of Popular Culture*, 27, 3

Boehmer, Elleke. (Fall 1992) 'Transfiguring: Colonial Body into Postcolonial Narrative' in *Novel: A Forum for Fiction*, 26, 1

Bradlow, Edna. (1990) 'Running amok and its historical significance' in *CABO* 5,1

Brand, Dionne. (1996) 'No Language is Neutral' in (ed.) Birbalsingh, Frank, *Frontiers of Caribbean Literature in English*, London and Basingstoke, Macmillan

Brantlinger, P. (1985) 'Victorians and Africans: The Genealogy of the Myth of the Dark Continent' in (ed.) Gates, H. L., *'Race', Writing and Difference*, Chicago, University of Chicago Press

Brass, Paul. (1974) *Language, Religion and Politics in North India*, New York, Cambridge University Press

Brasse Vannie Kaap. (1998) *BVK*, South Africa, Ghetto Ruff

– (2000) *Yskoud,* South Africa, Ghetto Ruff, EMI

Brathwaite, E. (1971) *The Development of Creole Society in Jamaica, 1770-1820*, Oxford, Clarendon Press

Burgess, A. and Dikeni, S. (1995) 'Kleurling Jeug Toyi-Toyi uit die ANC' in *Die Suid-Afrikaan*, 53

Butler, Judith. (1997) *The psychic life of power: theories in subjection,* Stanford, Stanford University Press

Caliguire, D. (1996) 'Voices from the Communities' in (eds) James, W., Caliguire, D. and Cullinan, K. *Now that We are Free: Coloured Communities in a Democratic South Africa*, Cape Town, Idasa

Callinicos, Luli. (1989) ''We Are Not Alone' – The Making of a Mass Movement: 1950-1960' in *Staffrider*, 8, 3/4

Carby, Hazel. (Summer 1992) 'Policing the Black Woman's Body in an Urban Context' in *Critical Inquiry*, 18

Carrim, N. and Soudien, C. (1998) 'Critical Antiracism in South Africa' in (ed.) May, S., *Critical Multi-culturalism: Rethinking Multicultural and Antiracist Education*, London, Falmer Press

Chambers, I. and Curti, L. (eds) (1996) *The Post-colonial Question: Common Skies, Divided Horizons*, London and New York, Routledge

Chapman, Chris. (1988) 'Popular Music and the Markets of Apartheid' in *Staffrider*, 7, 2

Cliff, Michele. (1990) 'Object into Subject: Some Thoughts on the Work of Black Women Artists' in (ed.) Anzaldua, Gloria, *Making Face, Making Soul, Haciendo Caras: Creative and Critical Writings by Feminists of Color*, San Francisco, Aunt Lute

Clingman, Stephen. (1988) 'Beyond the Limit: the Social Relations of Madness in Southern African Fiction', African Studies Seminar Paper, University of the Witwatersrand

Coetzee, J.M. (1980) 'Blood, flaw, taint, degeneration: the case of Sarah Gertrude Millin' in *English studies in Africa,* Vol 23

– (1988) *White Writing: On the Culture of Letters in South Africa*, New Haven and London, Yale University Press

Coleman, P. (1986) *Ageing and Reminiscence Process, Social and Clinical Implications*, Chichester, John Wiley and Sons

Colomina, Beatriz. (ed.) (1992) *Sexuality and Space*, Princeton, Princeton Architectural Press

Connerton, P. (1989) *How Societies Remember*, Cambridge, Cambridge University Press

Connolly, William E. (1991) *Identity/Difference Democratic Negotiations of Political Paradox*, Ithaca, Cornell University Press

Coplan, David B. (1985) *In Township Tonight! South Africa's Black City Music and Theatre*, London and New York, Longman

Cornwall, Gareth. (1989) 'Race as science, race as language: A preliminary enquiry into origins' in *Pretexts*, 1,1

Crocker, Jen. (1999) 'A look into the Metaphorical Fire: The Interview' in *The Cape Times*, 22 January

Dabydeen, David (ed.). (1985) *The Black Presence in English Literature*, Manchester, Manchester University Press

– (forthcoming). 'Hogarth and the Canecutter' in (ed.) Hulme, Peter, *The Tempest and its Rewritings*

Davenport, T R H. (1977) *South Africa: A Modern History*. Toronto, University of Toronto Press

Davids, Achmat. (1980) *The mosques of the Bo-Kaap*. Athlone, Cape Town, South African Institute of Arabic and Islamic Research

Davies, Carole Boyce and Savory Fido, Elaine. (eds) (1990) *Out of the Kumbla: Caribbean Women and Literature*, Trenton, Africa World Press

Davis, Angela. (1982) *Women, Race and Class*, London, Women's Press

De Kiewiet, C. (1942) *A History of South Africa, Social and Economic*, Oxford, Oxford University Press

Decker, Jeffrey Louis. (Spring 1993) 'The State of Rap: Time and Place in Hip-Hop Nationalism' in *Social Text*, 34

Deleuze, Gilles and Guattari, Félix. (1988) (trans). *Capitalism and Schizophrenia*, Vol ii, London, Athlone

Derrida, Jacques. (1976) *Of Grammatology*, trans. Spivak, G, Baltimore and London, The John Hopkins University Press

– (1978) *Writing and Difference*, trans. Bass, Alan, London, Routledge

– (1985) 'Racism's Last Word' in (ed.) Gates, Henry Louis, *'Race', Writing and Difference*, Chicago, University of Chicago Press

– (1991) *A Derrida Reader. Between the Blinds*, (ed.) Kamuf, Peggy, New York, Columbia University Press

– (Autumn 1986) 'But beyond ... (Open Letter to Anne McClintock and Rob Nixon)', trans. Kamuf, Peggy in *Critical Inquiry*, 13

Dirks, Nicholas B. and Ortner, Sherry B. (eds) (1994) *A Reader in Contemporary Social Theory*, New Jersey, Princeton University Press

Dirlik, Arif. (Winter 1994) 'The Postcolonial Aura: Third World Criticism in the Age of Global Capitalism' in *Critical Inquiry*, 20, 2

Djebar, Assia. (1985) *Fantasia: An Algerian Cavalcade*, London, Quartet

Dlamini, Jacob. (1995) 'Prophets R Coming, South Africa' in *Sunday Times*, 12 November

Doherty, Thomas. (Winter 1989-90) 'Do the Right Thing' in *Film Quarterly*, 43,2

Donald, J. and Rattansi, A. (eds) (1992) *'Race', Culture and Difference*, London, Sage

Driver, Dorothy. (1996) 'Transformation Through Art: Writing, Representation and Subjectivity in Recent South African Fiction' in *World Literature Today*, 70, 1

Dubois, Dominique. (Autumn 1998) 'Wilson Harris's "Infinite Rehearsal"' in *Commonwealth*, 21,1

Dubow, S. (1995) *Scientific Racism in Modern South Africa,* England, Cambridge University Press

Duncan, N. (1996) in Fakier, Y. 'A debate coloured by race' in *Cape Times*, 11 December

Du Plessis, Izak David. (1935) *Die Bydrae van die Maleier volkslied tot die Afrikaanse volkslied*, Cape Town, Nasionale Pers

– (1944) *The Cape Malays*, Cape Town, Maskew Miller

– (1975) *Aantekeninge uit Tuynstraat,* Cape Town, Balkema

Du Plessis, Izak David & Luckhoff, C. A. (1953) *The Malay Quarter and its people,* Cape Town, Union of South Africa Department of Interior, Race Relations serial publication 1.

Edwards, Paul and Walvin, James. (1983) *Black Personalities in the Era of the Slave Trade*, London and Basingstoke, MacMillan

Eichenberger, Beryl. (1999) 'Review of *The Slave Book*' in *The Cape Times*, 22 January

Eldredge, E. and Morton, F. (1994) *Slavery in South Africa: Captive Labour on the Dutch Frontier*, Pietermaritzburg, University of Natal Press

Elphick, R. and Shell, R. (1989) 'Intergroup relations: Khoikhoi, Settlers, Slaves, and Free Blacks, 1652-1795' in (eds) Elphick, Richard and Giliomee, Hermann, *The Shaping of South African Society, 1652-1840*, Johannesburg, Maskew Miller Longman

Elphick, R. (1985) *Khoikhoi and the Founding of White South Africa*, Johannesburg, Ravan

Encyclopaedie van Nederlandsch-Indie (1917) Leiden, E. J. Brill, Vol 1

Erasmus, Z. & Pieterse, E. (1999) 'Conceptualising Coloured Identities in the Western Cape Province of South Africa' in (ed.) Palmberg, M. *National Identity and Democracy in Africa*, Pretoria, The Human Sciences Research Council of South Africa, The Mayibuye Centre at the University of the Western Cape, The Nordic African Institute

Erasmus, Z. (2000a) 'Same Kind of White, Some Kind of Black: Living the Moments of Entanglement in South Africa and its Academy' in (ed.) Hesse, B. *Un/Settled Multiculturalisms: Diasporas, Entanglements, Transruptions*, London, Zed Books

– (2000b) 'Recognition through Pleasure, Recognition through Violence: Gendered Coloured Subjectivities in South Africa' in *Current Sociology*, 48, 3

– (2000c) 'Hair politics' in (eds) Nuttal, S. and Michael, C. *Senses of Culture: South African Cultural Studies*, Cape Town, Oxford University Press

Erskine, B. (1996) 'Loss and Grief in Oral History' in *Oral History Association of Australia Journal*, 18

Evans, Maurice. (1911) *Black and White in South East Africa: A Study in Sociology*, London, Longmans, Green & Co

Fakier, Y. (1996) 'A debate coloured by race' in *The Cape Times*, 11 December

Fanon, Frantz. (1986) *Black Skin, White Masks*, London, Pluto

February, Vernon. (1981) *Mind Your Colour: The 'Coloured' Stereotype in South African Literature*, London and Boston, Kegan Paul

Field, S. (1990) 'The Politics of Exclusion: A Case Study of the Factreton Area', unpublished Masters thesis, University of Cape Town

– (1996) 'The Power of Exclusion: Moving Memories from Windermere to the Cape Flats, 1920s–1990s', unpublished PhD dissertation, University of Essex

– (1998) 'From the "Peaceful Past" to the "Violent Present": Memory, Myth and Identity in Guguletu' in (eds) Norval, A. and Howarth, D. *South Africa in Transition*, London, Macmillan Press

Figueroa, John J. (1986) 'The Relevance of West Indian Literature to Caribbean

Heritage People Living in Britain' in (ed.) Brock, Colin, *The Caribbean in Europe: Aspects of West Indian Experience in Britain, France and the Netherlands*, London, Frank Cass

Finnegan, W. (1994) 'The Election Mandela Lost' in *The New York Times*, 20 October

Flax, J. (1993) *Disputed Subjects. Essays on Psychoanalysis, Philosophy and Politics*, London, Routledge

Forman, Murray. (1994) '"Movin' to an Independent Funk": Black Feminist Theory, Standpoint and Women in Rap' in *Women's Studies*, 23, 1

Fortune, L. (1996) *The House on Tyne Street: Childhood Memories of District Six*, Kwela, Cape Town

Foster, D. (1993) 'On Racism: Virulent Mythologies and Fragile Threads' in (ed) L. Nicholas, *Psychology and Oppression: Critiques and Proposals*, Johannesburg, Skotaville Publishers

Foucault, Michel. (1984) *Foucault Reader*, (ed.) Paul Rabinow, New York, Pantheon Books

Freedberg, J. (1987) 'Changing Political Identity of the 'Coloured' People of South Africa: A Political History, 1652-1982', unpublished PhD thesis, University of California

Fuss, D. (1989) *Essentially Speaking: Feminism, Nature and Difference*, New York and London, Routledge

Gates, Henry Louis. (ed.) (1985) *'Race', Writing and Difference*, Chicago, University of Chicago Press

– (1987) *Figures in Black. Words, Signs and the 'Racial' Self*, New York and Oxford, Oxford University Press

– (1988) *The Signifying Monkey. A Theory of Afro-American Literary Criticism*. New York and Oxford, Oxford University Press

Gillborn, D. (1995) *Racism and Antiracism in Real Schools*, Buckingham, Open University Press

Gilman, S. (1985a) *Difference and Pathology: Stereotypes of Sexuality, Race, and Madness*, Ithaca, Cornell University Press

– (1985b) 'Black Bodies, White Bodies: Toward an Iconography of Female Sexuality in Late Nineteenth-Century Art, Medicine, and Literature' in (ed.) Gates, Henry Louis, *'Race', Writing and Difference*, Chicago, University of Chicago Press

Gilroy, P. (1993) 'It ain't where you're from, it's where you're at' in Gilroy, P. *Small Acts*, London, Serpent's Tail

– (1993) *The Black Atlantic, Modernity and Double Consciousness*, London, Verso

Glissant, E. (1992) *Caribbean Discourse: Selected Essays*, Charlottesville, Caraf Books, University Press of Virginia

Goldin, I. (1987) *Making Race, The Politics and Economics of Coloured Identity in South Africa*, London, Maskew Miller Longman

Gordon, Robert. (1988) 'Apartheid's Anthropologists: the Genealogy of Afrikaner Anthropology' in *American Ethnologist*, 15, 3

– (1990) 'Early social anthropology in South Africa' in *African studies,* 49, 1

Gordon, Lady Duff. (1927, 1820) *Letters from the Cape*, Oxford, Oxford University Press

Gould, Janice. (1990) 'We Exist' in (ed.) Anzaldua, Gloria, *Making Face, Making Soul, Haciendo Caras: Creative and Critical Writings by Feminists of Color*, San Francisco, Aunt Lute

Griffin, Gabriele. (1993) ''Writing the Body': Reading Joan Riley, Grace Nichols and Ntozakhe Shange' in (ed.) Wisker, Gina, *Black Women's Writing*, New York, St Martin's

Grosz, Elizabeth. (1995) *Space, Time and Perversion*, London and New York, Routledge

Halbwachs, Maurice. (1992) *On Collective Memory*, (ed. and trans.) Coser, Lewis A, Chicago and London, Chicago University Press

Hall, S. (1990) 'Cultural Identity and Diaspora' in (ed.) Rutherford, J, *Identity: Community Culture, Difference*, London, Lawrence and Wishart

– (1992) 'New Ethnicities' in (eds) Donald, J. and Rattansi, A. *'Race', Culture and Difference*, London, Sage

– (1996) 'Introduction: Who Needs 'Identity'?' in (eds) Hall, S. and Du Gay, P. *Questions of Cultural Identity*, London, Sage

– (1996) 'Politics of Identity' in (eds) Ranger, Terence, Samad, Yunus and Stuart, Ossie, *Culture, Identity and Politics,* Aldershot, Avebury

– (1996) 'Cultural Identity and Diaspora' in (ed.) Mongia, Padmini, *Contemporary Postcolonial Theory: A Reader*, London and New York, Arnold

Hambridge, Joan. (1998) 'Roman Oor Slawe Tref met Uitbeelding' in *Rapport*, 6 December

Hart, D. (1990) 'Political Manipulation of Urban Space: The Razing of District Six, Cape Town' in (eds) Jeppie, S. and Soudien, C. *The Struggle for District Six: Past and Present*, Cape Town, Buchu Books

Haupt, Adam and Christopher Roper. (September 1996) 'Stifled Noise in the South African Music Box: Prophets of da City and the Struggle for Public Space' in *South African Theatre Journal*, 10, 2

Haupt, Adam. (1994) 'Power to da People: An Interview with Prophets of da City', Masters video project, Bellville, University of the Western Cape

– (1995) 'Rap and the Articulation of Resistance: An exploration of subversive cultural production during the early 90's, with particular reference to Prophets of da City', Masters mini-thesis, Bellville, University of the Western Cape

– (26 June 2000), 'POC's Still Bouncing', *Friedjam.com* http://www.friedjam.com/news_artist_archive_details.asp?id=11

– (2000) 'Roer Daai Potjie, Brasse!' in *Mail & Guardian*, 3 August

– (30 March 2000) 'Brave New World' in *Friedjam.com* http://www.friedjam.com/news_archive_details.asp?id=49
– (April 1996) 'Prophets of da City: Bek Uitspoel with Afrika's Hip-hop Koppe' in *Student Life*, 3, 3
– (March 1999) 'Brasse Vannie Kaap' in *Y*, 2, 2
– (March 1999) 'Is this the Real Hip Hop?' in *Y*, 2, 2
– (September 1998) 'Die Brasse Vertaal' in *Student Life*, 5, 8
Hayden, D. (1995) *The Power of Place, Urban Landscapes as Public History*, Cambridge Massachusetts, MIT Press
Hebdige, Dick. (1987) *Subculture. The Meaning of Style*, London and New York, Routledge
Hendricks, C. (2000) ' "We Knew our Place": A Study of the Constructions of Coloured Identity', PhD thesis, University of South Carolina
Hobsbawm, Eric & Ranger, Terence. (1986) *The Invention of Tradition* Cambridge, Cambridge University Press
Hooks, bell. (1984) *Feminist Theory: From Margin to Center*, Boston, South End
– (1991) *Yearning: Race, Gender and Cultural Politics*, London, Turnaround
– (1992) 'Representing Whiteness in the Black Imagination' in (eds) Grossberg, Lawrence, et al *Cultural Studies*, New York, Routledge
Horrel, Muriel. (1978) *Laws Affecting Race Relations in South Africa*, Johannesburg, Institute of South African Race Relations
Hurgronje, C. Snouck. (1931) *Mekka in the latter part of the nineteenth century*, (trans. by J.H. Monahan), Leyden, E. J. Brill
Hutcheon, Linda. (1989) *The Politics of Postmodernism*, London and New York, Routledge

Jacobs, Rayda. (1998) *The Slave Book*, Cape Town, Kwela
Jaggar, Alison & Bordo, Susan R. (eds) (1989) *Gender/Body/Knowledge: Feminist Reconstructions of Being and Knowing*, New Brunswick, Rutgers University Press
James, W. (1996) 'The devil who keeps promises' in (eds) James, W, Caliguire, D and Cullinan, K, *Now that We are Free: Coloured Communities in a Democratic South Africa*, Cape Town, Idasa
James, W, Caliguire, D and Cullinan, K. (eds) (1996) *Now That We Are Free: Coloured communities in a democratic South Africa*, Cape Town, Idasa
Jameson, Frederic. (1988) 'Postmodernism and Consumer Society' in *Postmodernism and its Discontents: Theories, Practices*, London and New York, Verso
Jan Mohamed, A. (1985) 'The Economy of the Manichean Allegory: The Function of Racial Difference in Colonialist Literature' in (eds) Gates, Henry Louis, *'Race', Writing and Difference*, Chicago, University of Chicago Press
Jeppie, Shamil. (1990) 'Aspects of the popular culture of inner-city Cape Town', M. A. Thesis, University of Cape Town

(1996) 'Commemoration and identities' in Tamara Sonn (ed.), *Islam and the Question of Minorities,* Atlanta, Scholar's Press

Johnson, Victoria E. (Winter 1993-94) 'Polyphony and Cultural Expression. Interpreting Musical Traditions in "Do the Right Thing"' in *Film Quarterly*, 47, 2

Jones, Tim Trengrove. (1999) 'Book of Week: From the Outside Looking Back to the Present' in *Sunday Times*, 25 April

Karon, Tony. (*Desember 1992/Januarie 1993)* 'Woorde in Woede. Rap en hip-hop is Amerikaanse modeverskysensels wat hierheen oorgewaai het en gou 'n inheemse politieke karakter ontwikkel het' in *Die Suid-Afrikaan*

Kavanagh, Robert Mshengu. (1985).*Theatre and Cultural Struggle in South Africa*, London, Zed Books

Keegan, T. (1996) *Colonial South Africa and the Origins of the Racial Order*, Cape Town, David Philip

Kirby, R.P. (1939) 'Musical instruments of the Cape Malays' in *South African Journal of Science*, Vol 36

Kritzinger, M.S.B. (1980) *Beknopte Verklarende Woordeboek*, Cape Town, Van Schaik

Kuper, Leo and M.G. Smith. (eds) (1969) *Pluralism in Africa*, Berkeley, University of California Press

Kuzwayo, Ellen. (1985) *Call Me Woman*, Johannesburg, Ravan

Laclau, E. (1990) *New Reflections on the Revolution of Our Time*, London, Verso

Laforest, Marie Helene. (1996) 'Black Cultures in Difference' in (eds) Chambers, I and Curti, L, *The Post-colonial Question: Common Skies, Divided Horizons*, London and New York, Routledge

Lamming, George. (1996) 'Concepts of the Caribbean' in (ed.) Birbalsingh, Frank, *Frontiers of Caribbean Literature in English*, London and Basingstoke, Macmillan

Landry, Donna and Maclean, Gerald. (1996) *The Spivak Reader*, New York and London, Routledge

Latifa, Queen. (1993) *Black Reign*, USA, Motown Record Company

Lee, Spike. (1989) *Do The Right Thing*, USA, Universal City Studios

Levi-Strauss, Claude. (1952) *The Race Question in Modern Science*, UNESCO

Lewis, Bernard. (1961) *The Emergence of Modern Turkey*, 2nd edition Oxford, Oxford University Press

Lewis, David. (1949) 'Religion of the Cape Malays' in E. Hellman & L. Abrahams (eds), *Handbook of Race Relations in South Africa*, Cape Town, South African Institute of Race Relations

Lewis, G. (1987) *Between the Wire and the Wall. A History of South African Politics,* Cape Town and Johannesburg, David Philip

Loram, C.T. (1917) *The Education of the South African Native*, London, Longmans, Green & Co

Lowenthal, D. (1985) *The Past is a Foreign Country,* Cambridge, Cambridge University Press

Lutz, C. and Abu-Lughod, L. (eds) (1990) *Language and the Politics of Emotion,* Cambridge, Cambridge University Press

MacCrone, I.D. (1937) *Race Attitudes in South Africa: Historical, Experimental, and Psychological Studies*, Johannesburg, Witwatersrand University Press

Macmillan, W.M. (1927) *The Cape Colour Question: A Historical Survey*, London, Faver and Gwyer

Magona, Sindiwe. (1990) *To My Children's Children*, Cape Town, David Philip

Mama, A. (1995) *Beyond the Masks: Race, Gender and Subjectivity*, London, Routledge

Maqagi, Sisi. (1989) 'Who Theorises' in *Current Writing*, 2

Marais, Sue. (1995) 'Getting Lost in Cape Town: Spatial and Temporal Dislocations in the South African Fiction Cycle' in *English in Africa*, 22, 2

Martin, D. (1999) *Coon Carnival: New Year in Cape Town, Past and Present*, Cape Town, David Philip

Martin, Denis-Constant. (1998) 'What's in the Name "Coloured"' in *Social Identities*, 4, 3

– (1992) 'Music Beyond Apartheid?' in (ed.) Reebee Garofalo, *Rockin' the Boat. Mass Music and Mass Movements*, London, South End Press

Marx, A. (1998) *Making Race and Nation: A Comparison of the United States, South Africa, and Brazil*, Cambridge, Cambridge University Press

Mattes, R. (1995) *The Election Book: Judgement and Choice in South Africa's 1994 Election*, Cape Town, Idasa

Mayson, John, S. (1861) *The Malays of Cape Town*, Manchester, Transactions of the Manchester Statistical Society

McClintock, A. (1995) *Imperial Leather: Race, Gender and Sexuality in the Colonial Contest*, New York and London, Routledge

McClintock, Anne. (1994) 'The Angel of Progress: Pitfalls of the Term "Post-colonialism"' in (eds) Williams, Patrick and Chrisman, Laura, *Colonial Discourse and Post-Colonial Theory. A Reader*, New York, London, Sydney, Toronto, Tokyo, Singapore, Harvester Wheatsheaf

McCormick, Kathleen Mary. (1989) 'English and Afrikaans in *District Six: A Sociolinguistic Study*', unpublished PhD thesis, University of Cape Town

McCormick, Kay. (1990) 'The Vernacular of District Six' in (eds) Jeppie, Shamiel and Soudien, Crain, *The Struggle for District Six: Past and Present*, Cape Town, Buchu Books

Mignolo, Walter D. (1994) 'Signs and their Transmission: The Question of the Book in the New World' in (eds) Hill Boone, Elizabeth and Mignolo, Walter D. *Writing Without Words: Alternative Literacies in Mesoamerica and the Andes*, Durham and London, Duke University Press

Millin, S. (1951) *The People of South Africa*, Johannesburg, Central News Agency

Millin, Sarah Gertrude. (1924) *God's Stepchildren*, Cape Town, A.D. Donker

Minh-ha, Trinh T. (1990) 'Commitment from the Mirror-Writing Box' in (ed.) Anzaldua, Gloria, *Making Face, Making Soul, Haciendo Caras: Creative and Critical Writings by Feminists of Color*, San Francisco, Aunt Lute

– (1990) 'Not You/Like you: Post-Colonial Women and Interlocking Questions of Identity and Difference' in (ed.) Anzaldua, Gloria, *Making Face, Making Soul, Haciendo Caras: Creative and Critical Writings by Feminists of Color*, San Francisco, Aunt Lute

– (in conversation with Annamaria Morelli). (1996) 'The Undone Interval' in (eds) Chambers, I and Curti, L, *The Post-colonial Question: Common Skies, Divided Horizons*, London and New York, Routledge

– (1996) 'The Undone Interval' in (eds) Chambers, I and Curti, L, *The Post-colonial Question: Common Skies, Divided Horizons*, London and New York, Routledge

Mishra, Vijay and Hodge, Bob. (1994) 'What is Post(-)colonialism?' in (eds) Williams, Patrick and Chrisman, Laura, *Colonial Discourse and Post-Colonial Theory. A Reader*, New York, London, Toronto, Sydney, Tokyo, Singapore, Harvester Wheatsheaf

Mitchell, Timothy. (1986) *Colonizing Egypt*, Cambridge, Cambridge University Press

Mongia, P. (ed.) (1996) *Contemporary Postcolonial Theory*, London, St Martins Press

Mukherjee, Arun P. (Autumn 1990) 'Whose Post-Colonialism and Whose Postmodernism?' in *World Literature Written in English*, 30, 2

Mukherjee, Bharati. (1987) 'They Never Wanted to Be Themselves', review of *You Can't Get Lost in Cape Town* in *New York Times Book Review*, 24 May

Ndebele, Njabulo. (1984) 'Turkish Tales and Some Thoughts on S.A. Fiction' in *Staffrider*, 6, 1

– (1994) 'Liberation and the Crisis of Culture' in (eds) Boehmer, Elleke et al, *Altered States: Writing and South Africa*, Sydney, Dangaroo

– (1994) *South African Literature and Culture: Rediscovery of the Ordinary*, Manchester and New York, Manchester University Press

Nkosi, Lewis. (1965) 'The Fabulous Decade' in *Home and Exile and other Selections*, Harlow, Longman

Norval, A. (1996) *Deconstructing Apartheid Discourse*, London, Verso

Ozinsky, M. and Rasool, E. (1993) 'Developing a Strategic Perspective for the Coloured Areas in the Western Cape' in *African Communist*, Second Quarter

Papastergiadis, Nikos. (1997) 'Tracing Hybridity in Theory' in (eds) Werbner, Pnina and Modood, Tariq, *Debating Cultural Hybrdity*, London, Zed

Pateman, Carole. (1988) *The Sexual Contract*, Cambridge, Polity Press

Pateman, Carole. (1989) *The Disorder of Women: Democracy, Feminism and Poltical Theory*, Cambridge, Polity Press

Pecheux, Michel. (1982) *Language, Semantics and Ideology*, London, Macmillan

Peterson, Bhekizizwe. (1994) 'Apartheid and the Political Imagination in Black South African Theatre' in (ed.) Gunner, Liz, *Politics and Performance. Theatre, Poetry and Song in South Africa*, Johannesburg, Witwatersrand University Press

Phillip, Marlene Nourbese. (1990) 'The Absence of Writing or How I Almost Became A Spy' in (eds) Boyce Davies, Carole and Savory Fido, Elaine, *Out of the Kumbla: Caribbean Women and Literature*, Trenton, Africa World Press

Pieterse, J. N. (1992) *White on Black: Images of Africa and Blacks in Western Popular Culture*, New Haven, Yale University Press

Pinnock, Don. (1984) *The Brotherhoods: Street Gangs and State Control in Cape Town*, Cape Town, David Philip

Plomer, W. (1926) *Turbott Wolfe*, London, Ad Donker

– (1984) *Selected Stories*. (ed.) Stephen Gray, Cape Town, David Philip

Plummer, Robert. (1999) 'Fascinating and Unexplored Slice of our History' in *The Sunday Independent*, 7 March

Podrey, Joe. (1990) 'Of Human Bondage' in *Financial Mail*, 9 April

Population Registration Act No 30 of 1950, *Statutes of the Union of South Africa* (1950)

Posel, Deborah. (1991) *The Making of Apartheid 1948-1961: Conflict and Compromise*, Oxford, Clarendon Press

Prakash, Gyan. (1990) 'Writing Post-Orientalist Histories of the Third World: Perspectives in Indian Historiography' in *Contemporary Studies in Society and History*

– (1995) *After Colonialism: Imperial Histories and Postcolonial Displacements*, Princeton, Princeton University Press

Pratt, M.L. (1985) 'Scratches on the Face of the Country; or, What Mr. Barrow Saw in the Land of the Bushmen' in (eds) Gates, Henry Louis, *'Race', Writing and Difference*, Chicago, University of Chicago Press

Prophets of da City. (1990) *Our World*, South Africa, Teal Trutone

– (1991) *Boom Style*, South Africa, Teal Trutone

– (1993) *Age of Truth*, South Africa, Tusk Music Co

– (1995) *Phunk Phlow*, South Africa, Ku Shu Shu

– (1996) *Ghetto Code*. South Africa, Ghetto Ruff

Public Enemy. (1990) *Fear of a Black Planet*, USA, CBS Records

Rassool, E. (1996) 'Unveiling the Heart of Fear' in (eds) James, W, Caliguire, D and Cullinan, K, *Now that We are Free: Coloured Communities in a Democratic South Africa*, Cape Town, Idasa

Rathbone, Gary. (1988) 'Contemporary Popular Music In South Africa: The State of Things' in *Staffrider*, 7, 1

Raven-Hart, R. (1967) *Before Van Riebeeck: Callers at South Africa from 1488 to 1652*, Cape Town, Struik

– (1971). *Cape Good Hope 1652-1702: The First Fifty Years of Dutch Colonisation as Seen by Callers*, Vol 1, Cape Town, A.A Balkema

Reddy, T. (1995) 'Hegemony and Resistance: The Construction of Subaltern Subjects as Other in South Africa', unpublished PhD thesis, University of Washington

Report of the Commission on Mixed Marriages (1939)

Rex, John and Mason, David. (eds) (1986) *Theories of Race and Ethnic Relations*, Cambridge, Cambridge University Press

Reynard, James and Haupt, Adam. (19 June 2000) 'BVK Goes *Yskoud*', *Friedjam.com*, http://www.friedjam.com/news_artist_archive_details.asp?id=16

Ridd, R. (forthcoming) 'The Marion Institute', Mimeograph

Rive, R. (1990) 'District Six: Fact and Fiction' in (eds) Jeppie, S. and Soudien, C. *The Struggle for District Six: Past and Present*, Cape Town, Buchu Books

Rive, Richard. (1981) *Writing Black*, Cape Town, David Philip

Rose, Tricia. (1994) *Black Noise. Rap Music and Black Culture in Contemporary America*, Hanover and London, Wesleyan University Press

Ross, Andrew. (Spring 1990) 'Ballots, Bullets or Batmen: Can Cultural Studies Do the Right Thing?' in *Screen*, 31, 1

Ross, Robert. (1979) 'Oppression, Sexuality and Slavery at the Cape of Good Hope' in *Historical Reflections*, Vol 6, 2

– (1983) *Cape of Torments: Slavery and Resistance in South Africa*, London, Routledge and Kegan Paul

Russell, K. et al. (1993) *The Colour Complex: The Politics of Skin Color Among African Americans*, New York, Anchor Books

Said, Edward. (1979) *Orientalism*, New York, Vintage

– (1983) *The World, the Text and the Critic*. Cambridge, Cambridge University Press

– (1995) *Culture and Imperialism*, New York, Vintage

Samuel, R. and Thompson, P. (1990) *The Myths We Live By*, London and New York, Routledge

Saunders, Christopher. (1988) *The Making of the South African Past: Major Historians on Race and Class,* Cape Town and Johannesburg, David Phillip

Scarry, E. (1985) *The Body in Pain, The Making and Unmaking of the World*, Oxford, Oxford University Press

Schermerhorn, Richard A. (1970) *Comparative Ethnic Relations*, New York, Random House

Schumacher, Thomas G. (April 1995) '"This is a Sampling Sport": Digital Sampling, Rap Music and the Law in Cultural Production' in *Media, Culture and Society*, 17, 2

Scully, P. (April 1995) 'Rape, Race, and Colonial Culture: The Sexual Politics of Identity in the Nineteenth-Century Cape Colony, South Africa' in *American Historical Review*

– (1997) *Liberating the Family? Gender and British Slave Emancipation in the Rural Western Cape, South Africa, 1823-1853*, Cape Town, David Philip

Sepamla, Sipho. (1981) *A Ride on the Whirlwind*, Johannesburg, Donker

Serote, Mongane. (1981) *To Every Birth Its Blood*, Johannesburg, Ravan

Sharp, John. (1981) 'The roots and development of *volkekunde* in South Africa' in *Journal of Southern African Studies*, 8, 1

Sharpley-Whiting, T.D. (1999) *Black Venus: Sexualized Savages, Primal Fears, and Primitive Narratives in French*, USA, Duke University Press

Shava, Piniel. (1989) *A People's Voice: Black South African Writing in the Twentieth Century*, London, Zed

Shell, R. (1994a) *Children of Bondage: A Social History of the Slave Society at the Cape of Good Hope, 1652-1838*, London, Weslyan University Press

– (1994b) 'The Tower of Babel: The Slave Trade and Creolization at the Cape, 1652 – 1834' in (eds) Eldredge, Elizabeth and Morton, Fred, *Slavery in South Africa: Captive Labor on the Dutch Frontier*, San Francisco, Westview Press

Sherman, Jessica. (1989) 'Liberation Songs and Popular Culture' in *Staffrider*, 8, 3

Shusterman, Richard. (Summer 1991) 'The Fine Art of Rap' in *New Literary History*, 22, 3

Sicherman, Carol. (1993) 'Zoe Wicomb's "You Can't Get Lost in Cape Town": The Narrator's Identity' in (ed.) Fletcher, Pauline, *Black/White Writing: Essays on South African Literature*, London and Toronto, Associated University Press

Smith, Ashley. (1998) 'Drug Dealer "Not Afraid to Die"' in *Cape Argus*, 29 April

Smith, Valerie. (1998) *Not Just Race, Not Just Class*, New York and London, Routledge

Sony, Warrick. (1991) 'Strange Business: The Independent Music Culture in South Africa' in *Staffrider*, 9, 4

Soudien, C and Meltzer, L. (1996) 'Representation and Struggle' in *District Six: Image and Representation*, Cape Town, South African National Gallery

South African Native Affairs Commission 1903-5 (1905) Vol 1, Cape Town, Cape Times Ltd

Soyinka, Wole. (1999) *The Burden of Memory, the Muse of Forgiveness*, New York, Oxford University Press

Spivak, G. (1988) 'Can the Subaltern Speak? Speculations on Widow Sacrifice' in (eds) Nelson, Cary and Grossberg, Lawrence, *Marxism and the Interpretation of Culture*, London, Macmillan

Spivak, G. (1988) *In Other Worlds*, New York, Routledge

Statutes of the Union of South Africa (1950) Parow, Government Printer

Steadman, Ian. (1994) 'Towards Popular Theatre in South Africa' in (ed.) Gunner, Liz, *Politics and Performance. Theatre, Poetry and Song in Southern Africa*, Johannesburg, Witwatersrand University Press

Stepan, N. 'Race and Gender: The Role of Analogy in Science' in (ed.) D. Goldberg, *Anatomy of Racism*, Minneapolis, University of Minnesota Press

Stoler, A. (1991) 'Carnal Knowledge and Imperial Power: Gender, Race, and Morality in Colonial Asia' in (ed.) di Leonardo, Micaela, *Gender at the Crossroads of Knowledge: Feminist Anthropology in the Postmodern Era*, Berkeley, University of California Press

– (1997a). 'Making Empire Respectable: The Politics of Race and Sexual Morality in Twentieth-Century Colonial Cultures' in (eds) McClintock, Anne, Mufti, Aamir, and Shohat, Ella, *Dangerous Liaisons: Gender, Nation, and Postcolonial Perspectives*, Minneapolis, University of Minnesota Press

– (1997b) 'Sexual Affronts and Racial Frontiers: European Identities and the Cultural Politics of Exclusion in Colonial Southeast Asia' in (ed.) Gates, Nathanial, *Critical Race Theory: Essays on the Social Construction of Race*, London, Garland Publishing Inc

Strother, Z.S. (1999) 'Display of the Body Hottentot' in (ed.) Lindfors, Berth, *Africans on Stage: Studies in Ethnological Show Business*, Bloomington, Indiana University Press

Swanson, M. (1977) 'The Sanitation Syndrome: Bubonic Plague and Urban Native Policy in the Cape Colony, 1900-1909' in *Journal of African History*, Vol 18, 3

Thornton, Robert. (1983) 'Narrative ethnography in Africa, 1850-1920: the creation and capture of an appropriate domain for anthropology' in *Man*, 18,1

Tijerina, Aleticia. (1990) 'Notes on Oppression and Violence' in (ed.) Anzaldua, Gloria, *Making Face, Making Soul, Haciendo Caras: Creative and Critical Writings by Feminists of Color*, San Francisco, Aunt Lute

Tlali, Miriam. (1980) *Amandla*, Johannesburg, Ravan

Van den Berghe, Pierre (1965) *South Africa: A Study in Conflict*, Berkeley, University of California Press

– (1987) *The Ethnic Phenomenon*, New York, Praeger

Van Der Ross, R.E. (1986) *The Rise and Decline of Apartheid: A Study of Political Movements Among the Coloured People of South Africa, 1880-1985*, Cape Town, Tafelberg

Van Heyningen, E. (1984) 'The Social Evil in the Cape Colony 1868-1902: Prostitution and the Contagious Diseases Acts' in *Journal of Southern African Studies*, Vol 10, 2

Van Kessel, I. (1994) 'Grassroots: from community paper to activist playground', paper presented at the conference of the *Journal for Southern African Studies*, 9-11 September, York

Van Vuuren, Helize. (1999) 'Puik Roman Oor Slawe Tref met Uitbeelding' in *Die Burger*, 7 April

Vergani, Linda. (1993) 'Rapping for Democracy in South Africa. University enlists the aid of music group in campaign to educate first-time voters' in *Chronicle of Higher Education*, A43, 3 November

Wallace, Michele. (1990) *Invisibility Blues: From Pop to Theory*, London and New York, Verso

Walvin, James. (1986) *England, Slaves and Freedom*, Basingstoke, MacMillan

Ware, Vron. (1996) 'Defining Forces: 'Race', Gender and Memories of Empire' in (eds) Chambers, I and Curti, L, *The Post-Colonial Question: Common Skies, Divided Horizons*, London and New York, Routledge

Warner, M. (1994) *Six Myths of Our Time, Managing Monsters*, London, The Reith Lectures

Watts, Jane. (1989) *Black Writers From South Africa*, London, Macmillan

Weeks, J. (1991) *Against Nature. Essays on History, Sexuality and Identity*, London, Rivers Oram Press

Werbner, P. and Modood, T. (eds) (1997) *Debating Cultural Hybridity: Multi-Cultural Identities and the Politics of Anti-Racism*, London, Zed Books

Werbner, Pnina. (1997) 'The Dialectics of Cultural Hybridity', in (eds) Werbner, Pnina and Modood, Tariq, *Debating Cultural Hybridity*, London Zed Books

Western, J. (1981) *Outcast: Cape Town*, London, George Allen and Unwin

Wetherell, M. and Potter J. (1992) *Mapping the Language of Racism: Discourse and the Legitimation of Exploitation*, New York, Harvester Wheatsheaf

White, Hayden. (1978) 'Historicism, History and the Figurative Imagination' in *Tropics of Discourse: Essays in Cultural Criticism*, Baltimore, John Hopkins University Press

Wicomb, Z. (1987) *You Can't Get Lost in Cape Town*, London, Virago

– (1990) 'Another Story' in (eds) Lefanu, Sarah and Hayward, Stephen, *Colours of a New Day: Writing for South Africa*, Johannesburg, Ravan Press

– (1996) 'Postcoloniality and Postmodernity: The case of the coloured in South Africa' in (eds) Wittenberg, H. and Nas, L, *AUETSA 96. Proceedings of the Conference of the Association of University English Teachers of South Africa, UWC, 30 June-5 July*, Cape Town, University of the Western Cape

– (1998) 'Shame and identity: the case of the coloured in South Africa' in (eds) Attridge, D, and Jolly, R, *Writing South Africa: Literature, Apartheid, and Democracy, 1970-1995*, Cambridge, Cambridge University Press

Williams, B. (1996) 'The Power of Propaganda' in (eds) James, W, Caliguire, D. and Cullinan, K. *Now that We are Free: Coloured Communities in a Democratic South Africa*, Cape Town, Idasa

Williams, Raymond. (1976) *Keywords: a Vocabulary of Culture and Society* London, Fontana

Willis, Susan. (Winter 1993) 'Hardcore: Subculture American Style' in *Critical Inquiry*, 19

Wilson, James. (1998) *The Earth Shall Weep: A History of Native America*, London and Basingstoke, Picador

Winberg, Christine. (1992) 'Satire, slavery and the *ghoemaliedjies* of the Cape Muslims' in *New Contrast*, 76, 19

Young, James E. (1997) 'Between History and Memory' in *History and Memory: Studies in Representations of the Past*, 9,1/2, Fall

Young, R. (1990) *White Mythologies: Writing History and the West*, London, Routledge

– (1995) *Colonial Desire: Hybridity in Theory, Culture and Race*, London, Routledge

Zerubavel, Eviatar. (Summer 1998) 'Language and Memory: "Pre-Columbian" America and the Logic of Periodization' in *Social Research*, 65, 2

Zook, Kristal Bent. (1990) 'Light skinned-ded Naps' in (ed.) Anzaldua, Gloria, *Making Face, Making Soul, Haciendo Caras: Creative and Critical Writings by Feminists of Color*, San Francisco, Aunt Lute

Index

D

E

S

X

Y

Z